Thoreau's
Redemptive Imagination

THE GOTHAM LIBRARY
OF THE NEW YORK UNIVERSITY PRESS

The Gotham Library is a series of original works and critical studies published in paperback primarily for student use. The Gotham hardcover edition is primarily for use by libraries and the general reader. Devoted to significant works and major authors and to literary topics of enduring importance, Gotham Library texts offer the best in literature and criticism.

Comparative and Foreign Language Literature:
Robert J. Clements, Editor
Comparative and English Language Literature:
James W. Tuttleton, Editor

Thoreau's Redemptive Imagination

Frederick Garber

New York · New York University Press · 1977

Copyright © 1977 by New York University
Library of Congress Catalog Card Number: 77-73031
ISBN: 0-8147-2965-7 (cloth)
    0-8147-2966-5 (paper)

Library of Congress Cataloging in Publication Data

Garber, Frederick.
  Thoreau's redemptive imagination.

  (The Gotham library of New York University
Press)
  Includes bibliographical references and index.
  1. Thoreau, Henry David, 1817-1862—Criticism
and interpretation. I. Title.
PS3054.G3   818'.3'09   77-73031
ISBN 0-8147-2965-7
ISBN 0-8147-2966-5 pbk.

Manufactured in the United States of America

Preface

This book grew out of a long-term interest in Thoreau and particularly in the place he occupies in the Romantic movement as a whole. Thoreau is distinctively, even blatantly, chauvinistic, a position which informs his perception of the world at every level of his experience. At the same time he shares essential concerns and attitudes with many of the Anglo-European Romantics; indeed, he shares them with some of the same figures whom he attacks, in an occasional moment of strategic excess, as barren and stultified. Though I weighed the possibility of a comparative study which would place Thoreau within the entire Romantic context, I found that his modes of organizing his experience of the world were so fascinating and intricate in themselves that they needed and deserved an entire study of their own. A reading of Thoreau in his Romantic context will come at a later point. However, I frequently indicate analogies between Thoreau and other Romantic figures, particularly Rousseau, whose *Cinquième Promenade* is a touchstone of a number of central Romantic interests.

I have concentrated primarily on those texts which most clearly illuminate the successes and frustrations of Thoreau's redemptive imagination as it seeks to make a place for the self in American nature. Since this struggle is repetitive and takes the same forms time after time, I have chosen to examine the most crucial and revealing stages and patterns in Thoreau's perception of experience. *The Maine Woods* and "Walking" are more critical in that context than are *Cape Cod* and even the lovely "Autumnal Tints." My method is both topical and chronological. I begin at the point of absolute beginning, the center of the ordering consciousness, and move out from there to all that is outside that center—other men, Concord, America, the world. At the same time there is a chronological base to my reading because there is development within the modes of Thoreau's imagination even though its struggles are, in great part, always the same. Therefore I end with an examination of the conclusion of "Walking," the richest and most compelling of Thoreau's late essays. Ultimately I seek to illuminate the ways in which the order of his mind tried continually to adjust itself, but to retain its essential duties, as the world changed for him.

The biographical studies of Walter Harding and Joseph Wood Krutch, the textual work of J. Lyndon Shanley and the editors of the Princeton edition of Thoreau, the critical essays of Charles Anderson and Sherman Paul—all these most prominently but not exclusively—have helped me in my own thinking about Thoreau. Several recent studies which appeared when my essay was already formed have confirmed, directly and indirectly, some of my own conclusions. I should cite in particular Lawrence Buell's *Literary Transcendentalism,* James McIntosh's *Thoreau as Romantic Naturalist,* and especially Stanley Cavell's *The Senses of Walden.*

—Frederick Garber

Contents

References

References to *A Week on the Concord and Merrimack Rivers,
Excursions,* and *Journals* are to the volumes in the Walden Edition,
The Writings of Henry David Thoreau (1906; rpt., New York: AMS
Press, 1968). *J* refers to the *Journals*. References to *Walden* and *The
Maine Woods* are to the volumes in the Princeton series, *The Writings
of Henry David Thoreau,* as follows: *Walden,* ed. J. Lyndon Shanley
(Princeton: Princeton University Press, 1971); *The Maine Woods,* ed.
Joseph J. Moldenhauer (Princeton: Princeton University Press,
1972). The letters are quoted from *Correspondence,* ed. Carl Bode and
Walter Harding (New York: New York University Press, 1958). I
have also used *Consciousness in Concord; the text of Thoreau's hitherto
"lost journal," 1840-1841,* ed. Perry Miller (Boston: Houghton
Mifflin, 1958).

I am grateful to the following libraries for permission to quote
from manuscripts in their possession:

The Concord Free Public Library for an excerpt from the
manuscript of "Walking";

The Huntington Library, San Marino, California, for materials from HM 924, the "E" text of *Walden,* and HM 13195, *A Week on the Concord and Merrimack Rivers;*

The Houghton Library, Harvard University, for materials from MS. bms Am 278.5, Thoreau's "Manuscript Fragments."

Mr. Kenneth W. Cameron has given me permission to quote passages from my essay "Unity and Diversity in 'Walking' " in *New Approaches to Thoreau: A Symposium,* ed. William Bysshe Stein (Hartford: Transcendental Books, 1969).

1.

A Clearing in the Forest

In a passage from the chapter on "Solitude" in *Walden* Thoreau comments on a peculiar order of consciousness which shows that "we are not wholly involved in Nature" (*Walden*, 135). The order comprises "a certain doubleness by which I can stand as remote from myself as from another." There is, it would seem, an aspect of the self which does not take an immediate part in experience but looks on as the rest partakes; and then "when the play, it may be the tragedy, of life is over, the spectator goes his way. It was a kind of fiction, a work of the imagination only, so far as he was concerned." The spectator is not the artist who created the spectacle but a detached viewer who witnesses the work of a theatrical imagination. Thoreau transformed the old metaphor about men's lives and the stage into an observation on the duplicity of our relationship to nature, ending with a hint that the impassive onlooker has an immortal life ahead of him and is not at all bound to terrestrial things. Of course the truly whole self contains earthly and unearthly parts; but to specify that the spiritual is merely an observer involves, at the least, an extraordinarily complex view of the activities of consciousness. Emerson touched on such doubleness frequently, but Thoreau's own emphasis falls as much on the spectatorial aspects of the order as on what Emerson stressed, the dichotomy between the elements.

The fact of aloofness seemed to fascinate Thoreau. The earliest state of the passage from *Walden* appears in the journal for August 8, 1852, while he was working toward the final version of the book. Six years later, on November 1, 1858, he showed himself to be a fully accomplished observer, practicing a mature interplay of distancing and involvement. He looked out at the November twilight:

> It appeared like a part of a panorama. . . . Just such a piece of art merely, though infinitely sweet and grand, did it appear to me, and just as little were any active duties required of me. We are independent on all that we see. The hangman whom I have *seen* cannot hang me. The earth which I have *seen* cannot bury me. Such doubleness and distance does sight prove. Only the rich and such as are troubled with ennui are implicated in the maze of phenomena. You cannot see anything until you are clear of it. (*J*, XI, 273)

The most successful seeing requires a withdrawal from entanglement in the intricacies (the "maze") of phenomenal activity. That part of his role is pure hedging, a holding back. Here the self is a singular audience watching "a piece of art merely," and there is nothing said about acting or partaking. But he does speak again of "doubleness," showing that Thoreau still knows that a part of the self must have a direct and immediate relationship with experience or the observer will have nothing at all to see. Thoreau is now so well practiced that all the implications of duplicity are contained in the word "doubleness." The assured tone of the passage speaks to the skill with which he was going about his spectatorial business, here near the end of his life. But in fact he had been speaking of aloofness and participation for nearly two decades. In a passage from the journal for November 1841 Thoreau said of the poet that "though more than any he stands in the midst of Nature, yet more than any he can stand aloof from her" (*J*, I, 289). The poet can participate or not, as he chooses. He is not necessarily bound to the nature which surrounds him.

This complex of activities is essential not only to Thoreau's understanding of the contract of mind and nature but also to the mind's own understanding of itself. It is, in part, an extension of the Transcendental distinction of genius and talent, derived from Coleridge's remarks on Reason and Understanding and elaborated by Emerson and others until it became standard matter for conversation in Concord idealist circles.[1] Thoreau put it precisely and cogently in 1840, when he was still very close to Emersonian thinking: "The perfect man has both genius and talent. The one is his head, the other his foot; by one he is, by the other he lives" (J, I, 119). There is an aspect of self which is close to or actually a part of Being: "by one he is," the verb of absolute existence denoting the proper activity of a central and reserved element, kept back from participation. Since it is the core of personal reality it must be cherished and protected. Later Thoreau was to call it the "interior and essential and sacred self" (J, IV, 290). The other aspect of self does the exterior work for the whole: "by the other he lives," makes participatory gestures, deals with natural experiences; that aspect is the practical agent of the total self. But there are implications here concerning not only the practices and structure of the order of consciousness but also the way in which that order abuts the world outside. If there is an untouchable center, withdrawn and observant, and a busy participant that does the exploring for the whole, there has to be a place where the world within ends and the outside begins. Further, the whole complex must have a shape that determines the order of those relationships. Thoreau had a number of ways of explaining what that shape was, and sometimes he did so through his own rendition of familiar Transcendental baggage relating to sphere, center, and circumference.

Thoreau's writings are full of spheres, a favorite image in Concord for the wholly effectual man. He could be as self-assuredly moralistic with a sphere as could any of his contemporaries, but he was also like them in stressing the use of spheres to indicate the centrality, that is, the godlikeness, of man in the universe: "the universe is a sphere whose center is wherever there is intelligence. The sun is not so central as a man" (Week, 373).[2]

Sometimes Thoreau used radii rather than spheres to make his point, and the effect was significantly different. Whenever he conceived of man as surrounded by a perfect sphere—which man reflected in his own perfection— he worked by and large in cosmic terms, that is, he would see the spheres as the bowl of the sky or some similar concavity: "Let us wander where we will, the universe is built round about us, and we are central still. If we look into the heavens they are concave, and if we were to look into a gulf as bottomless, it would be concave also" (*Week,* 353). But when he worked with radii by themselves he would see men in a terrestrial framework, with the lines radiating round them horizontally: "Wherever I sat, there I might live, and the landscape radiated from me accordingly" (*Walden,* 81).

In either case, however, all the lines that bisect experience shoot out from the site he occupies, which means that the position of the observer is the central point from which all directions flow. Genius, the element of pure Being, sits immovably at that still point, while talent moves out along the radii into the world of experience. Thoreau's conception of centrality is deeper than all the moral implications which a Transcendentalist would draw from it concerning man's key position in the universe. Indeed, the relation of centrality to some accepted Transcendental doctrines is only one factor in explaining its importance to him, and it is not the most important one. Thoreau's perception of the centrality of the self, or of an aspect of the self, was one of the major determining principles in the way his consciousness perceived and ordered experience, and it was so in a way that transcended local influences. All Thoreauvian perception begins from his awareness of the point of self shooting out radii, or from its alternate in which the point where consciousness begins is at the exact center of some enclosure, often but not exclusively a sphere. The variations on his use of that point of incipient perception are as extraordinary as its prevalence. He can be the smug egoist capable of mild self-mockery:

All things are up and down, east and west, to *me.* In me is the forum out of which go the Appian and Sacred ways, and a thousand beside, to the ends of the world. If I forget my centralness, and say a bean winds with or against the *sun*, and not right or left, it will not be true south of the equator. (*J*, I, 84)

Or he can be cognizant of both centrality and the multiplicity of centers:

> I am always struck by the centrality of the observer's position. He always stands fronting the middle of the arch, and does not suspect at first that a thousand observers on a thousand hills behold the sunset sky from equally favorable positions. (*J*, II, 296)

Or he can turn his surveyor's awareness of geometry into a lovely image of moral order:

> As all curves have reference to their centres or foci, so all beauty of character has reference to the soul, and is a graceful gesture of recognition or waving of the body toward it. (*J*, I, 332)

Or, finally, he can be aware that centrality is both portable and a point of support for his freedom and self-sufficiency:

> If a person lost would conclude that after all he is not lost, he is not beside himself, but standing in his own old shoes on the very spot where he is, and that for the time being he will live there; but the places that have known him, *they* are lost,—how much anxiety and danger would vanish. I am not alone if I stand by myself. (*Week*, 193)

As this last quotation makes especially clear, the point of centrality is locative: when I know where it is I can say that here is my pure center, this is where I am. But of course one faces the danger of wandering away from the point and losing sight of it; or—the fate of most men—one can forget where it is or that it exists at all: "For the most part, we are not where we are, but in a false position" (*Walden*, 327).[3] Our basic business, it would seem, is to find out where we are, though sometimes we grow smug and satisfied with the minimal exploration we have done. At the beginning of the chapter on "Reading" in *Walden* Thoreau points out that while he was working on his house and hoeing his bean patch he kept an *Iliad* on his table, but could glance at it only occasionally. At that time his business was not in Troy, though Homer was never very far from Thoreau's private center. Yet he did cheat somewhat: "I read one or two shallow books of travel in the intervals of my work, till that employment made me ashamed of myself, and I asked where it was then that *I* lived" (100). A similar query about his own home center had led Thoreau to his real job there, the purpose of his coming down from Concord to the side of the pond. The move to Walden Pond, the clearing of the land and the building of the house, was in great part an effort by Thoreau to find out where he *was*,—"where *I* lived." His imagination was extraordinarily visual and kinesthetic, which meant that when he wanted to locate his own place, or set up the process by which he could search for it, the activity of locating had to be put into graphic, physical terms. He had to build something and clear something else, to work hard on an object or place that could be seen by himself and others. Even when there were only the walls, the house he built specified his exact location: "This frame, so slightly clad, was a sort of crystallization around me" (85). With such a signpost, which he could feel in his hard-worked muscles, there was less danger of his wandering away from his own central point, of becoming like those who "for the most part . . . are not where [they] are, but in a false position."

Further, the point of centrality is organizational as well as locative. The landscape radiates from Thoreau wherever he is ("wherever I sat"), and all points of the compass start from him as center ("all things are up and down, east and west to *me*"). Though this literal egocentricity orders the world around him, it never becomes entirely solipsistic. Thoreau knows that there are centers other than his own, "a thousand observers on a thousand hills," and that each one's cosmos begins from himself and radiates out from there. Yet the experience at Walden did not involve the multiplicity of human centers but a natural center that stood over against his own, and that was Walden Pond. It too could organize a landscape, pulling everything else in sight into place around it.

What he says of Fair Haven Pond is true for all others: "The water or lake, from however distant a point seen, is always the centre of the landscape" (*J*, IV, 385). Fair Haven was more open than any of the others and could therefore be seen from more distant points, but since it was the paragon it established the principle of centrality for all.[4] Late in 1859 he thought of Walden Pond as a "blue navel" in the middle of the earth (*J*, XII, 378). In his continuing study of Walden Pond Thoreau saw that the organizational principle could go even further than locating a natural center. He mentions several times in *Walden* that on days when the pond is most perspicuous it reflects within itself both the earth and the sky: "Lying between the earth and the heavens, it partakes of the color of both" (*Walden*, 176). Nothing is more central or centrifying than this great eye that looks up to heaven as well as all around the horizontal landscape. The pond is a kind of omphalos, the navel of the earth or the universal center. Of course there is a sense in which he too can reflect within himself both the earth and the sky, the wild forest and the heaven above it, flesh and spirit: part of the activity in the *Week* and *Walden* involves a quest for images to make that point, to clarify the ability of the self to organize, in a coherent whole, both the physical and the spiritual orders.

In the world of *Walden* the two deep centers are his own and the pond's. And though he will sometimes think of himself as an omphalos he is also extremely sensitive to the multifaceted relationships between his own centered self and the enclosure of water just out there beyond where he sits. *Walden* explores a number of analogies of the pond and the self; for example: "they plainly fished much more in the Walden Pond of their own natures, and baited their hooks with darkness" (130). To stare into it is also to stare into oneself: "A lake is the landscape's most beautiful and expressive feature. It is earth's eye; looking into which the beholder measures the depth of his own nature" (186). But the analogy can also be tenuous and ironic: "Of all the characters I have known, perhaps Walden wears best, and best preserves its purity. Many men have been likened to it, but few deserve that honor" (192).

The landscape which radiated from wherever Thoreau sat was

in considerable part either a forest or some other kind of unenclosed land. The next move was out to the fields and woods of his immediate surroundings, which were encumbered to the degree that the fields usually belonged to individual farms, and some parts of the woods were owned by people like Emerson. Out of these surroundings and the geography of the North American continent Thoreau postulated a map for his imagination, and the precise cartographical accuracy of that postulate is far less important than its efficacy, that is, its usefulness for his imagination. He speaks frequently as if the North American wilderness began just at the edge of the boundaries of Concord and extended out from there in reaches which seemed infinite because they encompassed a major continent.

To get a sense of the map one has to conceive an immense and deep vastness, imaged nearly always as a wilderness. Within that immensity there are scattered dots of clearing, spaces that have been won from the open and unenclosed. After the fields and woods around Concord and other towns, areas of relative unrestrictiveness, the next step is to the rougher, more thickly packed and wilder landscape of Maine and Canada, where the cities as points of clearing give way to individual cabins, the cabins give way to camps, and then, beyond camps, there is only the infinite wilderness. (The imagery of the West has a separate though related set of meanings which I shall take up later.) This map, made by and for the imagination, is a grand *as if* that pervades Thoreau's work from his earliest journal entries to the last major statement in the final version of "Walking." On the other hand, the map is not merely a fictional construct, designed to help him get along in the complicated world of contemporary America. This bit of "home-cosmography" is a kind of language which tells certain truths about the relations between the American self and the nature around it, between Concord as a center of civilized amenities and the unamenable world that still covered much of America. Thoreau interpreted the givens of his experience, the raw data which reached him at home in Concord, into meanings for himself as American imaginative man. His private map of a country in the making created a field upon which he could specify locations for the work of his imagination, for what his consciousness had to do in making a place for itself in American experience.

In "A Walk to Wachusett" Thoreau tells of passing through the town of Sterling, to the west of which was a small village that was just beginning to get settled on the banks of the Stillwater: "We fancied that there was already a certain western look about this place, a smell of pines and roar of water, recently confined by dams, belying its name, which were exceedingly grateful"*(Excursions,* 140). The village, too new for a name or a post office, sat within a recently leveled piece of land "where the axe had encroached upon the edge of the forest." It is obvious that on Thoreau's map the outside of Sterling looks just like the outside of Concord, with the pines right up to the edge where the vastness begins. Immediately after this Thoreau mentions that he was greeted complacently, almost compassionately, by the inhabitants as he passed through the various small villages. He ends with a remark that was enlarged upon in *Walden* and says a great deal about his understanding of the relations of consciousness and experience: "So is each one's world but a clearing in the forest, so much open and inclosed ground." This whole passage shows how Thoreau's own surroundings fit into his postulated map; or, conversely, how the map leads him to read his surroundings. But, put together with the original journal entry from which some of its elements came, the passage also shows how useful the map was for clarifying his intuition of what was being done in America, and of what he had to do in it to make a place for his mind. "A Walk to Wachusett" is dated "Concord, July 19, 1842," while the journal entry containing the greeting by the villagers as well as the moral tag to which the whole passage leads is dated May 5, 1838. However, the entry does not refer to Sterling or a walk to Wachusett but, instead, to a trip through Maine: "Portland to Bath *via* Brunswick; Bath to Brunswick" (*J*, I, 47-48). The point here is not just in the flexibility of Thoreau's imagination—in that he had no peers in Concord and few anywhere else in America— but in the interchangeability of the observations and particularly of the generalization he came to from contemplating his map. Men had to clear places for themselves in the vastness just beyond Concord as well as in the wilds of Maine where such activities would seem to be more predictable.

Here is Thoreau describing a walk with Channing into Acton and Carlisle:

descending through swampy land [we] at length saw through
the trees and bushes into a small meadow completely surrounded by woods, in which was a man haying only eight or
ten rods off. We felt very much like Indians stealing upon an
early settler. (*J*, VI, 44)

Tame as this is, the scene has all the tensions of the raw and the
finished that Thoreau needed to define the event; and he adds the
threat of danger that in older and wilder cases gives the ultimate
tone. Of course this is partly play, but that is to keep the
imagination's consciousness of history in full and active stretch.
Maine may have been wilder than this, but it required the same
from men as did Massachusetts. In fact, since "each one's world is
but a clearing in the forest," it follows that one has to perform an
act of clearing, of winning one's world from the wild, wherever one
is. Clearing is an activity of consciousness basic to all men. The
actions through which we organize our relations to the world are
graphically imaged on the map which shows where Americans
have cleared spaces for themselves in the continental wilderness.
Pioneering in America, opening up either a piece of Concord's
woods or the unclaimed wilderness in Maine, is therefore an
extension of an essential, elemental enterprise, proper to all men as
functioning beings. That is why the comment on each one's world
was continued in *Walden*:

There is commonly sufficient space about us. Our horizon is
never quite at our elbows. The thick wood is not just at our
door, nor the pond, but somewhat is always clearing, familiar
and worn by us, appropriated and fenced in some way, and
reclaimed from Nature. (*Walden*, 130)

As cartographer for the imagination, then, Thoreau drew both the
vastness outside the clearings and also the areas of individual
clearing themselves. Within the clearings are those points from
which, for each one, "the landscape radiated from [him] accordingly." Outside and surrounding each point of centrality is a space
made for it, a piece of "inclosed ground" that is the home place,
the enclosure, within which the point functions. Thus the center
not only has a place in which it lives and has its being, but it also

has a protective area surrounding it so that there can be breathing room and a guarantee of freedom from encroachment.

Each space taken away ("reclaimed") from nature is a point of human reference within it, something that a man has made out of the undeveloped, the unencumbered, the unenclosed. (In certain of his moods Thoreau spoke of it as the unredeemed.) The act of clearing, then, is a distinctively human one: insofar as it is an act of consciousness, it is what all men do when they seek to make their worlds; insofar as it is a pioneer act in the literal wilderness it is what men do best when they are fully themselves, pitting their creative energies against the unredeemed vastness outside their private enclosures. Emerson, in "The American Scholar," put it much as Thoreau was to do throughout his own work, though with Emerson the phenomenon was one of a number of ways of phrasing the mind's relation with experience, while for Thoreau the act of clearing was a central concern of consciousness; in Emerson's words, "so much only of life as I know by experience, so much of the wilderness have I vanquished and planted, or so far have I extended my being, my dominion."[5] Clearing, we see, is an act through which the self comes to understand itself, its qualities and capacities. As Thoreau phrased it in a letter of 1855 to H. G. O. Blake, the self may learn much about the shape of its own moral order from the activity of clearing:

> To what end do I lead a simple life at all, pray? That I may teach others to simplify their lives? ... Or not, rather, that I may make use of the ground I have cleared, to live more worthily and profitably. (*Correspondence,*384)

The act is both a discovery about what the world is like (or ought to be) and what he himself is like. In the same act he organizes his perception of himself and of his world. A clearing in the forest is therefore not only an instance of what consciousness can do, redeeming a piece of nature; it is also an image of the redeeming consciousness itself, the cleared place within which one stands and does one's relating to experience. Furthermore, whatever consciousness gains through these creative acts leads to an increase in the content of the mind. When consciousness redeems nature, it transforms the world into itself:

Our stock in life, our real estate, is that amount of thought which we have had, which we have thought out. The ground we have thus created is forever pasturage for our thoughts. . . . If you have ever done any work with these finest tools, the imagination and fancy and reason, it is a new creation, independent on the world, and a possession forever. You have laid up something against a rainy day. You have to that extent cleared the wilderness. (*J,* IX, 350)

In this passage Thoreau's terms for the redeeming agent(s) are accepted Romantic ones, drawn from Coleridge and the tradition of Anglo-European Romanticism which informed American Transcendentalism. Indeed, the reclamation which he practices had long been an essential activity of the Romantic consciousness. The imagination is as redemptive in Thoreau as it is in Blake and Wordsworth. It is as assertive against surrounding chaos, the wilderness, as is the mind of Faust in its ultimate act, building dikes against the ever encroaching sea. Talent, we recall, is the part by which one lives, as opposed to genius, which is the center of personal being. It appears that when the activity of living is fullest and richest, the talent creates ground for the mind's pasturage, making a clearing out of part of the mindless wilderness which surrounds it.

Since the act of clearing sets up man against the chaos in his vicinity, to clear a space means to civilize, for civility is the antagonist of chaos, and the city or garden is the opposite of the wilderness. As he put it in 1857, "redeeming a swamp . . . comes pretty near to making a world" (*J,* IX, 311). Those poets who have a positive attitude toward wildness may well have mixed feelings about these issues: "The turning a swamp into a garden, though the poet may not think it an improvement, is at any rate an enterprise interesting to all men" (*J,* III, 328). But even with this grudging though good-humored qualification (Thoreau is far less complacent at other times), he acknowledged that the agricultural counterpart to the imagination's clearing of the wilderness is also redemptive. To enclose a piece of open ground is to establish the moral basis for the best fruits of civilization and, not coincidentally, for the best aspects of the one who clears the ground. The act pays off in heaven as it does on earth:

I take up a report on Farms by a committee of Middlesex Husbandmen, and read of the number of acres of bog that some farmer has redeemed ... and I feel as if I had got my foot down on to the solid and sunny earth, the basis of all philosophy, and poetry, and religion even. I have faith that the man who redeemed some acres of land the past summer redeemed also some parts of his character. (*J*, III, 327)

Redemption, then, can be subjective, an enrichment and cultivation of the world within as well as a reclamation of the world without. Those activities are counterparts and can have a considerable effect on each other, as this quotation evidences and as Thoreau affirmed when he was hoeing his bean field or surveying. Despite the poet's frequent uneasiness, transforming a bog into a garden means that one may clear a garden within oneself, a bit of subjective paradise that is enclosed and fruitful and civil. Thoreau's faith in the subjective potential of the farmer's business was based on the possibility of the collocation of inner and outer landscapes, and therefore he could not look upon the effort to civilize as being entirely negative, whatever his discomfort with the draining of bogs. Of course the subjective reclamation was no more than a possibility, something that could happen but most often did not because the inner materials were either reticent or simply not there. Once—during the meeting with John Field recorded in the "Baker Farm" chapter of *Walden*—Thoreau even rejected the collocation of landscapes in a moment of frustration. Field was an Irish immigrant who spent his time "bogging," clearing a farmer's meadow for a measly fee. Thoreau's awareness that Field was morally obtuse and unaffected by his work in the meadow led him to split up his usual alignment of inner and outer reclamation: "I should be glad if all the meadows on the earth were left in a wild state, if that were the consequence of men's beginning to redeem themselves" (*Walden*, 250). Ordinarily, though, Thoreau held on to the possibility of collocation, preferring to think that field work should be able to effect an increase in the capacities of consciousness, that civility could be fostered by clearing a piece of the wild. In fact, he contributed to the process of cultivation with his own business as a surveyor. One suspects more design than chance in Thoreau's choice of surveying as a mode of making a living: the job fit in too neatly with the kinds of patterning through which he regulated his reading of the world. The surveyor is the harbinger of the wild's redemption, the first sign of civility to reach the uncharted wilderness. The surveyor's tools are civilizing instruments, and his acts are efforts at reclamation. Thoreau took full advantage of the imaginative potential of the characteristics of the job, turning them into tools for his interpretation of American experience.

As a surveyor it was Thoreau's business to walk around perimeters, to perambulate the boundaries of clearings, and, at times, to delineate the contours of those boundaries. His talents as a surveyor, the commercial activity by which he lived and protected his genius, put him out at the line where the clearing ended. He was an explorer at the edge, the civil man performing a civilizing act, the agent of the Concord fathers and those farmers who wanted to pin down the exact location of the fields they had won from the bogs. Since he worked for those people only because he wanted to support his other perambulations, Thoreau occasionally complained about the need to walk around the edges of Concord simply for self-support. A week of "perambulating the bounds of the town" and immersing himself in the worldly and the trivial left him, on September 20, 1851, wandering in the fields looking for his tone and sanity and simplicity again (*J*, III, 5). But eight days earlier, on the twelfth, Thoreau had been looking forward to the week he was about to begin, and he had come to a full recognition of all that this exploration at the edge could mean. It was a magnificent moment in which what he had to do occasionally and what he wanted to do all the time came together in rare harmony. That had happened before and was to happen again, but hardly ever with such happy effect. The passage is worth quoting in full:

> On Monday, the 15th instant, I am going to perambulate the bounds of the town. As I am partial to across-lot routes, this appears to be a very proper duty for me to perform, for certainly no route can well be chosen which shall be more across-lot, since the roads in no case run round the town but ray out from its centre, and my course will lie across each one. It is almost as if I had undertaken to walk round the town at

the greatest distance from its centre and at the same time from
the surrounding villages. There is no public house near the
line. It is a sort of reconnaissance of its frontiers authorized by
the central government of the town, which will bring the
surveyor in contact with whatever wild inhabitant or wilderness its territory embraces. (*J*, II, 498-99) [6]

This passage is a pristine and nearly complete version of the
world at the center, including not only its full shape, and the
rhetoric associated with it, but also his pleasure in being the man
at the edge, touching at the wild. (It lacks only his ambivalence,
though that is an omission of considerable significance.) This time
the point from which the landscape radiates, the center protected
by a clearing and enclosed by a boundary which fronts the wild, is
a civil place, the place of harmony, Concord. The town is neither a
pasturage nor a likely place for the self's private discoveries about
its relations to experience. But—taken with all the other comments
on the clearing in the wild—the passage suggests analogies among
the orders of self, town, and meadow. They form mutually
reflective structures whose interconnections would seem to make
possible a considerable complexity of organization in Thoreau's
interpretation of his world around Concord. For example, all the
analogies indicate the importance of boundaries, how they seem to
be a necessary accompaniment to the awareness of centrality. The
paradigm quoted above shows how the boundary of the town, its
frontier, demarcated the end of the redeemed and the beginning of
the wilderness. Beyond the boundary was the area that had not yet
felt the efficacy of men's minds. But all clearings needed such an
edge where the foreign—perhaps the most encompassing word for
everything out there—could begin.[7] In an important sense the
clearings were never completed until their perimeters had been
precisely delineated. In some moods and for specific reasons
Thoreau wanted those lines to be sharp and exact: "Individuals,
like nations, must have suitable broad and natural boundaries,
even a considerable neutral ground between them" (*Walden,* 141).
We need those spaces and boundaries because the best in us is
"that in each of us which is without, or above, being spoken to,"
and our best can be heard only when we are far apart bodily.[8] The
best, of course, is the genius within each one, that by which one *is*.

Thoreau had already carried through this analogy of individuals and nations somewhat earlier in *Walden:* "Our life is like a German Confederacy, made up of petty states, with its boundary forever fluctuating, so that even a German cannot tell you how it is bounded at any moment" (*Walden,* 92). To make firm perimeters one has to "simplify, simplify," get rid of the baggage whose excess bursts our boundaries (91). The year after he published *Walden* Thoreau made the same point to H. G. O. Blake: simplification involves a clearing of ground for the self, that is, the establishment of the self's own place (see page 11 above). The result would be self-circumscription, the establishment of precise personal perimeters, the reenactment nearly a century later, and at the edge of the American wilderness, of Rousseau's prescription for the delineation of the bounds of the self: *"Commençons par redevenir nous, par nous concentrer en nous, par circonscrire notre ame des mêmes bornes que la nature a données à notre être."* [9] Within these bounds one can redeem spaces for one's private paradise, whether one is on an island in a Swiss lake, as Rousseau was for a brief but perfect period, or by the shores of an American one. It is a Romantic process, as valid for Wordsworth in the vale of Grasmere as for Rousseau or Thoreau. All the same, however, the variations and idiosyncrasies of landscape guarantee that there will be significant differences among the particulars of all these Romantic paradises.

Outside Concord's perimeter is the wild, or at least the natural. Outside Thoreau's own circumference is not only the wild but Concord and the rest of the world, which includes all other men. Concord, the place of harmonious civility, had men within it with whom he would sometimes have things to do; and what the wild had within itself was both strange (other) and familiar (alike) but with a capacity for surprise that, at several points in Thoreau's experience, startled him into a profound uneasiness. Inside Thoreau's private configuration there was only himself, a fact that created a considerable ambivalence with which he could not always come to terms. He learned very quickly that the shape of the structure through which his consciousness functioned was that of a prison as well as a paradise. It kept other men out while it kept part of him in, however much he wanted to make that part available now and then. These complications in his relations with others revealed limitations in what he could do with consciousness, and those restrictions were to find their parallels in his work with everything else outside his private perimeter. Thoreau discovered more enforced separateness, and at more levels, than the conventional pieties of Concord would recognize or accept. He came to see that the desires of the redemptive imagination had to take all of these paradoxes into consideration, and he found it necessary to organize the work of his consciousness accordingly.

One of the most persistent activities in Thoreau's life was the putting of spaces between himself and other men, making those "suitable broad and natural boundaries" that seemed necessary for the best kinds of relationship (*Walden*, 141). The visual, spatial configurations with which he patterned his understanding of the self were therefore embodiments of desire, that is, exact specifications of the way he wanted experience to be. It was good that the places men carved out of the surrounding bogs had both a cleared area around their center and also a boundary around the clearing, because in that way other men could be kept distant, within their own proper spheres. Through that form he could also keep off other demands associated with civility—"any work whether of the head or hands"—when he needed to: "I love a broad margin to my life" was his comment describing the conditions under which he could enjoy a morning-long Rousseauesque reverie, unaware of time or most disturbances from outside (111).[10] Consciousness had to have free and open spaces around itself in order to do its business. The image of margins can be extended and played with so as to include all manner of personal and social economies:

> as every man, in respect to material wealth, aims to become independent or wealthy, so, in respect to our spirits and imagination, we should have some spare capital and superfluous vigor, have some margin and leeway in which to move. (*J*, X, 6)

The margins are, at once, the surplus of capital which is our strength and the spaces we occupy when we exercise it, those same spaces which keep other men away.

Obviously the kind of work Thoreau did at Walden and elsewhere had to be done alone. As much as other men were occasionally welcome, they could never be around during the long periods in which one transacted one's private business. This is, of course, the familiar Thoreau, the creation not only of the Thoreauvians who quite properly took him at his word but of Thoreau himself, for whom the fostering of a public image was a necessary aspect of the business by which he ordered his life. The accuracy of the public image was based to a considerable extent upon Thoreau's sense of a community of intellect in which no one had to—indeed, no one ever could—stand alone. All men for whom thinking was more than a peripheral or incidental employment took part in a community that recognized no boundaries of self as well as no separations in space or time. The mind could make out of its activity an image of eternal and shared identity: "Sadi entertained once identically the same thought that I do, and thereafter I can find no essential difference between Sadi and myself. ... By the identity of his thoughts with mine he still survives" (*J*, IV, 290). The requisite contrary to that community is the separation from his contemporaries which the thinker feels at the same time that he dives into the timeless society of thought: "A man thinking or working is always alone, let him be where he will" (*Walden*, 135). He is alone, of course, but only to the extent that he is separate from those he can see. In the *Week* Thoreau had said that he was never really alone when he was by himself (193); thus, in the company of Sadi, he could espouse separateness from his palpable contemporaries.

In his deepest work Thoreau could keep himself aloof while various aspects of consciousness were occupied with the most elemental forms of association. He could have his boundaries and transcend them at the same time. In such moods Thoreau was as self-sufficient as Rousseau in his *Rêveries*, and for the same reason: each argued that he had reached a state of absolute self-contain-ment, in which nothing more was needed from other men since na-ture and the self-creating activities of consciousness would suffice for every necessary occupation. Thoreau's version (and Rousseau's as well) was far more intensely worked out and more concerned with pure states of existence than Emerson's Self-Reliance. Rou-sseau and Thoreau had their exact counterparts elsewhere, in other instances of the Romantic enclosure of the self which asserted that the mind is its own place. But the state was no more unalloyed for those two than it was for Byron's Manfred.

As it turns out, the boundaries are necessary for other reasons, and they come very near to contradicting the ones we have been inspecting. Thoreau argued that the broad distances between himself and other men were there for the protection of what is best in each of them. But there is also considerable evidence that he saw the dividing spaces as being forced upon men by the inexplicable nature of things. Thoreau indicates repeatedly and over a long period of time that the center of each man's self cannot be reached by anyone else even if one should want it to be touched: "I cannot make a disclosure—you should see my secret.—Let me open my doors never so wide, still within and behind them, where it is unopened, does the sun rise and set—and day and night alternate.—No fruit will ripen on the common" *(Consciousness in Concord,* 176-77). This is one of the most disturbing paradoxes in the often contradictory order of Thoreau's consciousness: the most desirable form of relationship he can establish between himself and other men permits him to reach out and contact them but only when he wants to, and at a distance. And yet there is also an enforced separateness that continually unnerved him and that called into question all his proud assertions about his *will* toward seclusion, about that privacy which he *chose* consciously because only in such a state could he do his best work. (All of Theoreau's strained comments about friendship, a frustrated lifelong preoccupation, come to mind at this point.) There is a border between men that, with all the good will possible, can never be breached. "How alone must our life be lived," he remarked in 1841, beginning a sentimentalized passage based on the old imagery of travels and pilgrims *(J,* I, 239). The question of tone is important because for many years Thoreau tried to put the point accurately. He wanted the most exact formulation for speaking about the sometimes painful inaccessibility of the deep center within each one.

Several years before that attempt in 1841, that is, in the notes from a lecture on "Society" delivered in April 1838, Thoreau had worked out a rich and succinct expression of the problem: "That which properly constitutes the life of every man is a profound secret. Yet this is what every one would give most to know, but is himself most backward to impart" *(J,* I, 36).[11] The cool clarity of the phrasing cannot quite hide the sense of defeat. By "backward" Thoreau could mean "shy," but he surely means "unskilled" or "unable" as well. What properly constitutes our lives is, of course, the genius that lies at the center of our being. One of Thoreau's maturest diagnoses of the issue came, in *Walden*, in a context describing the discoveries of genius:

> Perhaps the facts most astounding and most real are never communicated by man to man. The true harvest of my daily life is somewhat as intangible and indescribable as the tints of morning and evening. It is a little star-dust caught, a segment of the rainbow which I have clutched. *(Walden*, 216-17)

It seems, after all, that the boundaries we choose to establish between ourselves and other men are the same which, like it or not, we are forced to have.

By the time he wrote *Walden* Thoreau had come to see that this issue of enforced separateness was crucial to his true business. He began the book by pointing the problem out and implying that the mode of what was to follow had its basis in a requisite privacy which needed to be acknowledged before the narrative could begin: "I should not talk so much about myself if there were any body else whom I knew as well. Unfortunately, I am confined to this theme by the narrowness of my experience" (*Walden*, 3). That last bit of irony shows that he had reached some control over the situation. And control had to be a major concern here because the recognition of enforced separateness meant an awareness of defeat, however partial. The issue became a question of the imagination's adequacy: if one cannot really know other men, then how are other men to understand oneself at those levels that matter most? How can one communicate an experience which had touched at the deepest strata of the self when those strata could never be opened to others? In the *Week*, Thoreau found a form through which the patterns of the mind's meditations, the ways in which consciousness operated, could be connected with the events that all men have to go through in the patterns of their lives. He tried the mode of the spiritual journey, the going out and return which allied his narrative with Romantic travel books as well as most forms of imaginative travel since at least the *Odyssey*. His success in that book was partial at best, but that was not due to the matter of radical isolation, which never came up in the *Week*.

Walden was clearly a different story, as the first page makes evident. It is, above all, a narrative of the imagination's struggles to redeem itself, to find its home in a world which resisted many of its efforts to clear a place of its own in experience. Among the resisting elements were other men; nature; and "the narrowness of my experience," that is, the privacy of each one's life in the forest of the world. One way to begin overcoming the resistance of the latter was to acknowledge the possibility of rebuff, to show how the issue is going to shape the mode of what is to follow. Such an argument had been made before, in similar terms, by Rousseau and others like him who saw the same potential conflicts of desire and capability. Most Romantics, at one point or another in their experience, faced the question of self-redemption (redemption of their own selves as well as of others') in terms similar to Thoreau's, however differently they may have valued the elements of self, society, and nature. Their attempts to find adequate forms through which the imagination could handle redemption did much to determine the working modes of expression from the men of feeling down to Melville and Baudelaire, as well as the Decadents at the end of the nineteenth century. In a sketch for what was to become the introductory pages of his *Confessions* Rousseau qualifies Enlightenment doctrine about universals with the observation that most men judge others by what they know of themselves, yet they know themselves only imperfectly. In an act of unparalleled generosity Jean-Jacques offers to reveal himself to other men so that they can make use of another model than themselves, and will therefore be able to judge from more than the instance afforded by their own sublime egotism. What he offers them can be offered only by himself: *"Nul ne peut écrire la vie d'un homme que lui-même. Sa manière d'être intérieure, sa véritable vie n'est connue que de lui."* [12] How, then, to communicate what only oneself can know? At the least he will require a new language of infinite subtlety and malleability, able to handle the extraordinary complexity at the center of subjective experience:

> *Il faudroit pour ce que j'ai à dire inventer un langage aussi nouveau que mon projet: car quel ton, quel style prendre pour débrouiller ce cahos immense de sentimens si divers, si contradictoires, souvent si vils et quelquefois si sublimes dont je fus san cesse agité?* [13]

Rousseau recognized that what Thoreau was to call "the inexpressible privacy of a life" required the extension of our capacities for expression. Though Rousseau cherished his subjective forms and flaunted their idiosyncrasy, the *Confessions* and *Rêveries* show how much he wanted (or claimed he wanted) to make contact with others, to make himself transparent, while realizing that the center of self revealed in the *Cinquième Promenade* and near the end of the *Confessions* was thoroughly (and perhaps happily) untouchable and inexpressible. He knew that he could never be reached at that point within consciousness where, in the *Cinquième Promenade,* he was aware only of the stasis of self and the sound of moving water. Thoreau had much the same sort of experience and cherished it as much as Rousseau did, but at the same time he too had to acknowledge that the enclosure of the self could be a form of felicitous incarceration. In *Walden* he wanted to speak of the ways in which his talent helped his own unreachable genius to explore its profundities. To speak in those terms he had to show that he was both subject and witness of himself, the self-conscious exemplar always aware of his consciousness going through whatever it was that he was experiencing. And he was his own witness in large part because, like Rousseau, he could not study such matters in anyone else: "Who shall say what prospect life offers to another? Could a greater miracle take place than for us to look through each other's eyes for an instant?" (*Walden,* 10). That point had been made several years before in the *Week:* "How can we *know* what we are *told* merely? Each man can interpret another's experience only by his own" (*Week,* 389). In 1857 it recurred in a bitter comment on lecturegoers: "I never yet recognized, nor was recognized by, a crowd of men. I was never assured of their existence, nor they of mine" (*J*, IX, 215).

Thoreau's assurance of the conditions of his own existence created the mode of *Walden.* The book is an autobiographical narrative, exemplary in intent, archetypal in structure. It offers a model by which those who wish to follow can achieve self-redemption; or as Thoreau terms the result early in the book, "self-emancipation even in the West Indian provinces of the fancy and imagination" (*Walden,* 7-8). Of course every limitation has to be acknowledged: both the process and the book are forced to face the problem that "it is, after all, always the first person that is speaking," and that barrier to knowledge has to create some enormous difficulties when one is examining a model of desirable experience. But Thoreau's introductory paragraph, which is a topic statement for the entire narrative, is so organized that a way of working with the limitations is implicit from the beginning. The sequence of components in the first sentence of the book is the crucial point: he begins with a description of his existential state ("I lived alone"); follows it with a generalized locative statement ("in the woods"); intensifies the description of his aloneness ("a mile from any neighbor"); adds the element of self-sufficiency ("in a house which I had built myself"); and only then tells of the specific place in which this happened ("on the shore of Walden Pond, in Concord, Massachusetts"). It is obvious that the qualities of Thoreau's experience are more significant than the precise place in which it occurred. In fact, the reference to Concord is a limiting factor, because without it the statement would apply to any man who had been living independently, away from civilization and his neighbors; that is, it could exemplify a state which men can achieve anywhere. The remarks on the obstructions to knowledge, which follow immediately after, are also statements about universal experience, though the difficulties Thoreau describes in the second paragraph are inescapable, whereas the existential state referred to in the first has to be willed. The full meaning of this juxtaposition becomes evident in the succeeding paragraphs. In effect, Thoreau argues that though he cannot talk about "I" or "Thou" because their deepest reaches are unassailable or incommunicable, he can talk about "We." Using his own experience of "self-emancipation" as a concrete universal, an event which took place in Concord ("I have travelled a good deal in Concord") but could equally well have occurred in Bangor or Worcester, Thoreau makes his autobiographical narrative into an exemplum for all those who are enslaved by encumbrances. He talks about "I" because he has to (whom else can he know as well?) and because he wants to (you cannot know me in my profound genius, but you can do what I have done). If "each one's world is but a clearing in the forest," then Thoreau's small clearing which was redeemed from the woods beside Walden images what he can communicate of his own efforts at self-reclamation. The efforts are graphic, as befits an exemplary narrative, but their purport is subjective, clearing "the

West Indian provinces of the fancy and the imagination." Though parts of his own mind may be private, he can, after all, affect the minds of others.

For some Romantics the conditions of partly enforced privacy confirmed the need for a public feast of images (what Hölderlin calls a *Friedensfeier*) in which all men could participate. Private experiences can be sent across the perimeters of self through the reflection of subjective events in public analogies. The *"langage aussi nouveau que mon projet"* which Rousseau looked for also had to have areas in it where other men could meet him, however unparalleled his experiences; but Rousseau was no mythographer and depended on precision of statement to communicate the idiosyncrasies of selfhood. His aim, so he claimed, was absolute self-revelation, the total disclosure of that which only he could know. Yet such pure exposure was neither possible nor (given the polemical intent of his various confessions) entirely desirable. The result was both less and more, a withholding and reshaping that turned autobiographical narrative into an order of high artifice, with a persona through whom Rousseau could satisfy every impulse. At the opposite extreme were mythographers of immense ambition such as Blake and Hölderlin. Their systems were syncretic, with some components that were self-generated along with others drawn from universal experience; but in both cases the systems were based on radical archetypes which were more or less available to the skilled and erudite reader. Each system was informed by an idiosyncrasy of vision that sought to enliven the universal as well as give body to the most private modes of seeing. In each the forms of expression (e.g., the language of Hölderlin's late hymns or the organization of Blake's pantheon) made evident the awesome struggle to open up and give a voice to the least accessible areas of the self.

Thoreau shared qualities with both of the extremes. Like Rousseau, he shaped the givens of subjective reality into a narrative that is as much a loaded statement as it is an autobiography. But if Thoreau was more concerned with the exemplariness of his actions than with their uniqueness, he was also less confident than Rousseau that the deepest intimacies could be made available. He therefore looked for modes of delineating his experience which could encompass the accessible experiences of others as well as his own. There are several related quests in *Walden*: one is a hunt for those images which could bring to the bright surface of open experience all that went on in "in the Walden Pond of [Thoreau's] own nature." At the beginning of *Walden* he announces the difficulties of privacy and then proceeds to build his book on the most universal of all archetypes, the analogy of natural cycles with the rhythms of human life. The result is a magnificently imagined counterpoint of private and public language in which the imagery of depth, of solitude, and of the inwardness of the center of self is woven in with the universal cycles of day and season. The play-off of these masses, all of which share an identical form, is one of the activities which gives to *Walden* its most profound and stirring life. (I shall discuss the homology of these forms in the final chapter.) And that counterpoint, we now see, is based on a pervasive Thoreauvian paradox: his insistence upon contacting others but at a distance—"The value of a man is not in his skin, that we should touch him" (*Walden*, 136)—is counteracted by his recognition that such contacts may not occur at those levels where we are most ourselves. We *can* meet through the cycles, however, and from there each of us can go back to the areas which are peculiarly his own. Of course there is always that community of scholars which acts in a world beyond time and place; but theirs is a communion within consciousness, and that is not the sort in which one can live always. *Walden* itself pictured an exemplary instance, not a permanent mode of being. Thoreau could no more make a life out of that instance than he could live continually in the unbounded community of consciousness. When he left the pond he still had to live with and within himself— because he wanted to and because he was forced to—and he still had to seek out ways in which the redemptive imagination could work productively with what was just outside the edge of his own private perimeter—other men, Concord, and nature.

The problem was to express the copresence of necessity and desire in the self's relation to experience, and to do so in a manner that fulfilled the possibilities of a Transcendental consciousness. On the whole, Throreau seemed to find less difficulty when he worked with nature (as opposed to other men or Concord), perhaps because he felt less need to be concerned about the requisite spaces when he was dealing with natural objects. One of his mind's finest tricks came from the Transcendental impulse to look for analogies of consciousness in nature. In Emersonian terms, this meant that the mind used nature to understand itself; that is, it redeemed a piece of nature for man. On occasion Thoreau could do this to perfection. In a journal entry for January 23, 1841, he shaped out an image of desire which seemed so apt that he used it again the following year in "The Natural History of Massachusetts":

> When I detect a beauty in any of the recesses of nature, I am reminded, by the serene and retired spirit in which it requires to be contemplated, of the inexpressible privacy of a life,—how silent and unambitious it is. The beauty there is in mosses will have to be considered from the holiest, quietest nook. (*J*, I, 174)

Here is a satisfactory (if unconsciously poignant) analogy in which both seclusion and contact are present and perfectly balanced. Each element stays sequestered within its own enclosure, where it is naturally at home; in this case they are the recess within nature and his "holiest, quietest nook." When he is within his private place, contact with the other comes through contemplation, an activity which requires of him "a serene a retired spirit," a calm, comfortable withdrawal from the rest of experience. The inexpressible privacy of this life, as it turns out, is necessary for the finest kind of contemplation. Nothing is there but the two nooks and their inhabitants—the observer and his object. There is no question of nature reaching out to meet him. What he saw set his analogical imagination actively to work doing what consciousness likes to do best, transforming the world into images of itself. His mind jumps from the object to the state of consciousness he has to assume in order to see it properly; and that state, "serene and retired," echoes the conditions of the natural recess. From there his imagination, excited by analogies, goes deep into the sequestered self at the center of being, a position which also reflects the conditions of the recess, but at the most profound reaches of subjectivity. Then he moves upward and outward to the nook, the final analogy to the natural recess, and a necessary one because, to complete the system of analogies, the place of contemplation has to match the place to be contemplated.

This passage shows how the mind can be itself, give full respect to its own organization, and still redeem nature for men in general as well as for itself in particular. Thoreau accomplished this by establishing a series of echoing structures whose repetitions would indicate a basic link between the order of consciousness and what is outside of it. The process is exactly like that in Coleridge's "Frost at Midnight" in which "the idling Spirit . . . every where/ Echo or mirror seeking of itself . . . makes a toy of Thought." In Coleridge's poem, and all the other Conversation poems, consciousness looks for such echoes in order to fulfill its role as arbiter between the self and experience. What Coleridge calls at one point "the self-watching subtilizing mind" brings the world and the self together by finding the self in the world; a process which, in effect, transforms the world into the self.[14] (It is the failure of that process which is recorded in "Dejection.") Thoreau goes about it in a manner best described in the rhetoric of American Transcendentalism. He put the quest for echoes this way in 1853:

> He is the richest who has most use for nature as raw material of tropes and symbols with which to describe his life. (*J*, V, 135)

> Is it not as language that all natural objects affect the poet? He sees a flower or other object, and it is beautiful or affecting to him because it is a symbol of his thought, and what he indistinctly feels or perceives is matured in some other organization. The objects I behold correspond to my mood. (*J*, V, 359)

Success in this process of turning fact into subjective reality indicated that the imagination was adequate to its redemptive job, that it could face up to what was required of it, whatever it happened to meet outside. But the various limitations of consciousness ensured that the adequacy of Thoreau's imagination would always be under challenge. Certainly its efficacy had been called into question by his repeated recognition of the inaccessibility at the center of self. The order of self which he had generated out of his private experience and the wildness of his surroundings did not always suffice to bridge those gaps between desire and capability. In fact, though the clearing in the forest imaged the ability of the mind to win a piece of experience for itself, this order of the self contained problems inherent in its very structure; for example, the center could well be too far from the edge where the rest of the world began, sunk too deeply within the structure that housed it. When that happened the order defeated itself, and the imagination was shown to be, to some degree, inadequate. The order explained how the imagination could build a home for a self-sufficient consciousness out of the facts of American experience, but the imagination could encounter an impasse when Thoreau wanted to qualify self-sufficiency in his meetings with other men. Meetings with nature, however, seemed to be another matter: there it looked as though he would encounter no such rebuff because he would not ask from nature what he could sometimes hope for from men.

The passage on the natural recess is a fine instance of analogical wit successfully at work. His consciousness runs through a series of interlocking mirrors which takes him from the observation of external nature to the deep recesses of the self and then out again, when the requisite attitude is established, to the equivalent nook from which he can watch natural beauty being itself in delightful sequestration. There is no sense of struggle while he finds a place for himself in nature and nature in himself. All the counterparts click comfortably into place as though he were tracing their activities on a map; and that of course is just what he was doing, playing again at his survey of the American spirit as he charts the landscape shared by American consciousness and American scenery. At this point the adequacy is perfect.

But there are other kinds of demands to be made upon the imagination that confronts nature, other challenges and requirements to be met. On the day following the entry about the nook Thoreau theorized, in rather straightforward Emersonian terms, about the primacy of spirit: "It is more proper for a spiritual fact to have suggested an analogous natural one, than for the natural fact to have preceded the spiritual in our minds" (*J,* I, 175). Considering the hierarchy of spirit, it is better for consciousness to lead down toward that which is, in Emerson's words, "a remoter and

inferior incarnation of God, a projection of God in the unconscious." [15] This sounds as though nature should always yield easily
to mind, just as the tool should to the workman's talent. After all,
Emerson also said that "Nature is made to conspire with spirit to
emancipate us," which is his version of Thoreau's "self-emancipation even in the West Indian provinces of the fancy and
imagination." [16] Nature, in this view, is the silent, subordinate
partner in our redemption. But when Thoreau speaks of making a
clearing in the wilderness, he knows that he is robbing a piece of
itself from nature and that what is out there is, in part and in those
circumstances, an antagonist. At those times he speaks in a
language of struggle: "somewhat is always clearing, familiar and
worn by us, appropriated and fenced in some way, and reclaimed
from Nature" (*Walden*, 130). The mind appropriates nature
whether it uses the world as a source of lovely analogies or as the
field we reclaim in order to make our selves. But when Thoreau
had to carve a clearing out of nature his work was different in
mode and tone (i.e. in his awareness of resistance) than when he
made quiet nooks for sequestered contemplation. In the passage on
the recess there is no sense of the hard digging the mind had to go
through when it accomplished the spiritual equivalent of the
farmer's work. And these differing instances are only samplings of
the flexibility Thoreau had to keep continually in play if he
wanted the imagination to be adequate to all it could meet.

  Though there is a general progress in his overall development,
there is no single Thoreauvian stance vis-à-vis nature and therefore
no one, unvaried mode of the redemptive imagination. The
movements of his imaginative life show a continual series of
struggles (most of them met with delight) because he was aware of
nature's infinite variability and he wanted to face every fluctuation
with the mode which it required of him. Each voice that he heard
from nature demanded a slight shift in his own voice. And that
requirement is complicated by our wanderings because whenever
we move we bring a new nature into being: "The particular laws
[of nature] are as our points of view, as to the traveller, a mountain
outline varies with every step, and it has an infinite number of
profiles, though absolutely but one form" (*Walden*, 290-91). That is
one of the reasons why Thoreau will say, "I doubt if you can ever
get Nature to repeat herself exactly" (*J*, X, 97).[17] In his own work

this meant continual wariness and adaptation. There were moments of conflict and imposition, and others with calm suggestions leading to warm analogies. There were moments of eased floating down a stream and others containing a shocked stare at a terrestrial moonscape. Ultimately all these different contacts are events in a battle for primacy, whatever their mode and tone. They are always concerned with how the imagination makes a place for the self in the world, and how the self learns to get along within that place.

Thoreau is always aware of the kind of nature that happens to be out there at the perimeters of this being, the place where mind and nature meet. It is the business of the probing elements of consciousness to test the forms of nature that are out there. His extraordinary alertness, which is usually in a state of relaxed awareness, will then respond to that test and adjust his subjective modes according to the modes of the objects which face him. Since a different reading of nature requires a different aspect of the self to do it, the result at each event is a different view of the relations of self and nature. There were few Romantics anywhere who could match the fluidity and subtlety of these changes in Thoreau, though he shared that adaptability of self with Rousseau, Coleridge, and many others. In *Walden* Thoreau proves himself to be a master of such flexibility, an adept at responding to "the variety and capacity of that nature which is our common dwelling" (*Walden,* 124). Toward the end of the chapter on "Sounds," for example, Thoreau speaks of owls and the world of swamp and wood that surrounds them. During the day the race of daylight creatures expresses the meaning of nature appropriate to that race. But at twilight the creatures change, the quality of nature is transformed, and what it says of the human self (nature always speaks of the human self when a Transcendentalist listens) opens up the gray recesses of man's being:

> I rejoice that there are owls. Let them do the idiotic and maniacal hooting for men. It is a sound admirably suited to swamps and twilight woods which no day illustrates, suggesting a vast and undeveloped nature which men have not recognized. They represent the stark twilight and unsatisfied thoughts which all have. (*Walden,* 125)

There is nothing especially frightening about nature here, but the "idiotic and maniacal hooting" is unsettling, in part for what it points to in the analogous twilight depths of the human soul. In the original journal entry Thoreau had mentioned "the stark, twilight, unsatisfied thoughts I have" (*J*, III, 122-23). The change from the personal reference to an inclusive one ("which all have") made the recognition of the depths a bit more palatable; he is, after all, a representative figure. A few pages later, at the beginning of the chapter on "Solitude," Thoreau evokes a moment that is analogous to certain events Rousseau recorded in his *Rêveries* and occasionally in the *Confessions*. The difference lies in Thoreau's emphasis on sympathy with the external, a point about which Rousseau is more hesitant because, in his own version of these events, the directions of his interest tend to be more inner than outer. (Of course, in other kinds of occurrences, in the *Rêveries* and elsewhere, Rousseau can radiate sympathy.)

In this passage Thoreau moves around in nature with "a strange liberty," associating with nature as "a part of herself" (*Walden*, 129). Nothing particularly attracts him, yet "all the elements are unusually congenial to me." The association reaches such an intensity that he feels along with what he sees, his own state reflecting and offering a counterpoint to the fluttering and rippling which reach him from outside. However, though the qualities of his being balance the qualities outside, the outside does not supplant most of what had been in consciousness, as it did in the comparable event recorded in Rousseau's *Cinquième Promenade*.[18] With Rousseau the rhythms of the waves took the place of all other movements in his consciousness. But with Thoreau the inner reaches of consciousness are still kept somewhat aloof, even in this moment of exceptional closeness. The landscapes match, but they do not coalesce:

> Sympathy with the fluttering alder and poplar leaves almost takes away my breath; yet, like the lake, my serenity is rippled but not ruffled. These small waves raised by the evening wind are as remote from storm as the smooth reflecting surface.

This is not the gray, unsatisfied self of the passage on the owls because what meets him here requires a different attunement of the potential of consciousness. Thoreau has to stay in persistent alertness, shifting subjective rhythms as the rhythms from outside change pattern and contour. But sometimes the requisite attunement is so fine that a slight weakening of alertness can lead to disaster. Three pages later there is a modulation in tone which is actually a continuation of what he had done at the beginning of the chapter. He moves from ideas of sympathy and the counterpart flow of rhythm to àn assertion about a "sweet and beneficent society in nature ... an infinite and unaccountable friendliness" (*Walden*, 132). Here, where the pitch had to be exact, Thoreau went slightly off. The tone of the reciprocal landscapes turns from a surprised recognition of congruence to an embarrassing bathos: "Every little pine needle expanded and swelled with sympathy and befriended me." In justification one could say that in looking for every possible variation of relationship Thoreau had to come across this one too.

Finally (though this by no means exhausts the variations but only this set of examples) there can be disorientations in the matching of the landscapes, moments when the congruence suddenly breaks and the need to find it again leads to a new knowledge of self and its relationship to the world. Near the end of the chapter on "The Village" Thoreau speaks of going astray in the woods. The patterns of action are traditional, with quiet echoes of Dante mixed in among the modes of his own rhetoric. In our walks, he argues, we guide ourselves unconsciously by familiar points in the landscape. But our orientation, that is, our congruence with nature, is actually so tenuous that we can lose it with surprising ease; and only then do we truly see the kind of nature in which we have been walking: "not till we are completely lost, or turned round,—for a man needs only to be turned round once with his eyes shut in his world to be lost,—do we appreciate the vastness and strangeness of nature" (*Walden*, 171). Our relations are revealed to be contingent, and accidents can open up darker aspects of nature which go back to the swamps and woods of the maniacal owls. But there is no sense of personal disturbance in this passage, no fear of what the discomforting oddness out there beyond our periphery might point to in ourselves. Out of his disorientations come a rethinking of order, a new awareness of self-placement, a reshaping of relations at a level more complex than before the turnaround which revealed the strangeness of nature:

Every man has to learn the points of compass again as often as he awakes, whether from sleep or any abstraction. Not till we are lost, in other words, not till we have lost the world, do we begin to find ourselves, and realize where we are and the infinite extent of our relations. (*Walden,* 171)

The passage hints at something more than a return to congruence with the woods: "where we are" in this context is surely not where we were before, because the old world is not returned to but lost. The echo of New Testament renunciation ("not till we have lost the world") weaves in with the figure of the Dantean woods to make out of Concord what Thoreau always said it was, a place where archetypal occurrences are commonplace.

This last quotation asserts a superiority of the mind to place, that is, an ability of the mind to triumph over place and makes use of it for the purposes of self-understanding. An event which can occur in nature is taken up and described in language which, drawing on the previous context of that language, leads out of nature. In effect, we are told how we can use the world for our personal reclamation. Several years earlier than this, in a passage already quoted from the *Week* (see page 5 above), Thoreau prefigured these comments by displaying his confidence in the stability of individual being. When a person seems to be lost, it is not he but "the places that have known him, *they* are lost." The self is certain; the world is not. Though there is nothing in the passage from the *Week* about using the world, it is clear that both of these selections assume that the meeting of consciousness and nature is not an encounter of equals. But Thoreau could not settle comfortably into that implication, though he was very well aware of it and where it could lead. The passage in the *Week* on the self's superiority to place is countered by another which, by its very presence in the same book, shows that Thoreau knew what the problems were and was prepared to talk about them if not quite to solve them:

We would not always be soothing and taming nature, breaking the horse and the ox, but sometimes ride the horse wild and chase the buffalo. The Indian's intercourse with Nature is at least such as admits of the greatest independence of each. If he is somewhat of a stranger in her midst, the gardener is too much of a familiar. There is something vulgar and foul in the latter's closeness to his mistress, something noble and cleanly in the former's distance. (*Week*, 55-56)

These comments come in the midst of one of Thoreau's early meditations on wildness. A few lines before this he had reflected that "there may be an excess of cultivation as well as of anything else," and then he turned to the Indian, who "by the wary independence and aloofness of his dim forest life . . . preserves his intercourse with his native gods, and is admitted from time to time to a rare and peculiar society with Nature." Several lines after the comments about the gardener's excessive familiarity with nature Thoreau observes that "steel and blankets are strong temptations; but the Indian does well to continue Indian." Obviously he wanted for the Indian what he said he wanted for himself, an independence from those amenities to which one could become slavish. It is a far more complex thing, however, to have a relationship with *nature* that "admits of the greatest independence of each," allowing each to take up a productive role in relation to the other and yet retain its ability to stand alone and self-contained. This is the same balance of gift and withdrawal, of simultaneous aloofness and participation, which was often as necessary to Thoreau as it was painfully elusive. In his exemplification of this ideal pattern the Indian is not just a simplistic figure out of popular primitivism, and he is something more than even the self-sufficient savage who was built out of some hints from Montaigne and a muddy reading of Rousseau. The Indian's relation to nature, as Thoreau draws it here (he could work out a different picture of it at other times), is extraordinarily subtle: the Indian is respectful of all that is most to be protected within himself, and he is aware that nature has an independence and apartness that should be as inviolable as his own.

This observation on a sophisticated counterpoint of autonomy and participation had been made in a context that called for poems never heard in London or Boston: "There are other, savager and more primeval aspects of nature than our poets have sung. It is only white man's poetry" (*Week*, 56). Both nature and the Indian are radically savage and therefore keep up a perfect association. It surely follows, then, that white men will have difficulties because of their drive to cultivate; even garden plots are a violation of the integrity of man's natural partner. And there Thoreau ran into some prime difficulties. He was committed to the position that consciousness is assertive and redemptive, that is, necessarily aggressive because it is the business of mind to transform the world into the self. Whatever his views about nature, Thoreau never disavowed that elemental principle of Transcendentalism, however much he was impelled to qualify it at times. And whatever his disagreements with Emerson, Thoreau never gave up the idea that nature is made to conspire with us for our redemption, although his response to the facticity of nature was very different from that of Emerson. But if it is of the essence of mind to impose itself upon nature, if mind has to rob what is outside itself in order to build up its private stock—and Thoreau kept asserting these points throughout his life—then his desire to respect the independence of nature equally with his own had to run into trouble. The Indian whom Thoreau described seemed to have no such problems, and he was unlikely to share Thoreau's intense awareness of the impulse of consciousness to make a clearing for itself out of the forest which surrounds it.

Was Thoreau not, then, inferior to the Indian who could relate to nature under a condition which "admits of the greatest independence of each"? Thoreau could never play down the importance of the activities of consciousness or his joy in indulging them. Indeed, his life was spent in refining their possibilities in a daily practice which distilled and purified all the modes of relationship between nature and the mind. In that case, how could he permit nature to be itself and yet approach it with a consciousness whose very principles see the world as something that, however delightful, has to be used by man? How would it be possible to make the mind respectful, participatory, and redemptive all at once? Thoreau found it relatively simple to get out of Concord every day and to cleanse the town from himself by plunging into wildness; but he could find no obvious and clear solutions to the tensions between imposition and aloofness, and he put much of the force of his imaginative life into making those contraries productive. What he gathered of the Indian and what he knew of himself posed an immense challenge to the adequacy of his imagination.

2.

A Sort of Border Life

The wilderness Thoreau brooded on in the passage from the *Week* was the source of some of his most difficult problems as well as his subtlest joys. Though he could sentimentalize it as successfully as any of his Concord associates, the idea of wildness became for Thoreau the image (or the conduit) of a form of relationship between nature and the self that reached to levels of being which knew nothing of gardens and clearings. The relationship meant, among other things, that wildness and the imagination that reclaims could sometimes be at odds, though Thoreau knew that he needed them both. What wildness touches upon emerges on the first page of "Higher Laws" in *Walden,* in a passage so important to the understanding of Thoreau's imagination that I shall return to it a number of times. Though the passage fits into the context of wildness which permeates every aspect of Thoreau's work, there is nothing else in him which can match the depth of its atavism:

As I came home through the woods with my string of fish,

36

trailing my pole, it being now quite dark, I caught a glimpse of a woodchuck stealing across my path, and felt a strange thrill of savage delight, and was strongly tempted to seize and devour him raw; not that I was hungry then, except for that wildness which he represented. Once or twice, however, while I lived at the pond, I found myself ranging the woods, like a half-starved hound, with a strange abandonment, seeking some kind of venison which I might devour, and no morsel could have been too savage for me. The wildest scenes had become unaccountably familiar. (*Walden,* 210)

The meeting with the woodchuck is a moment of epiphany, the sudden opening out to Thoreau of a singular level of being he had known of and perhaps experienced but was unprepared to meet at that time and place. It is also a moment of temptation and an odd kind of hunger. Revelation, surprising or predicted, ought to be the fulfillment of desire, the full beholding of what one has always wanted to see; but this revelation offers no such satisfaction, since it only forces upon him an unresolved urge for contact. He does not devour the woodchuck raw though he would like to; and when he refers to his ravenous wanderings in the woods looking for some savage morsel, he does not say that he found any such food. This is no spiritual hunger, at least not in any sense which Emersonian or other orthodoxies would have condoned. Thoreau works with different affinities. The hunger is not only for the woodchuck's flesh, which is essentially a mediating element, but "for that wildness which he represented"; that is, Thoreau wants to eat the woodchuck so that he can absorb within himself both the wildness which is in the animal and the wildness which is symbolized by it. To eat the woodchuck, then, is to partake of the totemic animal. He would establish the most immediate kind of contact through absorption of the woodchuck and its wildness. Deep within the center of his own being is a wildness comparable in kind, though not in purity or intensity, to what he had glimpsed out there in all its furtiveness; in "Walking" Thoreau calls this subjective aspect the "wild savage in us" (*Excursions,* 237). His instinct for the proper mode of relationship with the woodchuck is therefore profound and exact: devouring would bring his own and the other wildness together in an intimacy so unparalleled that only totemism can offer it. This is not the sort of mystic union which rejects the body but, rather, one which celebrates flesh because flesh is the means toward union. The forms of intimacy with nature promulgated in the *Week* and the more complicated association at the beginning of the chapter on "Solitude" are of a very different order from the coalescence he wanted here. This primitivism goes deeper than all the delicacies of noble savagery, in part because of the accuracy of Thoreau's instinct in turning toward totemism, in part also because of the hunger for elemental contact which the instinct exemplifies.

But this is the center of wildness, not its entirety. The full scope touches on all that Thoreau imagined, from his map of the American spiritual landscape to the meaning of his occupation as a surveyor of the contours of Concord. His ideas about wildness include a peculiarly American parochialism, but, as I shall point out, they also reach to a level where chauvinism is transformed into a vision of international harmony. As the passage on the wood-chuck shows, Thoreau's sense of wildness implies an intricate order of the self and includes all that the self is and is not. Nothing about nature and its possibilities fascinated or unsettled him more than what consciousness could do with the forms of wildness.

Thoreau's fullest single statement about wildness is in "Walking," published a month after his death in 1862, though he had used versions of the text for lectures over the previous decade. The essay is a skillful collocation of various perceptions and modes of imagining which had appeared in the journals from the earliest entries, and in most of Thoreau's other essays and larger works. It shows that what had seemed to be a kaleidoscope of insights and revelations must have been unusually coherent at some level below immediate consciousness. But "Walking" is, finally, an insufficient piece, a brilliant statement made largely in Thoreau's public voice. It says nothing about what he knew of nature's otherness or, for that matter, about man's. Thoreau was aware that the essay was one-sided, and he cautioned the well-tuned reader in the second sentence: "I wish to make an extreme statement, if so I may make an emphatic one" *(Excursions,* 205). Some elements are going to be stressed beyond their legitimate proportions, with rhetoric displacing accepted standards of the reasonable. Thus, "Walking" takes much of its tone from exaggeration, what Thoreau usually called "extravagance"; that is, *extra-vagance,* wandering beyond the bounds of conventional experience. And that boundary-breaking is exactly that Thoreau does in the essay, though he never refers directly to the pun. Extravagance is one way of getting at the problem of adequacy, testing the imagination's capacity to stretch its limits and be up to all that is required of it. The full force of the pun emerges near the end of *Walden:*

> I fear chiefly lest my expression may not be *extra- vagant* enough, may not wander far enough beyond the narrow limits of my daily experience, so as to be adequate to the truth of which I have been convinced. *Extra vagance!* it depends on how you are yarded. ... I desire to speak somewhere *without* bounds. *(Walden,* 324)

The journal entry from which this passage is taken adds a remark about "wandering toward the more distant boundaries of a wider pasture" (*J,* VI, 100). These comments occur in 1854, in the middle of the decade when he was putting "Walking" together. It is possible that Thoreau ignored the pun in "Walking" because he had already made use of it in *Walden.* But there is no question that the essay's extraordinary wandering beyond the bounds, the breaking of the barriers which usually hem us in, is an attempt to do in rhetoric what he could not always do in life. That problem also emerges in the intricate structure of the essay itself. "Walking" has a remarkable organization and significant form. Its inner life grows from a number of interconnected movements that lead inevitably to the brilliant, if qualified, coda of the final pages.

The essay focuses on no particular walk but on the activity itself. Its interests are generic rather than specific, which means that Thoreau's imagination is led more directly than usual to the allegorical forms which so often control the shape of his movements. But he is pointedly particular about his direction. Thoreau indicates that in his walks he inevitably starts out toward the southwest, or at least "between west and south-southwest," a partly intuitive, partly canny choice that draws simultaneously on universal archetype, American myth, and Romantic precedent (217). The remark is one of Thoreau's usually sufficient signals that more than an ordinary point is being made. Coleridge's Mariner starts out in the same direction toward a similar form (though not result) of exploration and moves back again toward the place from which he came. He returns exactly as Thoreau does, renewed and somewhat more knowledgeable, though chastened and sociable in a way that is particular to his own case. In the general bent toward the west, however, there was no such return. "Walking" draws part of its paraphernalia from the current (and recurrent) American myth of westering, which by Thoreau's time had taken on specific, predictable contours, associated with Eden and a new, patriotic pastoralism. Thoreau's own movements reproduce a national impulse: "This is the prevailing tendency of my countrymen. I must walk toward Oregon, and not toward Europe" (218). But American images are themselves images of universal inclination, signifying, among other things, not only that America is in tune with the rhythms of mankind but that it is fulfilling the main business of all men: "And that way the nation is moving, and I may say that mankind progress from east to west" (218). And thus Thoreau stands in Concord as a home-grown concrete universal-ist, simultaneously parochial, patriotic, and archetypal. The ab-stractions are carefully organized over several pages so as to be increasingly inclusive. Their fusion is original to the degree that Thoreau bases it on the peculiarities of his own exploration: "I know not how significant it is, or how far it is an evidence of singularity, that an individual should thus consent in his pettiest walk with the general movement of his race" (218-19). It is indeed both singular and representative, based on Thoreau's idiosyncratic construction of the whole complex but indicative of perennial desire. And finally, Thoreau's personal explorations are themselves reiterations of a prevalent Romantic habit, that of making the breaking of new ground into a fertile image for the examination of self.

The newness which Thoreau breaks into is part of a series of interconnected perceptions which associate the new with the West and with wildness. They are also involved with forms of explora-tion that bring both essay and walker within sight of a new Elysium. Thoreau's series of associations echo those aspects of American myth which always put the pristine out in the wilder-ness, no matter how old and familiar the wild areas may have been to others. (Thoreau, like Cooper, was sometimes bothered by the fact that the wild was new only to white men, but he was never disturbed enough to shred his spiritual map.) Such American myths usually included some agent of the old who forced his way into the place of newness, so that his activity always kept him out beyond the boundary where the new and the wild began. In *A Yankee in Canada* Thoreau refers several times to the Canadian *coureurs de bois* who pushed into the western wilderness before anyone else, preceding even the American pioneers and giving the Americans the name for "prairie" *(Excursions,* 43; cf. 56 and 67-68). Those Canadians were far out and in deep, out at the edge of the known and beyond it, which brought them comfortably into the framework through which Thoreau structured the relations of the cleared and the unredeemed. His sense of analogy was busy with all these materials, finding out what he always wanted to find out about himself, that his activities were representative and brought together a myriad of levels of meaning within a single gesture:

> One who pressed forward incessantly and never rested from his labors, who grew fast and made infinite demands on life, would always find himself in a new country or wilderness, and surrounded by the raw material of life. He would be climbing over the prostrate stems of primitive forest-trees. *(Excursions,* 226)

The extravagant walker is one who pushes out boundaries. He is continually driving himself against the edge where the walked-upon or the cleared meets its opposite, forcing the perimeters of the known farther toward the west—a direction which was delightfully general and therefore useful to the cartography of the imagination since it could mean Maine, Montana, or the world just beyond Concord.

Considering the analogies of the self and the field, all those places cleared by the mind or the spade, we can see how walking becomes an activity of consciousness, indeed one of the primary tasks of the mind:

> The walker in the familiar fields which stretch around my native town sometimes finds himself in another land than is described in their owners' deeds, as it were in some far-away

field on the confines of the actual Concord, where her
jurisdiction ceases, and the idea which the word Concord
suggests ceases to be suggested. These farms which I have
myself surveyed, these bounds which I have set up, appear
dimly still as through a mist. (242)

Walking brings him to the edge where mind and nature meet; and
when he can be extra-vagant, it puts him out beyond all the old
boundaries: "For my part I feel that with regard to Nature I live a
sort of border life, on the confines of a world into which I make
occasional and transient forays only" (242).[1] Out there he can
know the new, even if such knowing means only to touch at
nature's vast strangeness. In his most successful walking he breaks
out of every kind of clearing, every place that has previously been
redeemed; and this includes not only those cleared areas he had to
perambulate in his business as surveyor—"these bounds which I
have set up"—but also those areas within consciousness into which
he had temporarily been confined because of the minor but
necessary business of making a living. Walking is a way of getting
out beyond personal limits, and walking into wildness is perhaps
the fullest possible way of making that happen. In *Walden* Thoreau
had been firm about the need to set up the requisite spaces, the
broad margins to his life, that make up the boundary between one
self and another. But with nature the situation was often very
different. At another point in the same book he turned the hunt for
wildness into a willful overstepping of personal perimeters: "We
need the tonic of wildness. . . . We need to witness our own limits
transgressed, and some life pasturing freely where we never
wander" *(Walden,* 317-18). Here a transgression is a move out of
the area of the reclaimed into wilder pastures, where another kind
of life crops its fodder in freedom. That is what comes of going
beyond perambulation into extravagance. The causes of Thoreau's
hunger for the woodchuck are becoming somewhat clearer as all
these images of desire come together in his elaborate wordplay.

   Thoreau's compulsion to know the new is as unique an
extension of the Romantic quest as is Baudelaire's similar desire to
probe *"au fond de l'inconnu pour trouver du* nouveau!" He knows how to
turn old forms into patterns for his own (and America's) case,

combining private idiosyncrasies with generic structures. Thus, though his exploratory consciousness acts out some well-established designs in English and European Romanticism, his ideas on wildness have little to do with any banal contrast of the wild with the urbane and the settled, though he brings in just enough of that distinction to ensure its presence as an underlying motif. Beyond the outer edges of the known is "the raw material of life," unused potential which has to be molded into a productive relationship with whatever is behind the walker *(Excursions,* 226). In back of him is the ordered world of the East with its finished forms; and the wild, after all, is the source from which civilization, the old and ordered, has always been made. Where a man meets the wild the future begins:

> I once came unexpectedly upon a solitary hunter's lodge, on the shore of a savage pond about 8 miles from Concord in whose (wild) garden patch a dead skunk and a loon were suspended for a scarecrow—and I sniffed the air with a frenzy of delight as if I were approaching the centre of a new civilization.—I scented the future from afar.[2]

Thus, if wildness and westering mean freedom for Thoreau ("Eastward I go only by force; but westward I go free"), they also draw heavily for some of their most complex implications on his reiterated association of the West with ideas about exceptional fertility (217). The West is the ground out of which new creations spring at a rate and with an abundance and intensity which are awesome to those whose focus is bound to the East. Thoreau follows current patterns of chauvinistic myth in making his associations hold on several levels, the view from east to west, from Europe to America, and from the American East Coast out toward the west: "Where on the globe can there be found an area of equal extent with that occupied by the bulk of our States, so fertile and so rich and varied in its productions, and at the same time so habitable by the European, as this is?" (220). Wildness comes to be imaged as primordial life not yet made into forms of civilization, but with an immense, somewhat ambiguous promise inherent in its burgeoning fertility. The civilized, the East, covers over the wild,

gets between us and the intense vitality within it ("The most alive
is the wildest" [226]); and this vitality comes from the energy
within the fertile world toward which the walker moves.

When civilization takes over and covers the wild with its
layers, the energy still springs out of the fructifying mold from
which the civilized world derives its sustenance. The layers on top
draw their life out of those below: "The civilized nations—Greece,
Rome, England—have been sustained by the primitive forest which
anciently rotted where they stand. They survive as long as the soil
is not exhausted" (229). Wildness, then, is aboriginal muck that is
used to create more advanced societies. It may be that the
American East Coast has followed Europe in using up the warm
life that lived before it and has been living on underneath it.
Thoreau is sometimes blatant in his association of the American
East with decadent Europe, a linkage which flattered no one.[3]
Usually, though, he was far more moderate, sounding much like
Whitman in the way he played with perspective in these matters:
in *A Yankee in Canada,* for example, he saw New England as a point
on the road between the Old World and the Far West *(Excursions,*
59). But whatever the tone of his attitude, Thoreau realized that
the further one goes toward the interior, the more the East Coast
fuses with the civilization that preceded it. Finally there are no
more distinctions between Boston and London, both of which may
well rest on barrenness.

"Walking" thus turns the static contrast of the urbane and the
unexplored into an interplay of varied movements, all of which are
dominated by one, the infinitely expansive impulse for westering.
As Thoreau frames it, there are no longer two fixed polarities, but
shifting points on a track that goes toward the west or southwest.
The points shift because whenever the explorer gets beyond the
wild that has been just ahead of him the wild changes character, or
at least ceases to be the only mode available. Civilization moves on
behind the one who walks ahead. It covers over the wild with
successive layers as culture follows the walker down the track
toward the west. This comes to mean that the further westward of
civilization one can stay, the closer one gets toward the source of
vitality, the ultimate stratum, the absolutely wild. The move
west—or into the Maine woods or even the woods around
Concord—is therefore a drive toward the creative center of being,

the warm hearth of absolute potential out of which all creativity
(culture and the civilized) emerges. *That* move is a radical gesture
of considerable import to the life of Thoreau's imagination.

In fact, many of Thoreau's movements, and particularly the
search for wildness, are variant forms of the essential quest for the
creative center of being. It is his need to be at the edges of
experience or to get out toward them and down toward the
beginnings of energy that drives Thoreau, the walker in his
microcosm, out of Concord toward the fields and swamps. A fan of
bogs and fens, he found hope and future in "the impervious and
quaking swamps," and he often discovered that when some
farmstead interested him, he "was attracted solely by a few square
rods of impermeable and unfathomable bog,—a natural sink in one
corner of it" *(Excursions,* 227). A lover of muck, he admired one of
his employers, the owner of three patches of swamp, whom he once
saw swimming desperately, up to his neck in his own property.
That same man also cherished the potential of another piece of
swampland that he owned: "he remarked to me, true to his
instincts, that he would not part with it for any consideration, on
account of the mud which it contained. And that man intends to
put a girdling ditch round the whole in the course of forty months,
and so redeem it by the magic of his spade" (230).

At this point Thoreau is edging up once again to some
paradoxes which we have seen him touch on before: his passion for
pristine wildness is countered by his admiration for those who
respect the possibilities for growth in the root sources of energy,
those who know its true value and would use it accordingly: "I
think that the farmer displaces the Indian even because he redeems
the meadow, and so makes himself stronger and in some respects
more natural" (230). The contrast to the passage from the *Week*
concerning the Indian's respect for his own and nature's independence is startling. It reveals with absolute clarity the basic tensions
between Thoreau's twin desires—one for radical wildness and
another for reclamation—and the paradoxes and contradictions to
which the tensions will lead him. Here as elsewhere the farmer is a
natural redeemer, whether of meadows or of swamps. He is the
counterpart in the fields to the one whose imagination works with
the swamps of the spiritual wilderness. For awhile Thoreau was
both: that is, his job in the sojourn at Walden was to bring

together the work of his arms and the work of consciousness, reclaiming a piece of land and at the same time getting down toward the center where all the warm life is. His feeling for swamps helped him to make that difficult job clearer to himself. In the swamps are "the strength, the marrow, of Nature" (228); and marrow is what savages like the Hottentots, with their admirable instinct for metaphor, find most delightful. He knew how to apply that finding to himself: "The Hottentots eagerly devour the marrow of the koodoo and other antelopes raw. . . . Give me a wildness whose glance no civilization can endure,—as if we lived on the marrow of koodoos devoured raw" (225). Thoreau knew all the meanings of marrow and how his move to the pond was profoundly connected with those meanings: "I went to the woods because I wished to live deliberately, to front only the essential facts of life. . . . I wanted to live deep and suck out all the marrow of life" *(Walden,* 90-91). "To front" was one of Thoreau's favorite verbs for confronting, for being up at the edge against something. It was what one did when one faced the elements of essential wildness.

Several pages after this comment about his designs at the pond Thoreau repeats the association of fronting and digging down toward the absolute "till we come to a hard bottom and rocks in place, which we can call *reality,* and say, This is, and no mistake" *(Walden,* 98). There he reaches the core of pure being, the place where he can only point and say "this is"—it exists. But he goes on to show that when one stands "fronting and face to face to a fact" that too is a pure confrontation, this time with the facticity of reality; and that encounter is so dangerous that it can lead to a joyous slaying: "you will see the sun glimmer on both its surfaces, as if it were a cimeter, and feel its sweet edge dividing you through the heart and marrow, and so you will happily conclude your mortal career." Confronting a fact, we discover, can result in an insight so piercing that the fact, in its turn, penetrates to his own marrow, where he is sweetest. Like Keats, he is conquered by the identity of truth and beauty in the actual. The fact exposes him as he exposes it, and that mutuality of revelation announces not only the most perfect form of congeniality with nature but the way in which a highly developed consciousness can open up all sorts of levels in every mode of reality, including his own.

If this enterprise has its risks, it also shows the mind performing some of its finest feats. Thoreau knew that those activities of consciousness which root toward the core of reality (or face it in a fact) are the most creative because they have worked out the difficult mode by which one gains access to the center of being. Since the encounter with the center is the most exacting task of all, it requires consciousness to operate at full stretch and with all the adequacy it can muster. Fronting is one of those activities of consciousness; opening a clearing beside the pond is another; and so too is the act of writing, the gesture by which consciousness seeks to make sense out of what it has learned about "the marrow of life." Thoreau thought over these attributes of writing early in 1842 and later entered the point among his meditations on composition in the *Week:* "The talent of composition is very dangerous,—the striking out the heart of life at a blow, as the Indian takes off a scalp. I feel as if my life had grown more outward when I can express it" *(Week,* 351; cf. *J,* I, 349). All of these associations of fronting, the digging toward reality, and the perils of a spiritual scalping had come together already in the *Week,* in a major passage which contains the germ of Thoreau's most basic activities, including his reasons for settling beside the pond:

> The frontiers are not east or west, north or south; but wherever a man *fronts* a fact, though that fact be his neighbor, there is an unsettled wilderness between him and Canada, between him and the setting sun, or, farther still, between him and *it.* Let him build himself a log house with the bark on where he is *fronting* IT, and wage there an Old French war for seven or seventy years, with Indians and Rangers, or whatever else may come between him and the reality, and save his scalp if he can. (323-24)

Those materials in *Walden* which echo this passage say little about the struggle outlined here. That may be because the passage is prospective and the specific act that it urges, building a cabin at the place of fronting, was already over by the time of the later book. Of course there were other quests for the wild center, none so extensive as the two years at the pond, but versions of it all the same. The act beside Walden was one of a number of similar gestures, more evident than its counterparts because it was the longest-lasting and most productive, as well as the one which went as close to the meaning of the whole activity as Thoreau could get in this life. But he had made the move even before the long fronting at the pond. The journey recorded in the *Week* had set the pattern: the goal of his quest, the place which Thoreau could reach only by a long ascent, was the fountainhead of the Merrimack River at the summit of Agiocochook. Like all of Thoreau's books, the *Week* embodied a search for the point of origin, the essential source. The digging for reality beside the pond (which he did while he was writing the *Week*) was the mirror image of this ascent; going down and within in search of the absolute is, for the Romantics, both equal (in result) and opposite (in form) to a spiritual ascent. (E. T. A. Hoffmann's heroes could find in a mine what Sénancour's Obermann found on a mountain.)

When Thoreau put together the material that was to go into *The Maine Woods,* he returned, in the essay on "Ktaadn," to the idea of the journey up the mountain; and that essay, first published in 1848, records a trip made during the period in which Thoreau lived at the cabin. It appears, then, that the climb to Ktaadn and the sojourn at the pond were willed alternatives, opportunities for the imagination to exercise itself in different directions though for the same purpose. The experiences in Maine, however, were unlike the others in a most significant way because he was being led into the center of wildness by someone else, Joe Polis, for example. For the fullest action he would have to go alone, finding his own way, as he usually did in the cabin or in his walking around home. Finally, the walks out of Concord into the surrounding swamps and woods, the diurnal activities discussed generically in "Walking," are shown to be not only a reproduction of national and international movements but, even more important, a daily *imitatio* of the major actions performed in New Hampshire, at Walden, and in the Maine woods. Whatever Thoreau was doing, he was always, ultimately, doing the same thing.

As acts of *imitatio* his walks were sacramental movements, gestures of diurnal redemption. Thoreau treats each one of the walks, as well as the larger movements after which they were patterned, as an opportunity to cleanse off the crust made by his life in the town. Walking in itself refreshes, but the journey westward toward the edge where the wild begins takes him further, into the area of renewal where he can restore from its bed underneath what the day and the town had covered over. He mocks the courage of the mechanics and shopkeepers who can still go on while he has to go out to the woods and cleanse himself. In effect, each of the townspeople who is still working in the afternoon has by that time divided his own consciousness, split himself into separate pieces of observer and observed. And that condition, as Thoreau sees it, is a grotesque parody of the spectatorial consciousness that he found useful elsewhere: "Bonaparte may talk of the three-o'clock-in-the-morning courage, but it is nothing to the courage which can sit down cheerfully at this hour in the afternoon over against one's self whom you have known all the morning" (*Excursions,* 208). Even here Thoreau's language works simultaneously at a number of levels: he speaks of his sin at coming out when it is "too late to redeem the day." The sound of his irony fades along with his memory of the townspeople as he goes out toward a ritual of renewal, a redemptive act which it is a sin *not* to perform, an act which is a regeneration because it taps the generative sources.

The walk itself is a movement out toward nature's own marrow, the sacred place where he can dis-cover what is most truly his: "When I would recreate myself, I seek the darkest wood, the thickest and most interminable and, to the citizen, most dismal swamp. I enter a swamp as a sacred place, a *sanctum sanctorum.* There is the strength, the marrow of nature" (228). The import of this passage leads back to the beginning of the chapter on "Higher Laws" in *Walden* and the momentary impulse to partake of the woodchuck. That too was a sacramental act, impelled by the desire to partake of the flesh of the totemic animal and therefore of his wildness. Here in the swamp he feels the urge to get at the sweet center of nature and therefore, as he points out, to share in nature's strength. The gesture through which one reaches out beyond the edges of the cleared world is an attempt at reconciliation as well as regeneration. It is a bid toward bringing oneself together with the core of wildness. More precisely, it is an attempt to affiliate the inmost layer of his own self, his private stratum of wildness and incipient fertility, with its counterpart outside. Thoreau was always looking for sufficient forms to define such strange impulses. "Walking" is paradigmatic, a compact and unusually dense summary of major patterns in Thoreau's perception, and it solves the problem of imaginative sufficiency through some complex relationships among those patterns. In the essay the movement westward into the wild is paralleled by another movement—interlocked, complementary, and yet paradoxically opposed—a motion within the self which goes down toward the wild underlying the layers of the civilized ego.[4] The pattern of identical gestures allies both of the movements which led Thoreau down toward the fertile core, balancing off the wildness outside by a subjective counterpart: "A familiar name cannot make a man less strange to me. It may be given to a savage who retains in secret his own wild title earned in the woods. We have a wild savage in us, and a savage name is perchance somewhere recorded as ours" (237). Our private, untamed name, the title of the essential self, is at best known only to intimates; as Thoreau puts it in the source passage from the journal, "I seem to hear pronounced by some of his kin at such a time his original wild name in some jaw-breaking or else melodious tongue" (*J*, II, 209-10).

Further, to keep all the well-established associations intact, Thoreau has to acknowledge that the wildness concealed within him and imaged by the name emerges from the source of all fertility, which is always to be found in a westerly direction. He shows his awareness of the need for subjective westering in a passage that ought to have been in "Walking": "Let us migrate interiorly without intermission, and pitch our tent each day nearer the western horizon. The really fertile soils and luxuriant prairies lie on this side the Alleghanies" (*J*, I, 131). The underworld, whether in its private or external segments, is therefore a prime source of rejuvenation for Thoreau. His trips down and within are nothing like those of Odysseus or Aeneas, who found the dark places to be full only of memories and anticipations. Thoreau's burrowings are the acts of a hungry consciousness which wants confirmation of the bedrock of reality and then a coalescence with it, a linkage of its wildness with his own. The way to self-understanding, which is also an understanding of universal fertility, leads below through layers imposed from above. If we want to grow we must always be groping toward the deepest place: "Every tree sends its fibres forth in search of the Wild" (224).

The homology of consciousness and nature, articulated in layers and cores, makes possible an intricate interplay of disparateness and identity which is brought out fully in "Walking." Because of the parallel structures we can protect the privacy and idiosyncrasy of genius and still, through the process of analogy, stay intimately tied to the world we find so fascinating. Thoreau looks for an association which, by its nature (or actually by *his*), cannot be permanent but will at least bring him together for awhile with vital depth. The town will dull his awareness of wildness, but he can "redeem the day," and therefore reclaim the wildness within the self, whenever he chooses. In effect, this means that he needs elastic or permeable boundaries, not fixed ones. They have to give under the drive of his hunger to partake of wildness, though in the end they draw back to their original shape, the perimeters of Concord and the self. The homology does not resolve the tensions between privacy and association, but it does contain them. It satisfies just so long as what we see out there is something we would not object to seeing in ourselves.

By this point it has become clear that Thoreau's reading of American experience cannot be separated from the qualities and organization of the mind that does the reading. His mind's awareness of its own order, and of the order and meaning of all that is outside it, led him to draw up the map that I have called, alternatively, imaginative or spiritual. (The extent to which Thoreau was aware of drawing it up is neither definable nor especially relevant.) The vast wildness, speckled with variously sized clearings, was an image not only of American physical and spiritual experience but of the landscape in which consciousness and nature faced off against each other. Certain forms of private experience were, in part, open and available for analysis because they were echoed in what men had been doing publicly in America. Thoreau's chart of his world gave him considerable control over the ramifications of his daily experience. It was clearly an adequate tool, sufficiently flexible, encompassing and accurate so that his travels (in and out of the mind) could be traced on it, and all the places that he reached could be located on it with a good deal of precision. If those travels included an occasional hunt to satisfy a craving for woodchuck meat, his sense of where he was located and where the woodchuck was located—that is, his sense of clearings, boundaries, and the wildness within and without—was given its shape by the contours sketched out on the chart. And if it appeared easier to reach over the edge toward wildness than it did to reach from the center of one clearing to the center of another, the chart would at least show him where the other clearings— Concord and other men—could be found, and that was something too.

While he was working over these contours Thoreau had to keep in mind that this landscape was a relatively new one to white faces. Thus, the fullest definition of its properties required an understanding of the ways in which it differed from old landscapes. From his earliest writings, even his college essays, Thoreau carried on a rather elaborate series of comments on non-American landscape, in part out of conventional jingoism, but also because he came to sense that the idiosyncrasies of the American landscape were profoundly connected with his own. Much of his commentary on the landscape of the European imagination is infused with an amused chauvinism. When Thoreau looked back over his shoulder at Anglo-European literature, he would speak at times with a warm, witty haughtiness, in the tones of a new Adam looking out from a fresh paradise at the old fallen world. He stood there in the carefully devised role of the privileged observer, commenting with a light mockery that was affectionate, though unsparing, about the tameness of its target. "Walking" was a model of this attitude:

> English literature, from the days of the minstrels to the Lake Poets,—Chaucer and Spenser and Milton, and even Shake-speare, included,—breathes no quite fresh and, in this sense, wild strain. It is an essentially tame and civilized literature, reflecting Greece and Rome. Her wilderness is a greenwood, her wild man a Robin Hood. There is plenty of genial love of Nature, but not so much of Nature herself. Her chronicles inform us when her wild animals, but not when the wild man in her, became extinct. (231)

"Wordsworth," he wrote in his journal in 1841, "is too tame for the Chippeway" (*J*, I, 273). He even doubts whether the European nightingale can match the "unexplored wildness and fertility" in the song of the American thrush (*J,* IV, 263). Thoreau applies exactly the same criteria to the forms of nature out of which both Wordsworth and the nightingale emerged. In a number of passages in the journal and elsewhere he compares the landscapes of Europe and America for their relative fertility and lushness, for the depths of the wildness within them. In those comparisons European nature always comes up short. It is arid as well as tame, while America is humid, fertile, and primitive; in Thoreau's description, it is never quite so lush as Chateaubriand had made it but has all the potency of a rank wildness that begins just outside the towns of New England (cf. *J,* II, 147).

Such comparisons of European and American potential had long been commonplace before Thoreau made them. But for the American Romantics, because they were Romantics, the particularities of the American landscape had an importance beyond their immediate glories. In his "Essay on American Scenery" (1835) Thomas Cole puts succinctly what Thoreau was later to elaborate; and at the same time Cole touches on the theory of mind and nature which lies behind his own and Thoreau's attitude toward the landscape of the European imagination. The "most distinctive, and perhaps the most impressive, characteristic of American scenery," Cole asserts, "is its wildness," a generalization which he anchors with the same tension between contrasting masses which frequently appears in his paintings of the American landscape: "American mountains are generally clothed to the summit by dense forests, while those of Europe are mostly bare, or merely tinted by grass or heath." [5] His sense of America's superior lushness was to be shared by Thoreau, though Cole was more likely than Thoreau to argue for the wilderness as "YET a fitting place to speak of God" (100). His essay has more in it of Burke and Gilpin, and of the sentimental religiosity that characterizes the late-eighteenth-century picturesque, than one would expect to find in an important talent in 1835.[6]

Yet Cole can go beyond such large-scale clichés and establish a precise, interlocking relationship between the Romantic self and the specifics of American landscape: "And Niagara! that wonder of the world!—where the sublime and beautiful are bound together in an indissoluble chain. In gazing on it we feel as though a great void had been filled in our minds—our conceptions expand—we become a part of what we behold!" (105). The point here is not in the conventional comment about sublimity expanding the mind but in the relation of that comment to the surprisingly Blakean statement ("we become a part of what we behold") about the attraction of subject to object. First, the external landscape forces itself within him, filling a void of consciousness; then the mind is amplified in order to balance, within its own dimensions, the scope of the immensity outside; finally, the inner and outer landscapes are matched up, and the interlocking and resultant identity take place. Though Cole does not spell them out, and perhaps never thought them out clearly, the steps in this process are implicit in the experience he describes, and they lead rigorously to a meshing of mind and world.

From at least the time of Rousseau, Romanticism had pored over varying versions of the mutual reflection and interpenetration of mind and nature, of the ways in which the landscape within the mind and the landscape outside it worked upon each other. Cole's remarks point to one kind of interpenetration, with an external landscape so overwhelming that it forces the observer to identify with it. In Cole's experience of Niagara the inner and outer landscapes come together and become the same through the enforced submission of one to another. But of course other, less shattering relationships are possible. In his fifth *Rêverie,* Rousseau reduces the activities of self so that the only disturbance within it comes from the sound of waters entering his consciousness and becoming an active part of him. His passivity appears to be somewhat like Cole's, but it does not have the conventionally sublime element of overwhelming awe. Most important, however, mind and world are actually equals in that *Rêverie,* and the sound of waters serves mainly to give Rousseau the requisite sense of contact with the world outside. He does not submit to nature but to the requirements of consciousness: without some kind of contact coming from outside, the self would have a disturbing sense of death and thus would find it impossible to achieve a state leading to reverie.[7] Rousseau unites, so to speak, with nothing but himself. Wordsworth, in quite a different form of activity, can hear the same kind of watery sounds when he stands on Mount Snowdon and turns the massiveness of mountains and mist into the image of a mind like his own. All of these instances indicate that the meeting of landscapes can be a loving embrace of contraries in which each forces itself upon the other in mutual imposition. Yet the examples also share a characteristic Romantic assertion, the insistence that such interpenetrating activities reveal a radical resemblance between the order of mind and the order of nature. Nature can be both analogue and antagonist, sometimes both simultaneously, and the man who stands over against it has to adjust his consciousness to handle each of those attitudes. Once again it is an issue of the imagination's adequacy and its capacity to adapt to all the demands made upon it.

Thoreau's own understanding of these activities of mind is so complex and manifold, and his practice of them is so repeated and diverse, that he touches on nearly every variation of both analogy and antagonism somewhere in his experience. *Walden* is an omnibus of his attitudes toward nature, a collective of possible responses. In that book, his reading of the qualities of self is modified repeatedly as his sense of what is out there in nature fluctuates from the welcoming to the impenetrably strange. And the later journals make very clear that, as he aged, it became easier for Thoreau to look at the facts of nature than to penetrate them. But he seems never to have lost his sense of analogy and potential identity, and his awareness of the ways in which mind and nature can interlock and flow into each other. He was always concerned with the resemblances of form and function between the inner and outer landscapes. Two relatively early examples will do to show differing versions:

I learned to-day that my ornithology had done me no service. The birds I heard, which fortunately did not come within the scope of my science, sung as freshly as if it had been the first morning of creation, and had for background to their song an untrodden wilderness, stretching through many a Carolina and Mexico of the soul. (*J*, I, 125-26)

In the spaces of thought are the reaches of land and water, where men go and come. The landscape lies far and fair within, and the deepest thinker is the farthest traveled. (*Excursions*, 135)

The first example, startling in its unexpected fusion of the wildernesses within and without, comes from a journal entry of March 4, 1840. Thoreau used it in an abbreviated form in "Natural History of Massachusetts," but he omitted any reference to the wild places in "a Carolina and Mexico of the soul," since they would have been inappropriate in that context *(Excursions,* 114). The second example appeared in the so-called lost journal in August 13, 1840, and was used nearly verbatim in "A Walk to Wachusett" two years later—less than a year after Thoreau had commented in his journal on Wordsworth's relative tameness *(Consciousness in Concord,* 135). But his ideas on interpenetration had appeared as early as a college essay written in 1836 (the year in which Emerson published *Nature),* where Thoreau contended that "nature accommodates herself to the soul of man. Hence his conceptions are as gigantic as her mountains." [8] And he continued this insistence over the years with his long-range examination of the moral significance of American wildness. Considering this perpetual interest in the interflow of mind and nature, it seems strange that Thoreau rarely touches on the inferences that can be drawn from his remarks on Anglo-European landscapes and poets. After all, Romantic arguments for certain areas of radical exchange between mind and nature had done much to determine the workings of the Transcendentalist imagination. But the implications of Thoreau's comments are clear all the same: the paucity of wildness in Anglo-European landscapes has to explain the relative blandness in the domesticated souls of these poets, the substitution of Robin Hood for the wild man, and the greenwood for the wilderness. "Why such pains in old countries to plant gardens and parks?" he asked in a journal entry in 1852 *(J,* III, 215; cf. *Excursions,* 228). The Chippeway and the Algonquin needed far more ferocity and unplumbed fecundity than Wordsworth could find even in the byways of Grasmere. And the "unexplored wildness and fertility" in the song of the American thrush would have to be reflections of the rich and untamed loam in the landscape out of which the bird sings. As for the birds across the water, Thoreau can only say that any European nightingale who could sing so excitingly "must itself have emigrated long ago" *(J,* IV, 263).[9]

Thoreau's sly flippancy in these matters ought to be handled very carefully. His sardonic comments on the poets, the tamed Robin Hoods of English literature, are obviously exaggerations and can be countered by other comments elsewhere in his work. They are extra-vagant maneuvers, willfully so; and at one of the most productive levels of his experience Thoreau knew that his role as exaggerator was involved with his extra-vagance and that both were essential to his business as an instructor of men. Stepping beyond boundaries was a very private act, but its results were widely reflected in his public affairs: "No truth was ever expressed but with this sort of emphasis. . . . You must speak loud to those who are hard of hearing; so you acquire a habit of speaking loud to those who are not" (*J*, I, 412). Thoreau's gibes at the Anglo-European poets, then, were only partly playful, since his observation about the relative wildness of European and American landscapes is a rich and repeated assertion that has considerable relevance to his view of the various orders of self which emerge in those landscapes. For Thoreau and others like Thomas Cole there was nothing more significant or more distinctive and special about the American landscape than the palpable and immediate presence of the frontier, of a pervasive wildness whose borders are coterminous with our own, just out there at the edge where mind and nature meet. Untamed European frontiers, if there were any at all, were special and scattered, not so easily accessible, present and actual *(actuel)*.

Whatever wildness the Old World Romanticists had spoken of was nearly always exotic, somewhere else than at home, or in a time other than their own. Indeed, that is the point of most discussions of wildness and untamed frontiers in European Romanticism. Savages and the wilderness that surrounded them were part of a frame of moral reference which was so different that it seemed, at times, to come out of a different order of being. Those landscapes made perfect sites for a comparison of the exotic and the immediate, for a critical look at what could not be offered by local European material, colorful or otherwise. That is, the point was in a stress on the *difference* of the exotic. The vision of wildness in Anglo-European Romanticism tends to be stereoscopic, superimposing what is theirs onto what is not theirs. Montaigne had mocked earlier versions of this mode of perception in "Des Cannibales," where he points out that we call actions different from our own "barbaric" because we take our criteria of reason and truth from our own usages. His strategy in the essay, however, is to hold onto the European sense of the term, with its implications of crudeness and brutality. With that meaning as a tool he can refer to instances of high-mindedness among the natives and of cruelty among the Europeans, ending with the wily proposal that only one or the other can be truly savage because *"il y a une merveilleuse distance entre leur forme et la nostre."* [10] Montaigne, then, based his moral examination of exoticism on his awareness of the complex relations between physical and moral distance. Rousseau based his own reading of the exotic on the relations between temporal distance and physical and moral strength. In the *Discourses* he argues that after an initial stage of self-sufficient stupidity, and a more satisfactory one of cautious cooperation, men have eased into a process of enervation, leading to the gradual disappearance of traits which were at least relatively admirable. With both Montaigne and Rousseau the moral points could be made only because the savage paragon was so far away: the sense of difference was compounded by a sense of distance. The case of Scott is somewhat more complicated. His Highlanders, who (along with Byron's Albanians) are perhaps closest to being contemporary European wild men, are just out there in the gray reaches where the Lowland amenities give out. But the equivocal foreignness of these strange cousins runs as a disconcerting motif through all of the Scottish novels. Scott makes the otherness of the Gaelic tribes the most distinctive feature about them.

Thoreau recognized and made much of this question of exoticism and immediacy, of that which can be embodied only in idyll and that which is felt daily and presently on the fingertips. In an early version of the passage from "Walking" about the tamed Robin Hoods he says, "there was need of America"; and the need was not only to counter European gardens with American swamps but, finally, to actualize the theoretical and put it into immediate and necessary practice. American literary men had received the best of European culture and were thoroughly acquainted with its traditions, including the European awareness of distant savagery. But if the physical and temporal gaps between European phenomena and the savage paragon were the basis on which Montaigne and Rousseau had built up their moral arguments, those gaps had been closed for the American intellectuals. In America the exotic became localized and had to be directly faced. Traditions and modes of consciousness that produced pastoral fictions about wildness had to be adjusted by literary men who stared out at a relatively close and actively present frontier. Their idiosyncratic surroundings became part of the landscape of the American imagination because the edge where wildness starts was a crucial demarcating principle in their country's social and moral geography. Of course there were hints of precedence in Scott, whose Highlanders stood just beyond the outworks of society, and in Byron, with his fondness for wild Albanians. Yet such instances were spotty and occasional, cut off in mountain pockets which could be reached only with considerable effort and will. Even the Ossianic figures for whom Thoreau had such praise in the *Week* were ostentatiously parochial, drawn off into a strange corner of European experience.[11] In America, though, the wild was available to Thoreau in Maine, Canada, and the West as well as in the woods around Concord. Wherever he found it, it was always just out beyond the edge where men had set themselves to front their analogue/antagonist. The first of the following exemplary passages is from *A Yankee in Canada*, the second from "Natural History of Massachusetts":

as it was a muddy day, we never got out of the mud, nor out of the village, unless we got over the fence; then, indeed, if it was on the north side, we were out of the civilized world. There were sometimes a few more houses near the church, it is true, but we had only to go a quarter of a mile from the road, to the top of the bank, to find ourselves on the verge of the uninhabited, and, for the most part, unexplored wilderness stretching toward Hudson's Bay. *(Excursions, 42; cf. 55, 60-61, 89)*

When our river overflows its banks in the spring, the wind from the meadows is laden with a strong scent of musk, and by its freshness advertises me of an unexplored wildness. Those backwoods are not far off then. *(Excursions, 114)*

The wild was ubiquitous and contemporary, and the presence

of both of these factors determined some of the major patterns of Thoreau's concern with the domestication of Romantic tradition. Those factors, in particular, were the grounds on which he built his chauvinism about American wildness. There is, then, a magnificent cultural irony in Thoreau's adaptation of European Romantic modes of consciousness. When he speaks of the analogies of inner and outer landscapes, and of their reflection and interpenetration, he uses as a weapon against Anglo-European Romanticism some ideas about the relations of mind and nature which the Americans themselves had drawn from Europe. Arguments about the order of Romantic mind, its imposition on natural forms and its subjection to them, its mirroring of itself in nature and of nature in itself, figured significantly in the work of most of the Anglo-Europeans (such as Coleridge and Novalis) who influenced American Romantic thought. But those meetings of European Romantic modes and the American imagination took place in a landscape for which the Americans could find no exact equivalent in European phenomena.

Obviously new equivalents were needed, and in his search for them Thoreau looked deeply into the meaning of old modes and their applicability to the American Romantic consciousness. Given what was facing him near the pond in Concord as well as out in the Maine woods, the presence of immediate wildness meant that he had to argue for a kind of Romantic self which was peculiarly and specifically American, beyond chauvinism or any of the conventional assertions about the superiority of the American fresh start. All the laws of internalization and analogy inherited from European Romanticism determined that he would inevitably come upon a stratum of radical wildness within himself which was in many ways an exact counterpart of the wildness in the unique landscape surrounding him. At the same time, that level of elemental primitivism would have to be—again by the laws of analogy—quite unlike anything he could find in the souls of the Romanticists of the Old World to the east of America. "Walking" was definitive here too, since it not only brought together a number of statements about wildness and analogy but also showed how they could be organized so as to clarify the specifics of American experience. If the order of the essay was circular, its central tension came out of the opposed but complementary movements toward the wildness in the West and the savage in the self. It was these identical movements westward and within which carried the American Romantic domestication of wildness to its furthest position. For we are compelled to recognize that the savage is not exotic but localized, that the primordial is present and palpable. And, following the laws of internalization and analogy, that localization in American experience balances the wildness of the immediate frontier with another wildness that is as local as it can get, deep within the inmost layers of the American self.

The self which lies inside, then, has at its core a wild centrality of being which is approached, necessarily, through the layers of the civilized ego. The radical structure which informs this model of the self, with its remarkable pre-Freudian organization, is pervasive in Thoreau's work, and it occurs whenever he speaks of the self as the locale of wildness. But the structure serves him elsewhere for other purposes, and it serves him in such a way that his perception of the wild self and his perception of the relations of civilization and wildness in American culture are seen to take shape through the same form. That is, with a slight shift in perspective which turns personal order into cultural order Thoreau can reshape his model of the wild self into a pattern of civilization and wildness which clarifies some peculiarities in American cultural geography. In fact, he has only to tip the model on its side, to speak of coasts rather than upper layers, and inland rather than depths of the soul, in order to come upon another version of the model spread out on the cultural map of eastern America. In a passage from *The Maine Woods* Thoreau sees the civilities and settlements of the East Coast as a thin shell and points out that even now, in some of the oldest eastern states, the strips of civilization on the coast border on an unexplored wildness within, one which is dark, strange, and virgin: "Like the English in New Holland, we live only on the shores of a continent even yet, and hardly know where the rivers come from which float our navy" *(Maine Woods,* 81). The city of Bangor is "the principal lumber depot on this continent," yet "only a few axemen have gone 'up river,' into the howling wilderness which feeds it," an unmapped country only sixty miles away (82-83; cf. *J,* I, 48-49). The congruence of this landscape with Thoreau's model of the self is exact and reverberative, implying a fertile promise in both the inner and the outer worlds. If Thoreau's perceptions were moral, they were also home-grown, for local consumption and edification. Some of his chauvinism was for show, though it was far less solemn than Emerson's; but much of it had to do with the purpose of the analogies and his role as the extravagant instructor of the local community.[12]

There are occasions, however, when Thoreau will universalize the wildness within and without, especially when he wants to speak of wildness as a vibrant core or area countering the thin surfaces of civilization which have spread out all over the world. In the *Week*, for example, Thoreau makes the Ossianic heroes into the symbol of a savage center of self still common to every man: "Inside the civilized man stand the savage still in the place of honor. We are those blue-eyed, yellow-haired Saxons, those slender, dark-haired Normans" (368). Of course this kind of universalism is an inconsistency, conflicting with Thoreau's usual argument that wild men have disappeared from immediate European experience. The wild is still there for all men, it would seem, personified in an archetypal savage inside. Thoreau is inconsistent here because he has given way to another impulse, his need to set off the debility of the world we have built for ourselves against the persistent strengths at the core of our being. All men, not just Americans, have had their energies smothered by the veneer of cultural fashions: "civilization does not dress men," he says in the same passage, and he made the point often when in a Carlylean mood. Yet Thoreau can bow to ancient European experience and still manage to indicate the superiority of the contemporary American version. A page earlier he had said that "Ossian reminds us of the most refined and rudest eras, of Homer, Pindar, Isaiah, and the American Indian"; and the American Indian, however tamed from his previous state, is the only one of these analogies still left and actively functioning in the life of contemporary men. Thus, although wildness may still simmer at the center of European being, Thoreau can continue to argue that there is nothing in contemporary Europe which can match the immediacies of American experience, nothing there which would permit the fruitful comparisons still visible and available in his own world.

Thoreau, like Emerson, saw himself as an American moralist, and both parts of that title have to be taken with equal weight. As a moralist he is compelled to make international moves because he knows that the problems which ought to concern us most are in no sense only parochial. As a moralist he speaks in archetypes, which means that his speech will now and then reach out to matters beyond the confines of Concord. And since those matters are universal and immortal, he can use any kind of exploration to body them forth, as long as that kind shows a move· into what is possibly desirable and is certainly wild and unknown. But as it turns out he nearly always uses the international to image matters that are the most immediate and local of all:

> What was the meaning of that South-Sea Exploring Expedition, with all its parade and expense, but an indirect recognition of the fact, that there are continents and seas in the moral world, to which every man is an isthmus or an inlet, yet unexplored by him. (*Walden,* 321)

There is a prevailing ironic pattern in which Thoreau, as moralist, appears to argue for universalism and then, as chauvinist, counters his own arguments with a simultaneous parochialism. Most universalism, moral or political, asserts that the qualities which are desirable locally can be found everywhere else, or should be propagated everywhere else. In a neat and incisive reversal, Thoreau, the master of the microcosm, finds the universal in America and a hemisphere in Concord. Unlike Melville, he was above all a local prophet, an explorer in place. When Thoreau breaks out of the parochial and immediate, he goes out only to clarify by succinct contrast all the contours of the most private issues.

The point is that all of Thoreau's images of travel, whatever their source, refer ultimately to the unremitting forward movement into the wild centers of man and nature. They are all figures for that nervous drive whose incessant push matches the vibrant activities of the core—his own or reality's—toward which it moves. But the core can be reached here in Concord as successfully as it can anywhere else: the live center is universally and therefore immediately available. Thus, he can practice exploration in place because his elemental impulse to drive toward the center fused with his awareness of the potential of local experience, whether the local is American or, more microcosmically, Concord. Of course there was a sense in which he carried his own center around with him wherever he went: "the secret of successful sauntering," he said in "Walking," is to be "equally at home everywhere," and Thoreau prided himself on the portability of self *(Excursions,* 205). Further, since the deep center of things was available everywhere, he could work out the requisite analogies wherever he went.

But Thoreau did not go to many places, and he always returned to the center at Concord, which seemed to offer the best frame for the most private activities of the self. His imagination would occasionally reach out toward foreign materials, but it always drew whatever it found back toward the core of his personal enclosure. It was Thoreau's habit to localize whatever conscious-ness could absorb, and since the most local was the selfhood within him, all alien materials ultimately ended up there. Thoreau's construction of experience (which is exactly parallel to that of Rousseau) placed his consciousness at the center of a concentric series of enclosures or clearings. Outside the self was Concord, and outside that was the wild and, finally, the world. Everything beyond Concord eventually had reference to the town, since it could be used for the town's understanding of itself: both London and the Maine woods had something to say which had meaning for Concord, and Thoreau made use of those meanings to establish the import of his American town. Beyond America was Europe, which Americans were happy to use as an instrument for the clarification of their own national experience. All of these external materials were grist for Thoreau. He could go out to the farthest reaches and carry back whatever he found through the American West and Concord until he came to the point of utmost centrality from which his genius looked out at the world:

> What does Africa,—what does the West stand for? Is not our own interior white on the chart? black though it may prove, like the coast, when discovered. Is it the source of the Nile, or the Niger, or the Mississippi, or a North-West Passage around this continent, that we would find? Are these the problems which most concern mankind? *(Walden,* 321)

Of course they are problems, but they are also analogies for the most pivotal of all issues—the exploration of each person's core of being. It has been said of the Divine Being that his center is everywhere and his circumference is nowhere. Thoreau had some very difficult problems with his personal circumference, but he knew that the deep center was universal and he knew also that exploration in place, in the parochial landscape of Concord, would probably find it. If Thoreau was literally provincial by circumstance (he seems to have had few opportunities to travel), he was imaginatively so only by choice, preferring to make a cosmos out of Concord. His occasional forays out of the field of American imagery could never be a sufficient source of the metaphors he needed when he looked at the particularities of his own and American experience. To define those particularities he needed ways to set West against East, the American present against the European past and present, the immediate and local against the foreign and exotic. He needed proximate wildness; or, rather, he needed to argue that wildness *was* proximate, just below the thin surface of American civilization and American skins, in Canada, Maine, and Concord.

3.

The Wild and the Good

Thoreau's occasional use of foreign metaphors to figure exploration into wild areas cannot match the breadth of Melville's performance. Melville was as obsessed with wildness as Thoreau was, but his tendency was the opposite of Thoreau's because he used American imagery to define universal experience. In his major study of elemental ferocity Melville evokes the exotic and the sea through images drawn from a home-grown idiom. In *Moby-Dick* the ocean is repeatedly identified with the American West. The whalemen set out to meet wildness, with some of them, like Ishmael, driven by a craving for the untamed and the imponderable, while others went out of greed or similar business. The meeting with wildness makes all of them into fit inhabitants of that landscape: "Long exile from Christendom and civilization inevitably restores a man to that condition in which God placed him, i.e. what is called savagery. Your true whale-hunter is as much a savage as an Iroquois."[1] Ahab is also properly at home in this sea of wild American metaphors. If the world inside him drives him to a mad marriage with what he seeks (it is in some respects his animal counterpart), the world he left at home serves as one source of imagery to define the qualities of self he brings to the quest. At one point he is likened, in a single paragraph, to both "the last of the Grisly Bears [who] lived in settled Missouri," and also "that wild Logan of the woods," referring to a particularly stubborn and defiant Indian chief (134). Elsewhere some other whale-hunting captains who went out to look for well-known killers are compared with "Captain Butler of old" who went into the Narragansett woods "to capture that notorious murderous savage Annawon, the headmost warrior of the Indian King Philip" (177).

But the center of the analogy of the sea and American wildness, as well as the most concentrated examination of the comparison, appears in the chapter on "The Whiteness of the Whale," and there Melville shows that his perception of wildness is in some ways very similar to that of Thoreau. Melville focuses all his ambivalence about whiteness and wildness in the figure of the White Steed of the Prairies, whose imperial grandeur and terrifying awesomeness are a localized counterpart of the qualities in the white whale of the western ocean. Nothing, it seems, can come close to matching Moby Dick in kind except the magnificent western horse which elicited both worship and terror from those who saw it. The horse is not surrounded by the rank and luxuriant eastern wildness with which Thoreau compared the fertility and potential in his own soul. The White Steed's home is broad, open, and terrifying, pristine and primitive. In this passage Melville holds on to the usual comparisons of the American West with the unfallen Adamic world but ironically makes his Adam into an awesome figure whose best analogy is not found in nature's fertile heart but in the stunning presence of the White Steed:

[The Steed was] a most imperial and archangelical apparition of that unfallen, western world, which to the eyes of the old trappers and hunters revived the glories of those primeval times when Adam walked majestic as a god, bluff-bowed and fearless as this mighty steed. (165)

The foil to this horse is the New England colt referred to a few pages later, who responds frantically to the shaking of a fresh buffalo robe behind him: "here thou beholdest even in a dumb brute, the instinct of the knowledge of the demonism in the world" (169). The brutes of the East, though with layers of tameness over their intuitive selves, find that primitive instincts can burst up through the layers upon sufficient provocation. Even for brutes the East is a place where civilized layers cover over their aboriginal awareness and fear of radical ferocity. And with perfect cultural appropriateness, the Vermont colt fears pure western wildness.[2] Melville clearly shares Thoreau's sense of elemental American forms: the order within the colt is the same as the order of tameness and proximate wildness in the society that supplies his fodder. But the differences are at least as significant as any structures held in common.

Thoreau's closest counterpart to the eastern colt is not a beast whose intuitive terrors are roused by the odor of wildness (Melville's parody of the odor of sanctity) but an eastern cow who appears in the last chapter of *Walden: "Extra vagance!* it depends on how you are yarded. The migrating buffalo, which seeks new pastures in another latitude, is not extravagant like the cow which kicks over the pail, leaps the cow-yard fence, and runs after her calf, in milking time" (324). The cow's wildness does not emerge in terror but in a characteristic Thoreauvian act, the spontaneous breaking of boundaries. The tone of this passage is typical: Thoreau was far more prone than Melville to the Romantic impulse for exploring with joy the counterpart activities of consciousness and the world. Melville could not exult in such analogies even when he saw them there because the shared content was rarely a cause for joy: what Ahab had in common with his quarry was potentially destructive of both. Still, Thoreau was not so naive as to ignore completely what Melville knew well. Thoreau was the only one of the Concord intellectuals to draw out most of the intricacies and implications in the meaning of American wildness. (As Sherman Paul puts it, "the Concord Circle wanted no Indians." [3]) Thus, it is not surprising that as Thoreau extended his understanding of wildness and the natural matter that embodied it he ran into areas that were, at the least, contradictory to what he usually saw and would have liked to see everywhere. The simple quantity of his explorations guaranteed that he would run into some disturbing negations. But Melville took a full, cold look at areas that Thoreau glimpsed only occasionally, and then with considerable unease. Those glimpses were sufficient to establish a permanent ambivalence in Thoreau that emerged in some remarkable qualifications to several basic public assertions. Melville's hard stares, on the other hand, were overt, persistent efforts to force out all the meaning of the disturbing analogies.

Melville was a builder of Edens who had the unsettling habit of setting up their opposites in conjunction with them. In *Typee* he portrayed a local idyll which, for the natives who were at home in it, never ceased to be paradisiacal. For others, however, it was an ambiguously ordered but definite failure, an Eden which appeared to carry its contrary within itself. Melville works carefully at establishing an equivocal tone for these islands. The landscape is warm, verdant, and gorgeous, a natural place for sentimental commonplaces about the correspondence between the soul and its surroundings. Toby, the sailor who later disappeared, draws an inevitable conclusion: "It is impossible that the inhabitants of such a lovely place as we saw can be anything else but good fellows." [4] The correspondence almost works: the natives are generally decent, their life—from their own point of view—a harmonious whole. If, from the narrator's perspective, their cannibalism is the disconcerting element that poisons paradise and drives him out, his reading of the situation is incomprehensible to them. What he sees as inimical is to the natives an element of natural order, though they do know that the whites cannot go along with their cannibalism and they therefore make some awkward stabs at hiding the evidence. Toby's initial sentimentalism turns into the narrator's sardonic recognition that the paradisiacal snake is within the human soul.

Melville argues that the relationship of nature and the soul (insofar as there is any) can be composed of contraries and cacophony as well as of all the predictable harmonies. The happy valley and its inhabitants exhibit a radical and perhaps inevitable human evil. As he played ironically with sentimental cultural myths in *Typee*, Melville accentuated the darkness that was present even in spite of the Edenic surroundings. In fact, it is only the sentimentalist who would say that the evil is there *in spite of* the lovely landscape. Melville and the narrator are more detached, and see that the natural surroundings neither forbid nor encourage evil, and may or may not reflect it. There are no neat demarcations of heaven and hell, no massive abysses between them. In effect, this meant that when he set up versions of the enclosure of the self, as he did in *Typee* and *Moby-Dick,* Melville was careful to show that the moral opposite of that enclosure was closely associated with it, and perhaps was even a part of it. And if the enclosure happened to be hellish within rather than paradisiacal, as it was in Ahab, Melville could show that there was a heaven right out there abutting it.

In *Moby-Dick,* whose structure and scope allowed for a complex interplay, Melville explored a variety of interchanges and contrasts between the evaluating consciousness and the values of external nature. Like *Walden,* the book is a collective of attitudes. For example, the White Steed of the Prairies, Moby Dick's western counterpart, shares the whale's violent drive and images the energy of both the sea and the West. In the section on the Steed, however, there is no direct suggestion of anything but his existential quality, his state as pure western wildness. There are no moral values attached to him; indeed, the main point is in his qualities of pure being. But Moby Dick himself is rendered in terms of those qualities and more, both a specific temper of being and also the values attached to it—though the values are negative and therefore (in combination with that temper) terrifying.

In the chapter on "The Whiteness of the Whale" it is only toward the end that the combination of being and value appears in relation to the West, in the shaking of the buffalo robe that startles the Vermont colt. Those latter pages are an evaluative finale, showing the full potential of the Steed's world, what can happen to his kind of being: though it is treated as pure, majestic energy and nothing more, the White Steed of the Prairies owns the same capacity for disinterested violence which pointedly characterizes the world of the whale, "the demoniac indifference with which the white whale tore his hunters, whether sinning or sinned against" (437). Yet this does not entirely settle the issue. It was never really possible for Melville to say that the evaluating consciousness had made a fully adequate reading of the world's wildness, or, for that matter, of anything else about the world (witness the uncertainties which shape the narrative of *The Confidence Man*). Melville's imagination is always ambiguous, even about the whale's undoubted ferocity. How much of it is "intelligent malignity" or "infernal afterthought of ferocity" (159)? How does the mind react to the immense grandeur and fearful symmetry of the demonic?

Melville had begun by seeing that the world was resistant to the desires of consciousness, if not always overtly malevolent, and *Typee* inaugurates a basic sense of ambivalence which his work never lost—which, indeed, became the radical tenor of his imagination. Thoreau's own wild landscapes have no exact corollary to the active, elemental malevolence which Melville reveals in wild people and places, but the possibility of nature's resistance did come upon him gradually, and with an immense, cumulative effect. Certainly there was nothing in Thoreau's early training to prepare him for any version of what Melville saw, particularly for a nature which could offer a strong rebuff. Emerson's *Nature* and similar work such as Orestes Brownson's essay on Victor Cousin gave no hint that the world external to the active, transforming consciousness can put up a serious, perhaps successful resistance. Whatever Thoreau may have thought of the abstractness of some of his contemporaries, compared with his own hard-won factuality, he carried into his later years the essential Transcendental mixture of correspondence and imposition which puts the mind at final advantage in relation to a nature which is willingly sufficient. If his confidence alternated with an increasing uncertainty and even skepticism, Thoreau always approached nature and its wildness with certain expectations about what they meant to him as a man. When those expectations were unsettled or flouted, he was more open to disturbance than Melville, who looked upon all Transcendental assertions with a fertile awareness of their ironic potential.

Thoreau's views on wildness and the reflecting orders of American nature and the wild American self are in several ways closer to Hawthorne than to Melville. Melville's international views are involved with the moral intricacies of all sorts of difficult personalities as well as with the equivalent complexities of an external nature that no one can understand. Thoreau's parochialism is aggressively positive and has far more to do with places and animals than with a recognition of the dark strata in the human order. Hawthorne shares Thoreau's parochialism to an extent, and he also has something of Thoreau's awe over the forests that surround the dots of clearing on the American coast: in *The Scarlet*

Letter he gives the chart of the landscape a Puritan moral framework, beginning with an awareness of "the few settlements of Europeans, scattered thinly along the seaboard." [5] Hawthorne's map is more literal than Thoreau's because it reflects an earlier state of settlement, but the components of the chart are exactly the same and have the same relationship to each other. In fact, Hawthorne is echoing an old pattern, what Richard Slotkin has called "the hedged-in Puritan concept of the coastal enclave." [6] But Hawthorne's attitude toward the few dots of clearing in the wilderness is combined with a dominating uneasiness concerning the Indian and the tangled darkness of the woods in which he is most at home. The Indian images the evil in the dark heart of the woods, and the woods themselves are the corollary of the black depths of the soul which one enters to undergo a struggle for self-purification. These too are Puritan patterns, old readings of the moral import of the New World, and Hawthorne uses them with exceptional skill to organize the reflecting structures of his inner and outer landscapes.[7] But the formal identity of this order with Thoreau's own cartography of American experience is countered by significant distinctions of interpretation.

Both Hawthorne and Thoreau use the wilderness as a place of work for the soul; but in Thoreau's usual readings of the wilderness it is not instinct with evil, nor is it the locale of a battle for the soul's salvation. Though both see the wilderness as a place for self-purification, in Hawthorne one has to struggle against what the wilderness holds, while in Thoreau one goes in it to look for the purity which only wildness has to offer. Much of the difference, of course, comes from the uses to which the redemptive imaginations of the Puritan Romantic and the Transcendental Romantic put the natural world. For Hawthorne the literal physicality of the wilderness has significance mainly for its duplication of tangled inner webs. He renders the resultant ambivalence in hints and images of dim paths and devils in the woods but most of all in his equivocal attitude toward Pearl, a product of Old World engendering and New World energies. Pearl does not see the forest as a moral wilderness but as a place of wild joy whose sympathy with her is elemental. And that communion identifies a moral demarcation of which both Hawthorne and the main characters are aware: " 'I have a strange fancy,' observed the sensitive minister, 'that this brook is the boundary between two worlds, and that thou canst never meet thy Pearl again' " (208). Pearl has an allegorical weight of the sort that Thoreau often balanced successfully, and his own public views of the relations between the European imagination and American wildness led him to a similar awareness (though from the other side of the brook) of that moral demarcation. Yet even though Hawthorne draws the lines between Europe and America with all the starkness of allegory, his views have none of the willful simplification of Thoreau's usual chauvinistic statements, the sort which appear throughout "Walking." If the clearings in Hawthorne's woods offer the possibility of redemption, they can also tempt the soul to devilish celebration, as in "Young Goodman Brown." And if Pearl's elemental wildness is new worldly, her mother's passion, imaged in the long black hair she rarely lets down, comes out of an old landscape which could find no proper moral frame for that passion.

Oddly enough, considering Thoreau's public chastisement of European tameness, there is considerable evidence that the Anglo-European Romantics shared Hawthorne's awareness of the need to adjust old landscapes to intense and potentially destructive energies. In the literature of the *Sturm und Drang,* for example, there is an extensive recognition of the extraordinary energies in both nature and the self, energies which are as alike in their intensity as they are equally difficult to control. With the awareness of those forces came an almost desperate sense of the possibility, the threat, of imminent anarchy in the self. Werther's struggle for an adequate structure of the self was waged against forces within himself; and his personal analogy for those forces was the stream which, under the pressure of overwhelming floods, broke up its enclosing banks and everything upon them. Hölderlin used a similar image of wild natural energies in *Der Rhein,* where the demigod-river, surging down out of the mountains in potentially lethal violence, becomes calmer and fructifying as it moves into its well-ordered course on the plains. Faust's shattering encounter with the *Erdgeist,* as well as the descent of Faust to the burgeoning creative center which contains *Die Mütter,* are still other instances of an awareness of the manifold possibilities in mundane energy; indeed, part of the progress in *Faust* lies in the hero's recognition that it is possible to work with, as well as against, the obscure potential of those forces.

And even in Scott there is an acknowledgment (e.g., in *Rob Roy*) of the uneasy analogy of natural and spiritual wildness which not only counters the extreme positions of Thoreau's chauvinism but adds an ironic historical qualification because of Scott's relationship to Cooper.

Thoreau knew some of this material very well, Goethe in particular, though he did not choose to follow through on all of its implications. Most of his remarks about Old World wildness were confined to a few examples out of England. When he said "European" or "old world," he ordinarily depended on a somewhat vague sense of the Continent, with less reference to postmedieval literature than to the ancient classics. He showed a somewhat more precise understanding when he spoke of the English landscape and its poets. But it is useless to complain about the limitations of Thoreau's chauvinism, since his purpose was to define, by easy and half-mocking contrasts, those qualities in the American imagination which he wanted to see drawn out and developed. He ought not to be treated as an easy mark, since he is not a fully serious one. Still, in his insistence upon taking so extreme an attitude toward Anglo-European Romanticism, Thoreau led himself into some dangerous simplifications—dangerous not because they were historically inaccurate (no serious American reader would have been fully taken in) but because in simplifying the issues he ignored the ambivalence in the European sense of self and its own relation to the wildness that was inside and out. A more objective reading would have shown him that his personal conception of wildness shared determining characteristics with the *Sturm und Drang* as well as several of their successors. Thoreau's intuitions about the association of wild energies with creative potential had been prefigured eighty years before "Walking" in the *Sturm und Drang* conception of the artist, even if Thoreau's versions take on a necessarily different form because of the special conditions of American experience. His sense of the uses and abuses of untamed energy is in essence a domestication of perceptions that Anglo-European Romantics had long been exploring, and with a complexity of awareness that we are only now beginning to understand. Ironically, there were events in Thoreau's own encounter with wildness and the materiality which embodied it that brought him closer than he would have wanted to be to the Anglo-European experience of untamed energies.

Goethe, Schlegel, and Byron realized that the forces of wild energy (both in and out of the soul) held a potential for total disorder and that the potential could be countered only by the capacities of consciousness to order experience. They knew, as a corollary, that the most severe challenge to consciousness came out of the same fertile energies which gave it its drive. Further, Byron in particular was deeply sensitive to the embodiment of those energies in mortal flesh, an association which engendered a severe but imaginatively fruitful ambivalence in himself. Had Thoreau given full attention to all these uneasy intuitions of proximate chaos, he would have had to qualify his chauvinism considerably. As it is, the difficulties of wildness and its material embodiment contained threats to the efficacy of consciousness—the adequacy of the imagination—which Thoreau could not ignore. Even though he continued to pipe his chauvinistic ditties about American wildness until the end of his life, he was reaching a lucid awareness of the possibilities of ambivalence in his own situation. What emerges from this challenge to consciousness is an imaginative achievement so complex and compelling that it can be matched by no other Transcendentalist. It finds its contemporary American equal only in the dense and vigorous world of Melville's fiction.

We can identify a number of points at which Thoreau's usual understanding of the relations of wildness and consciousness was shaken considerably, so much so that some basic patterns in the way he imagined his selfhood were seriously disturbed. One of those points, the first of his three trips to the Maine woods, came in late August and early September 1846, during the period when he lived in the cabin beside Walden Pond. Another takes its beginning from the encounter with the totemic woodchuck, which was recorded briefly and cryptically in the journal for August 23, 1845, early in his stay at Walden (*J*, I, 384-85). The experience in Maine was finished and self-contained, recorded soon in an accomplished narrative that became the first essay in *The Maine Woods*. Each of the essays in that book recounts a test of consciousness, a pitting of its capacities against the most resistant antagonist available. The first is the most concentrated in intensity and therefore the most dramatic, establishing the lineaments of the struggle; but all of the essays portray an extended version of the same activity, the drive toward the deep center of radical energy. The structural congruence of these trips and his business beside

Walden Pond is exact. But there are clashes and incongruities as well, essential differences between his explorations in place at home and his extensive examinations of an unfamiliar landscape in which he is a visiting alien. Those differences gave Thoreau some hard and unexpected lessons about the dependence of consciousness on its natural locale.

All of these moves toward the center, wherever they occur, reveal a gradual stripping-away of the surfaces that cover the stratum toward which one strives. The events at Walden Pond were designed to remove all encumbrances (a favorite word in *Walden*), anything that stood between Thoreau and the marrow of nature. In Maine there had been the same sloughing off of obstructions between himself and elemental wildness, but to call what was removed there an "encumbrance" is to miss all the ambivalence of Thoreau's attitude toward the process that was moving him toward Ktaadn. His trip was a departure from amenities (i.e., from the thin coastal edge of civilization which is the counterpart of the civilized ego) and toward areas which, when they finally end, have come down to the most elemental facts of human order. The beginning is at Bangor. The end of order is the point where the tracks leading out from the final logging camp give way to the woods, which absorb all orders into their own vastness. The last developed instance of man's presence in the woods is not even a dot of clearing but the ruts that emerge from one.

The move into the wilderness was a physical struggle, obviously, for no matter how good the shape Thoreau and his companions were in, they had to work against the resistance of the elementally physical—the speed and roughness of the rivers, the difficult ascents, the thickness of the woods, and the wetness of the swamps. But this resistance was, in terms of Transcendental modalities, only the corporeal stratum. Its correspondence was in the more stubborn opposition which the woods put up against the humanizing imagination, the attitude toward mind that had found its most influential substantiation in Emerson's *Nature*. Transcendental nature was supposed always to speak of man; but these travelers found that outside Bangor the woods said very little about men and said less and less as the group went along. Thoreau seems to have sensed the potential of that threat almost immediately. Near the beginning of their trip, while they were still close to the coast, he was confident enough to be mildly sardonic about an essential humanizing activity, the naming of places:

> At sundown, leaving the river-road awhile for shortness, we went by way of Enfield, where we stopped for the night. This, like most of the localities bearing names on this road, was a place to name, which, in the midst of the unnamed and unincorporated wilderness, was to make a distinction without a difference, it seemed to me. (8)

Such naming, as Thoreau knew well, is an assertive act of consciousness, a claim that what is now there has been annexed to the incorporated for the use of men. It is the Adamic act, given to a man to perform because everything else that partakes of mortality will be subservient to him. (All through *The Maine Woods* Thoreau asks about the Indian names of things.) But there is less admiration of these men in this comment than awe and badly disguised uneasiness at what Thoreau had already seen of the immensity of the unannexed wilderness. Intentionally or not, his arrogant and disquieted observation defines the conflict precisely and recognizes the qualities of the antagonists: naming is an assertion of the human through an act of consciousness, mind doing what it alone can do, and what it does best; but there is already a question of the extent to which the unnamed can be touched by it. Thoreau's remark is not so much misplaced mockery as an unwittingly ironic and self-protective gesture. After a few more miles he was to begin his own assertiveness about the human, rooting his acts in a more intense version of the mixture of wonder and discomfort seen here. Thoreau's combining of those elements so early in the trip indicates that he was already thinking over some basic problems about the confrontation of consciousness and the woods.[8]

His awareness that he was in an alien context, thus established near the beginning, increased in intensity as they went farther into the wilderness. Simply by responding to contrast, by comparing the scarcity of the houses with the immensity that surrounds them, Thoreau grows more impressed at the tenacity of the instinct to make clearings: "There were very few houses along the road, yet they did not altogether fail, as if the law by which men are dispersed over the globe were a very stringent one, and not to be resisted with impunity or for slight reasons" (10-11). But clearings are made out of their opposites, and here those alien elements are close, dense, and oppressive: "it was but a step on either hand to the grim untrodden wilderness, whose tangled labyrinth of living, fallen, and decaying trees,—only the deer and moose, the bear and wolf, can easily penetrate" (11). The wilderness, after all, seems impenetrable. It is obvious that Thoreau's confidence is less tenacious than the law about men's dispersal.

A short time after this, and in response to the scarcity of the products of consciousness as well as to the vastness of the unconscious, his sense of difference begins to establish an activity of its own, a counterpart to their party's movements away from the coast: as they went on he and his companions looked nervously for instances of the human or the domesticated, dwelling on them and turning them over and around as though reluctant to let them go by. If he could not find such things, he would make them for himself out of the workings of the imagination. And when he did find one, he deliberately made much out of little:

> Instead of water we got here a draught of beer, which, it was allowed, would be better; clear and thin, but strong and stringent as the cedar sap . . . a lumberer's drink, which would acclimate and naturalize a man at once—which would make him see green, and, if he slept, dream that he heard the wind sough among the pines. Here was a fife, praying to be played on, through which we breathed a few tuneful strains,— brought hither to tame wild beasts. (27-28)

There is still an aura of play about the workings of his mind as it goes over the imaginative potential of these artifacts. This is an attempt to balance a pair of man's products through antithetical imaginings about them: one drives man farther into nature, making him see green; the other pulls nature toward him, domesticating the exotic and wild. The beer and the fife (with its echoes of Orpheus) are artifacts shaped by the mind's skill; but the imaginative leap which Thoreau has just taken with them is also a product of what the mind can do best. The facility and the air of play show an awareness of command; but the subject matter and the sense of the surrounding woods show that, most of all, he is making a statement about what consciousness can do with every level of its product, whether drinkable, playable, or imaginable. At this point in the woods the houses are still relatively close-together. This one, Thomas Fowler's, is only four miles from the one before. There is no need for unusual nervousness yet, but Thoreau feels that he has to say something even here about the autonomy of consciousness.

After they left Fowler's, which was the last house, and they passed the camp which was "the last human habitation of any kind in this direction" (35), their subliminal uneasiness intensified, and it would surface and find release only when they came across fragments of the human: "I remember that I was strangely affected when we were returning, by the sight of a ring-bolt well drilled into a rock, and fastened with lead, at the head of this solitary Ambejijis Lake" (42). Later they were amused to find, deep in the wilderness, "a large flaming Oak Hall hand-bill, about two feet long, wrapped around the trunk of a pine, from which the bark had been stript, and to which it was fast glued by the pitch" (50). But just before that they had come across a single red brick and "some of us afterward regretted that we had not carried this on with us to the top of the mountain, to be left there for our mark. It would certainly have been a simple evidence of civilized man" (45). That mark would have made a point of human reference where they needed it most, at the top of Ktaadn. Just as Wallace Stevens's jar in Tennessee appeared to draw everything else up around it, the brick would have been one minuscule center of civilization in the midst of the wild. Yet the release these props afforded was only the momentary easing of a pressure that came in on the men again as they found nothing of their own kind or making to which to attach themselves. The ringbolt and handbill had nothing else near them but the thickness of the wilderness; but they were instances of the lives of men, correspondent images of those selves which were "but a clearing in the forest." (All through *The Maine Woods* clearings are associated with the order that only men can make: see, e.g., the comment on Waite's farm, 21.)

Between the camps and Ktaadn, Thoreau and his companions could find only these fragments by which to orient their sense of what men could do in (and against) the wild.

As Thoreau moved from the last logging tracks into the full expanse of the unredeemed, his anxiety was taking a toll. The atmosphere shook the stability of all that he had been building, and continued to build, about the order of self and its relation to the surrounding wilderness. The paucity of clearings threatened that order and challenged the creative capacities of the consciousness that had found it possible, in other circumstances, to recover a place for the self out of the foreign and unenclosed. The woods put into question the adequacy of the imagination because they held so little evidence of its working, and after awhile even that little disappeared.[9] When they started for the summit itself, Thoreau pointed out that "there was not the slightest trace of man to guide us further in this direction" (56).

By the time they were able to see the summit of Ktaadn, the resistance of the wilderness was making their progress exceptionally difficult: "It was the worst kind of travelling; sometimes like the densest scrub-oak patches with us" (59). But of course the summit was now there to be seen, and at that point the exhausted travelers looked for an early camp. While the others were settling in, Thoreau took his own private tour farther up the mountain, ascending a ravine which sloped upward at a forty-five-degree angle. With his sense of irony still in tow, Thoreau played with all the bizarrerie of the situation, emphasizing the extraordinary qualities of his ascent. He had to pull himself up ("and I mean to lay some emphasis on this word *up*") by the roots of firs and birches, for a long stretch "scrambling on all fours over the tops of ancient black spruce-trees, *(Abies nigra,)* old as the flood" (60). Those trees seemed remnants of the second chaos; and as he scrambled and walked he found room to compare himself a number of times, once through quotation, to Milton's Satan moving up through the original chaos. When he finally reached a mountainside, just before that point where the clouds obscure everything above, Thoreau came across some rocks. There, the quasi-satanic traveler turns himself by instant metamorphosis into God or Adam domesticating (by metamorphosing) the wild, finding (i.e., making) some familiar items out of the most basic pieces of this fantastic land where all scraps of the human have finally disappeared:

> Having slumped, scrambled, rolled, bounced, and walked, by turns, over this scraggy country, I arrived upon a side-hill, or rather side-mountain, where rocks, gray, silent rocks, were the flocks and herds that pastured, chewing a rocky cud at sunset. They looked at me with hard gray eyes, without a bleat or a low. This brought me to the skirt of a cloud, and bounded my walk that night. (61-62)

The temporary redemption of the rocks—rapid, instinctive, a fine instance of Coleridgean fancy—is a compulsive assertion of the sufficiency of mind to make a place in the wilderness for its own business. In *Nature* Emerson argued that the poet "invests dust and stones with humanity, and makes them the words of the Reason." [10] Though these sheep are not quite humanity, they are a giant step up the chain of being into the organic world, and they are also commonplace instances of domesticated wildness. Turning them into "the words of the Reason" makes them amenable to the activities of the mind, which can use them as language for its own expressive needs. In *Biographia Literaria* Coleridge pointed out that such acts were the necessary product of the mature imagination that confronts nature: "human associations had given both variety, and an additional interest to natural objects, which in the passion and appetite of the first love they had seemed to [Wordsworth] neither to need or permit." [11] At this point in the Maine woods Thoreau needed those associations urgently; more specifically, he needed to show that he could make such associations. This instance of the mind's sufficiency came in with perfect appropriateness at the last place where such action would be possible. After that the travelers moved into the field of elemental matter, where bare rocks were strewn about, lying there as potential building blocks for a planet and perhaps eventually for the imagination; but those rocks were not yet anything at all except themselves, that is, inert possibility: "They were the raw materials of a planet dropped from an unseen quarry, which the vast chemistry of nature would anon work up, or work down, into the smiling and verdant plains and valleys of earth" (63). Their presence—or rather, his reading of their presence—shows that he has taken still another step back toward radical beginnings.

The move upward, then, is both progressive and regressive, as are all other versions of Thoreau's drive toward centrality. But in no other instance—in the woods, in the swamps, at Walden, within himself—was there any sense that he was going beyond his appropriate boundaries into a place where he was, in effect, an interloper. After all, to go toward the center is to refresh oneself, to find again what (and where) one truly is. If he had to strip away the covering surfaces, that was only because they were impediments, pleasant or otherwise. Here, though, on the ascent toward the summit of Ktaadn, what is removed is all that is most precious and humane, and what one is moving toward is a place where no man can find an opportunity to be himself. The more he travels, the more the challenge to the capacities of consciousness turns into a threat. The closer he gets to the summit, the purer the threat becomes. What he moves toward is not the warm hearth which Heidegger finds as the point of centrality in Hölderlin but, instead, a land where perception is blocked and therefore the most basic activities of the imagination cannot go to work. As he ascended he reached a permanent cloud formation where he was "deep within the hostile ranks of clouds, and all objects were obscured by them" (63). Only occasionally does the mist break, and when it does all he can see is "a dark, damp crag to the right or left" (64). With an exact understanding of the relations between imagination and the landscape, Thoreau feels the primary qualities of his humanity dissipating under the pressure of his environment:

> Some part of the beholder, even some vital part, seems to escape through the loose grating of his ribs as he ascends. He is more lone than you can imagine. There is less of substantial thought and fair understanding in him, than in the plains where men inhabit. His reason is dispersed and shadowy, more thin and subtile like the air. Vast, Titanic, inhuman Nature has got him at disadvantage, caught him alone, and pilfers him of some of his divine Faculty. (64)

The threat has finally been fulfilled. Up there in the face of the ultimately unreasonable he has lost the solidity and contours of his finest faculty. Thoreau's ascent to the summit of Ktaadn forced a struggle for the values of consciousness similar to the Puritan struggle in the wilderness for the values of the soul. Though his encounter with his antithesis is not as starkly Manichean as Young Goodman Brown's, the effect is equally crippling. When thought, imagination, and understanding become vapid, he can do no more than look at things. Certainly he cannot make clear places with his mind. The rocks remain unredeemably rocks.

Still, Thoreau's redemptive instinct continues to fight for survival, its activities so reflexive and automatic that as he went down through some lands burned out by lightning fires he found himself "traversing them familiarly, like some pasture run to waste, or partially reclaimed by man" (70). Yet he is now so distanced from the compulsive imaginings of that instinct (though with words like "reclaimed" he still speaks in its rhetoric) that he can reject the imaginings immediately. Here, in the home of absolute reduction, he knows that there is only matter and no mind. Of course he is matter too, and even though reason has been dispersed he can still turn to the tangible part of his being. However much he has been reduced, there is still an identity between himself and the material facing him, though there can no longer be any thought of combing the material for correspondences. The activities through which Thoreau's consciousness ordered his world depended, for efficient functioning, on an interplay of difference and identity between himself and the world outside. Ordering was possible only because his Transcendental consciousness was superior to anything else in nature, while the organic materiality he shared with nature made him part of the context in which consciousness could do its work. But the experience at Ktaadn, when it made reason "dispersed and shadowy," threatened to obliterate the difference and emphasize the identity: with the full dispersal of reason he would be left only with his own materiality, and what would remain of himself then could hardly be acceptable or consoling. Pure matter (and only that) had become visible to him in this place of absolute strangeness, where men are transgressors. The fact of identity came home to him with astonishment: matter is what makes up his own materiality as well as that of the sterile rocks and burnt lands that form this strange moonscape. In a bleak vision his own body suddenly becomes strange to him, another foreign piece of the universe:

> I stand in awe of my body, this matter to which I am bound
> has become so strange to me. I fear not spirits, ghosts, of which
> I am one,—*that* my body might,—but I fear bodies, I tremble to
> meet them. What is this Titan that has possession of me? Talk
> of mysteries!—Think of our life in nature,—daily to be shown
> matter, to come in contact with it,—rocks, trees, wind on our
> cheeks! the *solid* earth! the *actual* world! the *common sense!*
> *Contact! Contact! Who* are we? *where* are we? (71)

This is a grotesque version of the acts of the spectatorial
consciousness, in which part of the subject is distanced from and
observant of another part of himself. In his most cogent analysis of
that movement of the mind Thoreau argues that "we are not
wholly involved in nature" because part of us can stand aside and
watch the rest in action *(Walden,* 135). Here at the top of Ktaadn
he can only stand aside from the materiality of his body and say
that he is, after all, very deeply involved in nature, awesomely so,
and that the daily encounter with natural matter is puzzling and
disturbing. The contact which he made on Ktaadn is clearly
beyond the control of the redemptive imagination. He can still
affirm spirit, indeed identify himself with it; but when, just after
that, he goes on to say that his body fears his spirit, he is in effect
positing a radical, unbridgeable split between his soul and his flesh.

By considering his own matter as strange and potentially
uncomfortable before his spirit Thoreau manages to recover the
combination of identity and difference, but he does so only by
making the distinctions harsher and more unnerving than before.
His body has more in common with "rocks, trees, wind on our
cheeks" than it does with the spirit which it houses. Such was the
cost of the experience on Ktaadn. He had begun the passage on the
spectatorial consciousness in *Walden* by saying that "with thinking
we may be beside ourselves in a sane sense." Here at Ktaadn he is
also beside himself, but the moment is not only not sane but,
chillingly, quite close to the reverse. He has encountered that
stratum of nature which is irreducible and—for nature and his
body—indispensable. His mind can do nothing with it except look
and wonder. In part the event is a kratophany, a revelation of "a
force not bound to be kind to man" (70). But it is also, and most
disturbingly, a moment of pure existential contact with elemental

materials, a realization of all that matter is and of what one facet of ourselves has to be.

Thoreau went up to Ktaadn with a set of established persuasions about the meaning of mountains to men. His instinct for archetype was always sensitive and dependable, and in the case of the mountains it was reinforced by a wide acquaintance with ancient tropes about the ascent toward transcendent experience. His suppositions were so firm that even Ktaadn could not obliterate them entirely, however much the events in Maine established a series of countervailing patterns to his habitual attitudes. The ascending of mountains was a counterpart of man's difficult and rewarding life in the world, a life that was rewarding to the degree that it was difficult. Thoreau made this ancient point as early as 1840: "If my path run on before me level and smooth, it is all a mirage; in reality it is steep and arduous as a chamois pass" (*J,* I, 152). On May 10, 1853, standing on Smith's Hill looking over the western landscape, he read the distant mountains as "terrene temples," "moral structures," "stepping-stones to heaven ... by which to mount when we would commence our pilgrimage to heaven; by which we gradually take our departure from earth" (*J,* V, 140-41). He put it more succinctly in 1857, saying that mountains "are meant to be a perpetual reminder to us, pointing out the way" (*J,* X, 162).

Thoreau enacted this trope several times before he went to Ktaadn. In 1839, during the trip recorded in the *Week,* he went up to the source of the Merrimack on the summit of Agiocochook in New Hampshire. At the final stage they left the boat and "trod the unyielding land like pilgrims" (*Week,* 324), arriving eventually at the top of the mountain and "the free air of Unappropriated Land" not yet annexed by man's artifice (334). Though this ascent is the climax of the book's order and the center point of its journey, there is a more elaborate and effective description of a pilgrimage up a mountain in the "Tuesday" chapter. It details a trip up Saddle-Back Mountain which occurred five years after the river journey of 1839 but is paradigmatic enough to contain the lineaments of most of Thoreau's other trips to the top of significant mountains. The route which he took up through the valley "seemed a road for the pilgrim to enter upon who would climb to the gates of heaven" (190). And Thoreau speculates that "he must be the most singular and heavenly-minded man whose dwelling stood highest up the valley" (191). The balance between literal and allegorical is neat and exact, with Thoreau aware, as usual, that his acts were acts of the creative and moral consciousness as well as events in which his body strained to accomplish its desires.

Of course such exertions of body and self were part of the long history of similar ascents, indeed were an important formal element in them; and to ensure that he carries through the formalities precisely, Thoreau rejects the better traveled and more comfortable approach up Saddle-Back for a steeper way through which there was no path. After a night's sleep at the top he looks out on a sea of mist that obliterates "the trivial places we name Massachusetts or Vermont or New York" (198). It seems a dream country, parallel in form to the world below but a paradisiacal transformation of it. He saw "an undulating country of clouds, answering in the varied swell of its surface to the terrestrial world it veiled," but it was unlike the world to which it was formally correspondent because "there was not the substance of impurity, no spot nor stain" (198). Like Wordsworth on Snowden, Thoreau reads into the mist an image of achieved desire. Now the earth below seems only the Pindaric dream of a shadow, and his post on the mountain looks like a halfway house on the road to the divine: "As I had climbed above storm and cloud, so by successive days' journeys I might reach the region of eternal day, beyond the tapering shadow of the earth" (198). The place he is in has been transformed into a country of pristine brightness and unassailable purity, perceptible from below only in faint reflections but seen here both in its own glory and as an echo of the glory still farther up. This foretaste has been sufficient to show him that only a linear continuation of his journey will get him beyond the earth's shadow, but the turnaround is, for now, inevitable. The letdown from such heights ("owing, as I think, to some unworthiness in myself" [199]) is gentler than in other cases; and, as one would expect, he cannot share even the memories of his vision: "[I] soon found myself in the region of cloud and drizzling rain, and the inhabitants affirmed that it had been a cloudy and drizzling day wholly" (200).

Thoreau's ascent to the top of Ktaadn forced him to rethink his attitude toward the old tropes about mountains. His first view

of Ktaadn elicited a stock response about mountains as midpoints
that link men to the divine. It looked like "a dark isthmus in that
quarter, connecting the heavens with the earth" (33). But by the
time he got to the top, it was seen to have a connection with the
divine which was not an invitation but a solemn warning:

> The tops of mountains are among the unfinished parts of the
> globe, whither it is a slight insult to the gods to climb and pry
> into their secrets, and try their effect on our humanity. Only
> daring and insolent men, perchance, go there. Simple races, as
> savages, do not climb mountains—their tops are sacred and
> mysterious tracts never visited by them. Pomola is always
> angry with those who climb to the summit of Ktaadn. (65)

Nearly twenty years later he was still talking of a mountaintop as a
temple and a sacred place "even to the minds of Indians," though
his later comment showed none of the distinct uneasiness of his
remarks about the summit of Ktaadn (see *J,* XIV, 305). In Maine
he had acknowledged the mountain's sacredness, but that statement was preceded by an admission of incapacity. This land was
not amenable to transformation by tropes. There was no suggestion that it was a halfway house on the road to the divine. Quite
the opposite, it was the far limit of materiality, the place where
matter was absolute and irreducible, most purely itself. Thoreau
quotes Book II of *Paradise Lost* with an apt and bitter irony,
protesting, in effect, against this mountain's denial of the meaning
of the old trope:

> Chaos and ancient Night, I come no spy
> With purpose to explore or to disturb
> The secrets of your realm, but . . .
> . . . as my way
> Lies through your spacious empire up to light.
> (64)

The landscape at the top of Ktaadn was entirely of the earth,
earthly, and there was no possibility that the imagination could
look out over it and turn it into a stainless reflection of paradise
pointing upward beyond itself. Ironically, the trip to the top had

satisfied the formal requirement of arduousness, and it had done so far more than any other comparable ascent; but whereas on Saddle-Back the redeeming imagination had been continually at play, allegorizing every move, on Ktaadn it had been under attack long before it got to the mountain, and it was defeated when it reached the top. Further, the passage about the taboo on mountaintops implies that Thoreau has violated a forbidden area, yet he also stresses that the prohibition in regard to Ktaadn is part of Indian spirituality, as exotic to him as he is to this strange landscape. He has insulted a god who is not his own by climbing this mountain and trying its "effect on our humanity." Though he shows all the awe that one ought to have when standing on a sacred place, he is still an alien presence (a point he makes all through *The Maine Woods*), and cannot participate fully in all the sanctity that Ktaadn has to offer. In a later passage he is somewhat harsher and separates himself even further from the place by peopling it with hypothetical inhabitants who are closer than his kind is to the hard and brute unconsciousness of nature: "It was a place for heathenism and superstitious rites,—to be inhabited by men nearer of kin to the rocks and to wild animals than me" (70-71). Perhaps, as he implies with the comment on the taboo, the disastrous effect on his humanity, the dissipation of his finest powers, has been his punishment for transgression. In any case, though Thoreau is obsessed by a form of dread he cannot put that emotion to use: his powers of transformation are held down by the very nature which fills him with awe. The limits of nature are also, paradoxically, the limits of the redemptive imagination.

Ktaadn, then, affected more than the use of old tropes. It challenged the subjective capacities that made use of those tropes and in doing so rubbed abrasively against Thoreau's understanding of what it means to be a man in encounter with nature. He could never separate being from doing, and therefore any event which hindered what some being has the power to do best was a rebuff to its essential order. Thoreau's sense of the center—a man's or nature's—was always involved with a radical potentiality for action. Below all the layers in the swamp was the source where nature's capacities began. His own center, the wild point within him that had a secret, savage name, was clearly of the same sort: it was the place from which his human strengths drew their potency.

The point of beginning was the ur-material, the fertile chaos before the beginning of division and order. In the ironic modes of Romanticism (e.g., in Schlegel and Byron) the subject of imitation was chaos, the complexity and fecund potential in the original state of things: *"Ironie ist klares Bewusstsein der ewigen Agilität, des unendlich vollen Chaos."* [12] The ironists saw consciousness as so adept that it could make an order which successfully mimics pure potency, creating a semblance of chaos whose artifice encompasses the most subtle modulations of order. Thoreau, equally convinced of the capacities of consciousness, was not concerned with imitating the modality of elemental potential but with drawing on its potency. He went into the swamp to revitalize himself, and dug down for the marrow of nature so as to partake of the vital center. The Maine woods, as a place of absolute wildness, were also a home of pristine energy, and he went into them to explore the source. But in Maine Thoreau found a literal chaos when he came upon radical nature, and it was so extreme and irreducible that his own creative potential, his private sources of energy, were severely thwarted. His redemptive skills were considerable but not irresistible. Their desperate self-assertion, which grew more apparent as he walked toward the mountain, was a sign that he was feeling the threat at the most profound levels of being.

The experience on Ktaadn reemphasizes the point that in Thoreau's relationship with nature the materials out there were always, simultaneously, both analogue and antagonist. They were instinct with spirit (if he was in a pure Emersonian mood) or with wildness (if he worked out of his own inclination); and in either case (they were not mutually exclusive) he saw in the world the same qualities that he saw in himself. If the world was also an antagonist, that was because he had a transforming consciousness whose business it was to turn the unconsciousness of nature, which never gave of itself easily, into tools for man's understanding of himself as well as the world. Each does what it does in the relationship because each is what it is; again, modes of activity imply qualities of being. Here on Ktaadn the structure of the relationship remained the same, with nature's similarity coexisting with its adversary stance. But this time the congruence between nature and himself had nothing to do with spirit or even with the energies of wildness: it was strictly concerned with the materiality of his flesh and those rocks, and it raised in him a surprise and implied repulsion that prefigure the existential chill of a Sartrean hero in confrontation with pure existence. The congruence was in an element that he could not control and that made the necessary resistance of nature all the more overpowering. He had little in himself with which to sway nature or to fight it off when its density began to move in on him. Thus his imagination became more insistent and urgent in its workings as its capacity to work became more and more intermittent. A familiar structure of relationship had been tipped absurdly out of balance, and it was not leaning askew for his or any man's benefit.

In fact, the structure was more than familiar to Thoreau. Its components, and their interrelationship, had long been ingrained in his perception and modes of constructing the world, and each of the components had a complex of associations attached to it. He connected all forms of openness, especially when specifically opposed to constrictions, with consciousness and civilization. Openness also included light, a perennial symbol for the acts and products of the mind. Constriction or closeness had to do with the opposites of all these, with darkness, the unconscious, and the wild. Thoreau was too deeply steeped in Romanticism to make easy moral demarcations out of the contrast of light and dark. Romanticists had worked overtly to undermine such assured categorizations, as Blake did with good and evil in *The Marriage of Heaven and Hell* and Hölderlin with the night and holy drunkenness in *Brot und Wein*. Thoreau probably knew Novalis well, and he found the night side of nature to have its own appropriate voices and content, which he expressed in the chapter on "Sounds" in *Walden* (see 125-26). Yet at the same time the pressures of too much constriction and darkness can become claustrophobic, and the emergence into openness, of whatever kind, can then be read as a welcome encounter with light and freedom.

Such events occur occasionally in *The Maine Woods,* where the components which served Thoreau in constructing his world are laid out in stark contrast with each other. The wild woods are broad and expansive, but they are also so jammed with trees and foliage that they can become overpoweringly dark and constrictive. To come out of them is to breathe easier; and through a series of complex associations, to leave them can also mean to move into an area that Thoreau calls civilized, even if it is no more a part of civilization than the woods themselves. Thoreau can work with such strange but irrefutable logic because of the profound brotherhood of clearings, civilization, and openness through which he had always ordered his world. For example, during his third trip to the Maine woods, recorded in "The Allegash and East Branch," he describes the pleasure of crossing a lake "after you have been shut up in the woods, not only on account of the greater expanse of water, but also of sky" (197-98). He then goes on to specify how openness and the wild can be opposites, how the spaciousness of lakes can enlarge the mind while the tightness of woods may constrict men into savagery:

> To look down, in this case, over eighteen miles of water, was liberating and civilizing even. No doubt, the short distance to which you can see in the woods, and the general twilight, would at length react on the inhabitants, and make them *salvages*. The lakes also reveal the mountains, and give ample scope and range to our thought. (198)

A few lines beyond this he remarks how "so quickly we changed the civilizing sky of Chesuncook for the dark wood of the Caucomgomoc" (198). Just after that he speaks of the lakes as "the oldest clearings ... great centres of light." Somewhat later in the same essay he observes that "the Chamberlain Farm is no doubt a cheerful opening in the woods, but such was the lateness of the hour that it has left but a dusky impression on my mind. As I have said, the influx of light merely is civilizing" (240). These patterns of perception and analysis are the same ones he uses to order the relations of self and world around Concord, though he uses them here to commit such apparent illogicalities as calling the sky civilized because it is clear, light, and open. But to see far is to participate in a clearing, which Thoreau, through long habit, identifies with the civilized, while to see only a short distance, and in perpetual twilight, is to become *salvage*. Thoreau's consistency is perfect, and it reveals how hard he was working to bring these difficult experiences into line with familiar patterns of organization and understanding. We can also see how this adds another element of clarification to Thoreau's concern about the hampering of his vision by the clouds near the top of Ktaadn. That too had been a constriction of the capacities of consciousness, the final step in the dissipation of his "substantial thought and fair understanding."

All of these examples show the self busy looking for means of accommodation in the foreign order of the Maine woods, whose wildness, which Thoreau was prepared to admire, was sometimes too much of a good thing. If his attempts at accommodation were often uneasy, and eventually imperfect, that is because he had been used to the efficacy of a creative, reclaiming consciousness, and its powers were severely reduced in these surroundings. Thoreau came to Ktaadn with well-settled expectations about the traditional meanings of mountains. He came with other presuppositions as well, less conscious because they were involved with instinctive forms of ordering experience. Since those forms were ingrained and elemental he could not give them up under any kind of pressure. What he did was to struggle with the discomfortingly dense wilderness of Maine, trying to make it fit with the structures and associations that had worked for him before. That he does make it fit at times is a triumph for the tenacity and flexibility of those forms. But Ktaadn had hit him so hard that the familiar patterns of order could not fully encompass it. The result was an ambivalence about himself and the Maine woods which emerged, at times, in unconscious irony and the derailment of expectations.

The ending of the essay is especially illuminating in this regard. As he moves into the summary pattern, preparing to look over the experiences in perspective, Thoreau turns to some of his most seasoned modes of rhetoric. Through them he attempts to fit his encounter with strangeness into established categories. He begins with a brief meditation on how a man can live "away here on the edge of the wilderness . . . in a new world, far in the dark of a continent," and he goes on to comment on how living at the edge of wildness can involve a move into the recesses of history (*Maine Woods*, 78-79). It is a well-made passage replete with the imagery of clearings and associated phenomena, all of which Thoreau could handle with admirable skill. This was, after all, his basic mode of organizing the challenges that the wild (and the world) made to the organizing consciousness. But Thoreau had learned enough out of his wilderness experiences to qualify—for this landscape, at least—the sufficiency of his own modes. Paddling up the stream is another sort of inhabitant "still more ancient and primitive . . . dim and misty . . . lost in space . . . the red face of man" (79). Deeper into history than his white counterpart, who is conscious of having pushed up to the edge of the unknown, the Indian carries his mysterious business so far into where the white man would like to go that there is no hope of more than the most elusive contact between them. What Thoreau can do is good but not good enough. The Indian is here and now but also in spaces of place and time which Thoreau, with the best he can accomplish, can never encompass.

In the passage which follows, Thoreau reveals in their pristine form all the components in the relationship of open areas and a dense, closed-in mass; but he also shows that he cannot quite come to terms with what he has seen:

> What is most striking in the Maine wilderness is, the continuousness of the forest, with fewer open intervals or glades than you had imagined. Except the few burnt lands, the narrow intervals on the rivers, the bare tops of the high mountains, and the lakes and streams, the forest is uninterrupted. It is even more grim and wild than you had anticipated. . . . The aspect of the country is indeed universally stern and savage, excepting the distant views of the forest from the hills, and the lake prospects, which are mild and civilizing in a degree. (80)

The forest is wild to the extent that it is uninterrupted. Where it is interrupted—"the open intervals or glades"—the wildness (or perhaps more accurately, his awareness of it) is toned down. This passage occurs only a few pages after Thoreau wrote of his shattering perception of absolute nature, pure wildness, at the top of Ktaadn. Thus, the handful of open spaces he refers to show a grim potential for paradox. Of the spaces listed, one, "the few burnt lands," has just been shown to be the object of some duplicity on the part of the redemptive imagination: those lands had seemed "like some pasture run to waste, or partially reclaimed by man" (70). Another set of open spaces, "the bare tops of the high mountains," could describe the summit of Ktaadn itself, where absolute wildness was shown to be absolutely ahuman, or at best fit for creatures who were far closer than he is to nature's unconsciousness. These were hardly clearings which could be comforting in terms of his usual associations, and the result is puzzlement and discomfort. Still, he does manage to temper and civilize the landscape "in a degree" through the broad openness of the views from the hills. The associations are still functioning at that general level, and he makes as much use of them as he can.

Each of these passages is a gesture at accommodation, and their components are treated with such lucidity that Thoreau can show himself, in utter candor, both making the gesture and realizing its insufficiency. What follows after these models of self-awareness is therefore all the more startling. It is so irrelevant to the experiences the essay describes, so glaringly false in this context, that it can be read only as an unconscious admission of incapacity:

> Who shall describe the inexpressible tenderness and immortal life of the grim forest, where Nature, though it be mid-winter, is ever in her spring, where the moss-grown and decaying trees are not old, but seem to enjoy a perpetual youth; and blissful, innocent Nature, like a serene infant, is too happy to make a noise, except by a few tinkling, lisping birds and trickling rills? (81)

There is no question of candor here, none of the qualifying ironies with which Thoreau had controlled his other attempts at making final sense out of the wilderness. The bathos is pure, and it stands as an astonishingly erroneous answer to the most difficult question of all, the nature of nature in the Maine wilderness. It is, in effect, a capitulation. In the following paragraphs, however, Thoreau recovers completely. They contain his fine description of the thin coastal strips of civilization and the contiguity of the massive darkness that enfolds the dense wilderness. At the end of the essay the accustomed modes of organization show that they can indeed work with complete success. He can point to the wilderness without analyzing or describing it, knowing that the gesture of location is sufficient to say all that he wants. It was a rare moment of victory.

The trip to the Maine woods tested the efficacy of other kinds of presuppositions as well, some of them having to do with Thoreau's attitude toward natural bleakness and what he could expect to find in it. If he had not heard or read about the configurations at the top of Ktaadn, Thoreau did speculate, as early as 1841, as to what such a place could be like, and he had his reaction well planned beforehand. In the journal for January 2, 1841, he sketched out a passage which was absorbed two years later into "A Winter Walk." This is the version from the essay:

> In the coldest and bleakest places, the warmest charities still maintain a foothold. A cold and searching wind drives away all contagion, and nothing can withstand it but what has a virtue in it, and accordingly, whatever we meet with in cold and bleak places, as the tops of mountains, we respect for a sort of sturdy innocence, a Puritan toughness. All things beside seem to be called in for shelter, and what stays put must be part of the original frame of the universe, and of such valor as God himself. *(Excursions,* 167)

In such "cold and bleak places, as the tops of mountains," natural things are pushed to a limit, but that limit is still within the field of his habitual experience. The rhetoric is conventional, even a bit tawdry. There are familiar elements of cant; for example, "a sort of sturdy innocence, a Puritan toughness." Particular emphasis is put on words customarily associated with power, such as "virtue" and "valor." The passage implies that even here in the area of the inhospitable the mind should be able to control its shaping of the world, drawing on prefabricated schemes and their attendant language. It can find a place for extremes which gives equal emphasis both to their extremeness and to their continuity with the defined and the predictable. Since the passage describes nothing which could disrupt the accepted patterns, Thoreau could have gone through his usual practice of reading the scene as an emblem for human experience: that is, men driven into such corners survive by virtue of their valor, innocence, and toughness. Certainly he had done that kind of moralizing frequently enough when similar material was at hand. Considering all that Thoreau had encountered in nature up through 1843, this passage was a good guess as to what natural bleakness on a mountaintop could mean. Though it deals with an extreme situation, it is like most other passages of its kind in its tone of assurance and its hint of the easy confidence which sometimes infected even wayward Transcendentalists. But at Ktaadn there was a vast lacuna, a break in the continuity of his experience which was so fundamental and divisive that only the ineffectual sputtering of his domesticating instinct could keep going. There, where old categories gave little direction, Thoreau could only press his own flesh in surprise and helplessness.

By the time of *Walden* Thoreau had modified his earlier subjectivism so that he could bring subject and object into a closer balance, achieving, because of this, a greater suppleness in his handling of the relations of nature and consciousness. But there was never any flexibility sufficient to take in Ktaadn. At times he looked for the specific words and modes with which to control it, but nothing ultimately successful ever came out of these attempts. On August 30, 1856, a year before his last trip to Maine and a decade after the first one, Thoreau tried to work with the materials of Ktaadn. He had found square rods in Middlesex County, he said, that were "little oases of wildness in the desert of our civilization, wild as a square rod on the moon." The proper attitude toward "such planetary matter" was "something akin to reverence"; stone worship was an old and valued form of respect:

> We are so different we admire each other, we healthily attract one another. I love it as a maiden. These spots are meteoric, aerolitic, and such matter has in all ages been worshipped. Aye, when we are lifted out of the slime and film of our habitual life, we see the whole globe to be an aerolite, and reverence it as such, and make pilgrimages to it, far off as it is. (*J,* IX, 45)

All of this is admirable but ineffectual, even a bit tricky. After all, Thoreau had run into such lunar materials elsewhere, and it was not just in tiny pockets surrounded by the gardens of Middlesex County (i.e., his home grounds) but in their own private place where he came and felt what only a stranger to it can experience. Up on Ktaadn he had encountered "hard matter in its home," and his role in the affair, like Satan's, was that of a transgressor *(Maine Woods,* 71). In other words, Thoreau makes it possible to face up to elemental matter only by reversing the facts of the original situation in which he had come upon Ktaadn's moonscape. Much of the rhetoric in this passage is the same he had used in the episode in the Maine woods, but now it is the rocks which are foreign to their surroundings; in Maine it was the redeemer who had been the outsider. Further, and equally important, the meeting with such "terrene, titanic matter extant in my day" does not come after a harrowing ascent in which he sloughs off most of his humane capacities but, instead, occurs as a surprise in a square rod just beyond some local cultivated fields. When he encounters the rock in Middlesex he has not been assaulted at the root levels of his creativity as he had been in Maine ten years before. Here his powers are fully at play, as they always were at home.

As an attempt to give a local habitation to Ktaadn, then, this passage has to fail. Thoreau ends it with the familiar language of domestication, arguing that we ought to reverence the rocks around us and not foreign meteorites: "Is not our broad back-door-stone as good as any corner-stone in heaven?" Of course it is, but that is not the point of the lunar landscape of Ktaadn, as Thoreau knew well. In order to overcome the shattering effects of his earlier experience with these materials he needed a more adequate mode than this, for this one was built on some basic falsifications.

The closest Thoreau ever came to adequacy in the use of the Ktaadn materials—and it is not nearly as close as it first appears— was in a journal entry of October 29, 1857 *(J,* X, 141-44). The passage holds a fascinating and somewhat bizarre combination of components: his usual ideas about mountains as a goal of spiritual ascent are interwoven with a description of a mountain summit which is a precise echo of his earlier pages about Ktaadn. Thoreau was led into this anomalous rhapsody by some comments on the equivocal reality of dreams and half-waking thoughts. To exemplify the problem he turns to his thought of that morning concerning "that mountain in the easterly part of our town (where no high hill actually is)," and he sets out to add to the morning vision with the content of some old related dreams. He used to ascend his imagined mountain through a dark wood (the echoes of Dante are firm and frequent) in which he would occasionally feel a shudder as he went along. Beyond the woods he came to "a rocky ridge half clad with stinted trees," what he later calls "the stinted wood (Nature subdued)." Somewhere in there he crosses an imaginary line of demarcation specifying the final point to which what are called hills (they are only "mere earth heaped up") can ever reach. By then, nature, the earthly, has been fully subdued. What rises after that line has to be called a mountain, and it is beyond the earthly ("superterranean"), awesome and sublime. At its summit are the features of the world he had encountered in Maine some eleven years before:

> What distinguishes that summit above the earthly line, is that it is unhandselled, awful, grand. It can never become familiar; you are lost the moment you set foot there. You know no path but wander, thrilled, over the bare and pathless rock, as if it were solidified air and cloud. That rocky, misty summit, secreted in the clouds, was far more thrillingly awful and sublime than the crater of a volcano spouting fire.

The divinity Thoreau had sensed at the top of Ktaadn becomes more evident here, the summit seeming like "the face of a god turned up," later described as "a hard-featured god reposing." Mulling over the mountain somewhat more, Thoreau realizes that he enters the dark wood through the gate of the Burying-Hill with its graves. He then goes on to remark that there are actually two ways to the summit: one through the wood and nature subdued; another, through a sunny pasture, obviously signifying an acceptance of the brightest and most pastoral passage through life. Thoreau's realization leads him to lament that "in the lives of men we hear more of the dark wood than of the sunny pasture," which is most likely an allusion to the annoying old insistence that one has to die to the natural world in order to ascend to the higher life. After this he compresses and abstracts his vision into a poem, whose main point is to affirm the insubstantiality of the vision and his inability to realize it in more than dream and waking thought. The mountain sinks each day because his aspirations are not yet sufficiently lofty for it. He had made the same point on Saddle-Back, attributing to some failure within himself the need to turn back and go down to the town. In the poem Thoreau clarifies the issue of his personal adequacy by identifying inner order with the road that goes up: "It is a spiral path within the pilgrim's soul/ Leads to this mountain's brow." The way out of the world actually wanders within oneself, but the way is not yet completed and the summit remains inaccessible.

Though Thoreau never expanded these outlines, they hold the potential for some marvelous feats of the imagination. His allegorical bent clearly relished the challenge to turn such enigmatic visions into the order of fable. He mixes literary allusions and old tropes with some personal memories and practiced jibes at dogmatic antinaturalism. As for the Ktaadn experience, it has been cleansed of its existential disturbances and transformed into a grand occasion for awe and pure sublime thoughts. And that is precisely the issue. Thoreau can use this old encounter only by ignoring what it was that he had encountered, what it was that "pilfer[ed] him of some of his divine faculty" and startled him into looking at his distant flesh with awe at its strangeness. There is nothing in this vision about pure nature, hard materiality, or unredeemable rocks. In fact, Thoreau succeeds in redeeming the Ktaadn landscape, what he called the home of "forever untameable *Nature*," only by reversing its character and making it a land beyond nature, a "superterranean" place, what he describes in the poem as "an unearthly ground." But if his encounter is not obsessed with raw natural materiality (his own and the world's), if it does not attempt to come to terms with the palpability of physical substance, then it may have some of the surface features of the Ktaadn experience, may include many of the details of the Maine landscape, but it does not partake of the full meaning *to him* of what he had experienced. The essential issues have not been faced. Nature subdued into unearthiness is part of the meaning of his old tropes of ascent, but it is diametrically opposed to the indomitable nature that had once unnerved him. Thoreau transcends the earthly only by ignoring what he had seen of its irreducible materiality, "the *solid* earth! the *actual* world!" On the evidence of this passage at least, pure nature would seem, after all, to be as untamable as he had found it in Maine.

Thoreau worked a few more times at combining the features of Ktaadn with the tropes of ascent and aspiration. Several trips to Monadnock in his later years gave occasion for attempting that fusion of literary and personal memories which clearly appealed to him because it brought together such extremely disparate elements of his experience. The journal entry for June 2, 1858, begins a long record of several days spent at the summit of Monadnock. As they approached the mountain he saw that it had a "brownish-gray, Ararat color . . . that gray color of antiquity," as befits its age and relation to other "crests of the earth" (*J*, X, 452-53). Put differently, the hue is "a terrene sky-color; solidified air with a tinge of earth," which signifies its role as a midpoint between men and their highest goals (453). Though there are mundane fragments of human business, such as newspapers and eggshells, up on the summit it is still "unhandselled [a key word that always denotes the Ktaadn phenomenon] and untouched. The natural terraces of rock are the steps of this temple" (458). This combination of the inchoate and the pious looks oxymoronic enough to be a successful concatenation of some of Thoreau's habitual concerns. Actually it is a skillful instance of those conventional versions of the sublime which fuse cragginess and religiosity into an affective pattern. (Some of the landscapes of Thomas Cole, especially when he was in a midway stage between pure landscape and religious allegory, show a similar combination of components.) Thoreau has toned down the potential of his materials to make them fit with a description of the summit of Monadnock, but he has kept the materials heightened enough to lend strangeness to this well-traveled mountain. The intensity of the individual elements is so well under control that the imagination finds a place for the unhandselled without giving it dominance over the holiness that is always part of the import of high places. The rocks of Monadnock are bare, ancient, and familiar, radically strange but not over-whelmingly so. They even have their voices. On the first evening Thoreau heard the nighthawks whose "supramundane" sounds "gave fit expression to this rocky mountain solitude. . . . It was a thrumming of the mountain's rocky chords; strains from the music of Chaos" (460). This is the same blending of chaos and the superterranean, the inchoate and the transcendent, which Thoreau had worked out when he went over his dreams and morning thoughts. Once again he makes echoes of Ktaadn amenable to the imagination by stripping them of their most essential meanings and the chill that went with the old encounter. The chaos up on

Ktaadn did not sing, though it seemed to tell him to go home. Thoreau, it appears, could neither make use of his memories in all their fullness nor put them entirely out of his mind. It was clear that they had to be used in this way—reduced in scale, domesticized, with the fear strained out—or they could not be used at all.[13]

Thus, Thoreau was defeated by the material of Ktaadn both before and after his first trip as well as on the summit itself. His early guess about the bleakness of summits had been unwittingly insufficient, while his late probings—though excellent in other ways—were too far from the truth. Because of its melodramatic atmosphere this experience and its numerous echoes emerge as outstanding examples of the mind's struggle to fully control all of the nature that was given to it; but they are by no means the only forms of that struggle or of the difficulties Thoreau's imagination had in taming and redeeming certain aspects of nature. We shall be looking at other versions throughout the remainder of this study. The issue was complicated by Thoreau's ability to carry, simultaneously, a variety of convictions and experiences which did not sit harmoniously with each other, and occasionally met in severe contradiction. There was a prominent aspect of Thoreau which could hold with Blake's assertion in *The Marriage of Heaven and Hell* that "where man is not, nature is barren." In the Argument to the *Marriage* the just man brings forth roses where there are thorn bushes, and puts honeybees out on the barren heath. Then he is driven away "into barren climes," presumably to resume the great cycle once again. Thoreau's own myths are neither so sustained nor so elaborate as Blake's, but the issue of natural barrenness is exactly the same, as in fact it was throughout most versions of Romantic epistemology. Thoreau is likely at almost any time to sound like Blake; and the latter's usual affirmation of the ultimate subservience of nature to the workings of consciousness was itself only one of the most extreme versions of a perennial Romantic position. Here, for example, are Thoreau in 1853 and Sénancour in 1804:

What is Nature unless there is an eventful human life passing within her? Many joys and many sorrows are the lights and shadows in which she shows most beautiful. (*J*, V, 472)

Que seriez-vous [monts superbes, etc.] à l'homme si vous ne lui parliez point des autres hommes? La nature serait muette, s'ils n'etaient plus.[14]

And the pattern goes on throughout Thoreau's life: in 1856 he said that "man is all in all, Nature nothing, but as she draws him out and reflects him" (*J*, IX, 121); in 1860 he asserted that "all nature is to be regarded as it concerns man" (*J*, XIV, 117). From these passages it would seem that nature's barrenness (the state when there is no mind working over it) comes from its pointlessness. It is a realm of unmeaning, without significance when it is untouched by man.

Sherman Paul has argued, with considerable persuasiveness, that Thoreau goes through an overall development from subjective to objective idealism, from a sense of nature's subservience to a more modest awareness of its toughness and density, as well as its independence from man.[15] The *Week* and *Walden* show the major stages in the sequence: if *Walden* stresses from its very first page that men are unbridgeably separate from each other, it ends having asserted that nature (though kindred and analogous) is separate from all of them and is always, to some degree, resistant. But Thoreau is as remarkable for his inconsistency in these matters as he is for an undoubted development out of the arrogance of consciousness to an acknowledgment of its limitations. He was capable of both evolution and fluctuation, and sometimes both within the same period of time. For example, from 1851 to 1853, when he was working over the final versions of *Walden*, Thoreau wrote into the journals a number of comments about the relations of consciousness and nature which show him at his most subjectively idealistic, as though he had never been repelled by the touch of matter at Ktaadn, or found a loon to be a fit symbol of nature's mocking inaccessibility. One passage will do as a model, since it was put down on May 23, 1853, during the final stages of the writing of *Walden:*

The poet must bring to Nature the smooth mirror in which she is to be reflected. He must be something superior to her, something more than natural. . . . No genius will excuse him from importing the ivory which is to be his material. (*J*, V, 184)

This echoes not only the stance of Emerson's *Nature* but the insistence in Coleridge's "Dejection" that "we receive but what we give,/And in our life alone does Nature live." Here is no meeting of equals but an association in which consciousness must dominate and give meaning or the relationship will have no valid result. Thoreau put it with less restraint a year before: "Nature must be viewed humanly to be viewed at all." Without an association with "humane affections . . . she ceases to be morally significant" (*J*, IV, 163). Yet the ending of *Walden*, already in developed form by the time of these comments, shows Thoreau exulting in the emergence of spring as a promise of man's recovery from the winters of the soul; and the nature which images that promise, though allied to him, is outside of and independent of himself, not merely a vehicle for the projection of desire. The presence of these differing and even contradictory assertions during the same period of time does not indicate retrogression or confusion but ambivalence, a fluctuation based on a compulsive struggle to integrate desire and capability. The echoes of that struggle are studded throughout the journals and continue with intense and stubborn persistence until the end of Thoreau's life.

The experience on Ktaadn may have had something to do with Thoreau's development toward a more objective idealism, forcing upon him a recognition of the otherness of nature.[16] But if it did he was unable to tame the experience itself. What it showed him of the relations of consciousness with the extremities of wildness, as well as its ironic reminder that he was, assuredly, at one with nature's materiality, remained a grim memory that Thoreau could never shake off. To put it another way, his experiences in Maine were in some respects quite the opposite of Blakean ideas about the barrenness of nature when it is independent of man. Thoreau saw, and at several points argued, that where man is not, nature may well be replete with fierce energies that have nothing to do with men. Of course the Blakean position does not deny the existence of nature's vitality (Vala's world is thick and green), but the significance of that quality outside the imagination. Thoreau holds the same position in his most subjectively idealistic moments. Yet Ktaadn showed him that there were powers in nature independent of the powers of his mind; and those natural energies were most dominant when he was least able to do anything with natural forms. That lesson did not die away in 1846. On his third and last trip to Maine, Thoreau states with impressive precision what it feels like to be in a world where Blake's assertions no longer hold:

> Only solemn bear-haunted mountains, with their great wooded slopes, were visible; where, as man is not, we suppose some other power to be. My imagination personified the slopes themselves, as if by their very length they would waylay you, and compel you to camp again on them before night. Some invisible glutton would seem to drop from the trees and gnaw at the heart of the solitary hunter who threaded those woods; and yet I was tempted to walk there. *(Maine Woods,* 184)

This was midsummer, 1857. These powers are a more aggressive, animistic version of the ones on the summit of Ktaadn; but in both cases the powers become apparent because consciousness cannot overcome the intensity of nature, and it is forced to take a markedly subsidiary role. Of course Thoreau does personify the natural energies he senses out there, and to that extent the imagination is at its proper business; but he personifies only to give form to the threat that those energies pose him. Thoreau's contradiction of the Blakean affirmation is exact: "where, as man is not, we suppose some other power to be." It seems that some kind of force has to be present in the world, and if man's consciousness is not viable, then another dominating power will necessarily emerge. Nature abhors a vacuum of energy and will fill the spaces itself if man cannot enter.

These observations in "The Allegash and East Branch" lock in with several letters Thoreau wrote to Harrison Blake in 1857, shortly after the final trip to Maine. On August 18 Thoreau recounts his business in Maine briefly and then goes on to several paragraphs of impressions. The first is about Indians and the woods, outlining his understanding of the meaning of Indian man in the wilderness. Thoreau goes up to the edge to which civilized men have pushed their probings and stops there, at the line where the wild begins: "I have made a short excursion into the new world which the Indian dwells in, or is. He begins where we leave off"

(Correspondence, 491). Beyond the edge, where there had seemed to be only elemental wildness, there is actually a form of human consciousness which is not white or civilized but is still human and therefore not brutish. He has discovered another instance of man's adequacy, and the effect of this discovery is to claim for mind what had always appeared to be out of its province: "I rejoice to find that intelligence flows in other channels than I knew. It redeems for me portions of what had seemed brutish before" (491). Yet this kind of adequacy is not exactly his own and is therefore not fully available to him. In the most general sense Thoreau has claimed the redemption for himself, as a man; but *he* is not in those woods, and the red men who are actually in it are of a kind whose business he cannot share. Further, he has at least a suspicion that the Indian's kind is closer to the woods themselves than to other men: the Indian not only lives in the woods but may *be* them: "the new world which the Indian dwells in, or is." Somewhat later Thoreau would report the strange affair in which Joe Polis, trying to attract a musquash, "seemed suddenly to have quite forsaken humanity, and gone over to the musquash side" *(Maine Woods,* 206-7). Indeed, at his first meeting with Polis, Thoreau speaks of "that strange remoteness in which the Indian ever dwells to the white man" *(Maine Woods,* 158). In the two later essays in *The Maine Woods* Thoreau transfers some of his awe about nature to the Indian, who partakes of areas of nature's secretive otherness which Thoreau could never hope to experience. The discovery about the new channels of intelligence in the woods is therefore not quite so comforting as it first seems. Thoreau's ambivalence does not undercut the revelation so much as qualify it into the most abstract sort of usefulness.

His ambivalence is somewhat starker in a letter written a month later, on November 16. Even on this third excursion north, and even with the recognition that some kind of man can make a place in the thickest wilderness, Thoreau cannot annul the touch of the first experience at Ktaadn. Under the prodding of the recent trip he brings to the surface the unnerving events of eleven years before. The old repulsion is partly palliated, but the disturbing separation from the flesh is still recapturable: "You must ascend a mountain to learn your relation to matter, and so to your own body, for *it* is at home there, though *you* are not . . . but your spirit inevitably comes away, and brings your body with it, if it lives" (*Correspondence,* 497). Perhaps because he does not have the rocks immediately before him, Thoreau turns his concentration more directly to himself and is now more specific than before about the segments of his body. He begins to dawdle over his fingers, "the funniest companions I have ever found." There is some echo of the earlier questioning as he toys with his fingers but there is also a new bit of bravado: *"Who* am I? What are they?—those little peaks—call them Madison, Jefferson, Lafayette. What is *the matter?"* His mind plays over the tips of his fingers with some decidedly nervous analogizing, masked as his usual play of wit.

In theme this image-making reaffirms the kinship of his own matter with that on the mountains. In mode it is the same kind of assertiveness to which he had given way when he made sheep out of rocks, and pasturage out of the burned lands. But on Ktaadn he brought the domestic to the wild, making objects from home out of objects that were distinctly strange. Here he reverses the process, making the most local material, his fingers, into pieces of the bleak world at the mountain's summit. This reversal is neither accidental nor a trick of the mind; rather, he is now under the pressure of a subliminal recognition which was not overtly stated in the essay about Ktaadn but emerges here after ten years of meditation on the experience. If his body was at home with the materials on Ktaadn, he has now come to see that it is equally at home with the local matter under his feet—an obvious but ominous fact which he had never before brought into the context of his disturbing experience in Maine. The body "might have been composed [on the mountain], and will have no farther to go to return to dust there, than in your garden. . . . Just as awful really, and as glorious, is your garden." The word "glorious" is new and not especially convincing: in "Ktaadn" he had spoken of nature as "savage and awful, though beautiful," but its beauty was less impressive than its massive materiality. More significant, because it serves to distinguish his spirit from the earth at home, is that identification of the matter in Concord with its bleak counterpart on the mountains. What sits on Ktaadn or Mount Washington is starker and therefore more glaring in its presence; but it shares materiality with the lush earth of the gardens at home.

This localization is new, and it exposes a complicated irony that had to be deeply disconcerting. We know that Thoreau and others had always asserted the relative tameness of European nature, arguing that genuine wildness was not part of contemporary European experience but was exotic, found only in foreign places. America, of course, was one of those places where the wild was truly at home, the product of local grounds. When Thoreau first went up to Ktaadn, however, he was unsettled by the *strangeness* of the nature up there, its separateness from his own snug and equally American surroundings. The strata of nature which were most purely wild, the strata which—before Ktaadn—had seemed to be local, turned out to be as exotic to his own domestic world as pure wildness was to a European. Up there he was in *its* home, and that was not at all like his own, though his imagination instinctively tried to make it so. If there had been any comfort on Ktaadn it was in the feeling that his own world was safely distinct from this bleak, oppressive, fascinating, and exotic landscape. He had put it this way in the first essay:

> Vast, Titanic, inhuman Nature . . . does not smile on [man] as in the plains. She seems to say sternly, why came ye here before your time? This ground is not prepared for you. Is it not enough that I smile in the valleys? I have never made this soil for thy feet, this air for thy breathing, these rocks for thy neighbors. I cannot pity nor fondle thee here, but forever relentlessly drive thee hence to where I *am* kind. (*Maine Woods,* 64)

And it went without saying that nature was kind (and kindred) around Concord. Its wildness was well within his control. But now, ten years later, Thoreau has come to acknowledge that there really is, after all, no essential difference between the strange chunks on the mountain and the lusher earth under his feet at home. Thus, in another complete turnaround Thoreau has reverted to his original position, admitting that the purest and most extreme wildness is indeed immediately present, in the shape of the elemental matter which his home turf has in common with the strange landscape on the mountain. The seemingly (and safely) exotic is actually part of what he can reach out and touch at home. That means, most of all, that the dense palpability which his flesh shares with the earth will be as apparent to him here at home as it was on the mountaintop. When he compared European and American nature, localization had been an arrogantly chauvinistic act. At this point in 1857 it was a disturbing admission that he could not evade. As it turns out, the frontier was only too proximate.[17]

Thoreau's studies of the American wild and of the place of his selfhood within the order of the American landscape had led him to put wildness at the utmost domestic point, deep within the radical strata of personality. Nothing could be more local than that submerged part of the self which has the secret savage name. Obviously this is something more than proximity, more than the sharing of a location with wildness. It is not a question of where we are, what is next to us, but of what we are, what is inside of us; and since it is also concerned with the identification of an aspect of ourselves with an element that is outside, the question came out to be a matter of continuity, not just of proximity. Thoreau ran through a related version of this recognition in the letter to Harrison Blake of November 16, 1857, but with an additional factor: the identity and continuity he was concerned with at that point were specifically objective and external, involved with the materiality he shared with Ktaadn's rocks. When he recognized that the substance of the Ktaadn landscape was no different in kind than what the earth held at home, he was also moved, once again, to identify the material of his fingers with that of the mountains in Maine. He saw that the complex included both the contiguous and the consubstantial, an awareness which was rare but exceptionally important for him when it occurred. The difficulty was in learning to control and shape that awareness, to find a way for the imagination to turn this hard knowledge into forms that would reveal the strength of consciousness in regard to the things of the world. His problem was intensified because when the memory of Ktaadn emerged again, his agitation had mellowed but was no less unsettling than before. Thus, Thoreau immediately set his imagination to work and came up with the bit of play about his fingers, but the nervousness of his wit disclosed the disturbance generated by these old and new recognitions.

This complex of continuity and proximity, flesh and spirit,

had so many complications and potential contradictions within it that Thoreau could avoid the built-in traps only by keeping the components of the complex separated. For example, when Thoreau was struck by the identity of his body and the earth, he could discharge the resultant tensions through the traditional likening of flesh and dust. All the Transcendentalists made use of that trope, perhaps because of the roots the movement had in the New England pulpits. In the letter to Blake, however, Thoreau builds a frame for the trope out of a specifically American landscape, localizing the analogy by making a home for it in the familiar places of American geography. Of course that is what Thoreau was always intent on doing, proving that all facets of the great world could be observed within the microcosm of Concord. On a grander continental scale this localization occurred in those forms of American chauvinism which saw the regeneration of ancient experience taking place all over the American landscape. To make it local meant that Thoreau could lock the revelations about matter into the order of imagery with which he was most at home. In the incident recorded in the letter, however, Thoreau fell into some subtle and incisive ironies: he had unwittingly achieved the localization he usually sought, but in a context that made the exploit nothing to congratulate oneself about.

Yet the issue is even more complex, and the ironies are multiple. If the ancient likening of flesh and earth could be comforting only to the most ascetic observers, the identity of the wildness within and the wildness without was one of the best hopes of contemporary America. Wildness represented a barely tapped source of energy (what he called in "Walking" "the springs of life") which every American could observe in his landscape and, insofar as he was Adamic and aware of his own vital center, in himself as well (*Excursions,* 209). When Thoreau located a slice of the wild within the enclosure of self, he gave it a place in the order of consciousness which was nearly as important as those of his genius and his talent. This was clearly a continuity to be trumpeted, not mulled over while staring nervously at the tips of one's fingers. But the revelations which grew out of the Ktaadn experience had shown Thoreau that wildness was inseparable from the materiality that embodied it, and if that fact was true of the top of a mountain it was true of himself as well. Men share not only in the innate energies at the core of things but also in the incarnation through which the energies have to function.

If the prevalent American myths were unrestrainedly optimistic about the potential of those energies, Thoreau's recognition of the necessary fleshly accompaniment could be unsettling and cacophonous, if not quite contradictory. Thoreau had once hoped that America would come up with a local version of the inspiring (and inspirited) eminence which most major cultures had found for themselves. He had mentioned that point in his essay about a trip to the top of Wachusett, perhaps the most consciously literary of all his ascents: "Who knows but this hill may one day be a Helvellyn, or even a Parnassus, and the Muses haunt here, and other Homers frequent the neighboring plains" *(Excursions,* 144). Ktaadn, as it turned out, was an anti-Olympus, a mountain which did not inspire the imagination but choked off all of its functions. It did, however, manage to localize an old analogy of flesh and earth, but that was not quite what Thoreau had in mind with his comments on Wachusett.

All these differing readings and evaluations of wildness reveal a profound, complex, and recurrent ambivalence which Thoreau would experience whenever all of the ramifications came home to him at once. Of course they did not always do so, and he managed to comment very often on wildness and its attendant energies without making the connection with flesh and all that an awareness of the flesh entailed. But the possibility of all the connections being made was always there, and when it did happen Thoreau responded with an ambivalence that had wide reverberations. There is weighty and considerable evidence that the whole set of associations came together often enough—sometimes obliquely, sometimes with full and direct force—to have a considerable effect upon the products of Thoreau's mature imagination.

But the components of this issue were not the discoveries of his mature imagination or even of the encounter on Ktaadn. It is possible to see them in juxtaposition much earlier in Thoreau's experience and to realize, as a result, that Thoreau had ascended Ktaadn with presuppositions about the flesh as well as the mind. The hunger for communion with wildness and the disturbance about one's own meat were already old issues by the time he went to Maine. What Ktaadn did was to bring together a series of related perceptions which Thoreau had been able to keep safely separate before that time. For example, in a journal entry for December 10, 1840, Thoreau reports his discovery of a track in the snow, which turns out to be that of a migrating otter. He reacts with a feeling of plenitude ("I am thus reminded that every chink and cranny of nature is full to overflowing") and with the startled but obviously comforting "assurance that the primeval nature is still working" *(Consciousness at Concord,* 187). He says nothing about hungering for the animal's meat as a way of getting through to a full association with the otter, though he was to refer to such hunger later in the analogous episode in "Higher Laws." Instead, Thoreau speaks only of the desire for a fusion with the essential wildness of the animal he nearly encountered: "Now I yearn toward him—and heaven to me consists in a complete communion with the otter nature." He ends this observation with a curious bit of uneasiness, expressed in the sentimentalism characteristic of the early Thoreau: "Mere innocence will tame any ferocity." Four days after this entry, on December 14, Thoreau spun out a long Baudelairean passage on the rankness of carrion. He finds the decay of flesh to be foul and sickening and wishes that man's carcass had the ability to die by dry rot, as a tree does, rather than putrefy and pollute the atmosphere around it. The tone of the first paragraph is typical of the whole:

> How may a man most cleanly and gracefully depart out of nature? At present his birth and death are offensive and unclean things. Disease kills him, and his carcass smells to heaven. It offends the bodily sense, only so much as his life offended the moral sense. It is the odor of sin. (188-89)

Yet it is not just the dead flesh but the flesh itself, living or dead, that is ultimately disgusting. The body was always mere meat: "It was no better than carrion before but just animated enough to keep off the crows" (189). Further, the separation from flesh does not fully guarantee the cleanliness of the soul as it rises to heaven: what was left behind is so impure in itself that the soul might well have been stained by it: "The guest is known by his leavings. . . . Will our spirits ascend pure and fragrant from our tainted carcasses?" (189).

The proximity of the entries of the tenth and the fourteenth is as important as the fact that they are in no way brought together, not to say reconciled. It may be that the proximity is a signal that at some level of awareness Thoreau recognized that they are related, if only through collision. The sentimentalism about ignorance and ferocity would seem to confirm that. A year later he was certainly aware of the association of flesh and wildness, as appears in the sentimental bravado of a letter to Lucy Brown on July 21, 1841:

> I grow savager and savager every day, as if fed on raw meat, and my tameness is only the repose of untamableness. I dream of looking abroad summer and winter, with free gaze, from some mountain-side, while my eyes revolve in an Egyptian slime of health,—I to be nature looking into nature with such easy sympathy as the blue-eyed grass in the meadow looks in the face of the sky. (*Correspondence,* 45)

Feeding on flesh is the sort of action that intensifies one's own wildness; and the increased personal savagery leads to a deeper sense of continuity with nature, a closeness that is so pure and concentrated that he becomes what he beholds: "I to be nature looking into nature." Communion can go no further in intimacy than the achievement of identity. Obviously there is nothing here about the rankness of carrion or the association of moral and physical rottenness.[18] If the journal entries of the year before were brought no closer together than fairly near neighbors, the letter links the issues of wildness and the flesh but ignores his earlier distaste for the body—which, even before death, was "no better than carrion." To force all these elements into a single complex would have created a disastrous ambivalence for which Thoreau had no solutions at that time. He had not yet developed imaginative forms through which he could attempt to handle all of the components at once. He solved the problem of adequacy simply by avoiding it.

Later, at Walden, the issues continued to come up. In the

chapter on "Economy" Thoreau announces that he had once devoured a woodchuck which had been eating through his bean field, but he was not especially pleased with the result: "though it afforded me a momentary enjoyment . . . I saw that the longest use would not make that a good practice" *(Walden,* 59). In order to feed his own substance he had given the woodchuck its freedom from earthliness, "effect[ed] its transmigration, as a Tartar would say." So went nature's balance, though not to the thorough satisfaction of either party. Thoreau gives no specific reasons for his distaste, though in the context of the other observations we have been inspecting his reasons are obvious enough. In the context of the chapter, the reference follows directly on the chart of his expenses for food, and it occurs among some supplementary remarks on the ways in which he eked out his slim budget with a mess of fish. Of course the whole chapter is ultimately concerned with the economy of the spirit, its care, feeding, and development. Thoreau absorbs himself in describing the specifics of his business at the pond, but "Economy" is one of the more obvious examples of his method of making a fact blossom into a truth. In this chapter economic problems develop into an implied structure of the relationship of flesh and spirit: there is a ratio through which the relative spareness of his budget for food is countered by the richness of its mirror image, the budget of the spirit. As the value of one goes up, the value of the other has to go down. That means that any act affecting the economy of either one will have an equivalent effect on the economy of the other. With the elimination of his flesh the woodchuck has been redeemed and transmigrated, becoming the woodchuck equivalent of spirit. It seems probable, then, considering Thoreau's recurrent comments, that the enrichment of his flesh through the ingestion of woodchuck meat resulted in a depletion of the budget of his spirit. This counterbalance of budgets was always delicate and, from all available evidence, rarely stable. All sorts of hunger could throw it off.

After his adolescence Thoreau gave up the usual kind of hunting and never scouted the woods for flesh simply to feed his body. (He tended to differentiate fish from meat and had less compunction about the former.) When he ate the woodchuck who had been ravaging his field it was "partly for experiment's sake," in

line with his inclination to make every possible test upon phenomena so as to discover the ways in which they could relate to
him *(Walden,* 53). It was an economical devouring which tested one
way of fusing with another form of being. Still, the animal was
killed and ingested and literally became a part of himself; and that
single fact about the action puts it at the opposite end of the
spectrum from the union he had wanted back in 1840 with the
essence of the muskrat who wandered through his yard. The best
way, the most encompassing form of communion with wildness,
would be able to accomplish every possibility in this spectrum:
that is, it would make literal devouring into a symbol of an act of
union that means more than a joining of the flesh. Thus, the
temptation toward the woodchuck described at the beginning of
"Higher Laws" represents the optimum mode of amalgamation, a
form of totemic relationship. This sacramental act would give
equal due to both the flesh and the essential wildness of nature
which is inseparable from the flesh. It would keep them in a
balance which seems neither tenuous nor tricky but designed to
respect all the natural economies which concern a man. The eating
of the woodchuck would have been an act of the flesh which was
not for the sake of the flesh but for what it could lead to: "[I] felt a
strange thrill of savage delight, and was strongly tempted to seize
and devour him raw; not that I was hungry then, except for that
wildness which he represented *(Walden,* 210).[19] By so demonstrating his continuity with wildness Thoreau would be doing everything that it was possible for a man to do with the immediate
presence of other phenomena. He would satisfy nature so admirably that his craving for it would be seen to be as worthy as the
craving for spiritual fulfillment, the other outstanding element in
the complex system of his desires. This means that there are two
equally valid continuities at play, and however different their
directions and goals, he can move out of the enclosure of the self
and travel successfully in both:

> I found in myself, and still find, an instinct toward a higher,
> or, as it is named, spiritual life, as do most men, and another
> toward a primitive rank and savage one, and I reverence them
> both. I love the wild not less than the good. (210)

His phrasing affirms that the equality was not momentary, not confined to the once or twice when he ranged the woods "like a half-starved hound" or to August 23, 1845, the day the woodchuck crossed in front of him (*J*, I, 384-85). Rather, he found the balance then and finds it still: the equal instincts have stayed with him.

This was a subtle and hard-won bit of juggling, and the fact that it works at all, even on this one page, is admirable. It works so long as neither element is neglected in any way; and neglect in this case could involve a slightly weightier leaning toward one side. Such leaning, if it were to exist, would perhaps be apparent in a tendency to evaluate one side more favorably than the other, an imbalance which would throw the whole structure awry. After all, "I reverence them both. I love the wild not less than the good." And with all the due reverence given to each side, with the hunting of the flesh undertaken only to establish continuity with a totem, Thoreau cannot manage to make a perfectly adequate structure. He gives himself away almost immediately, in the pairing, through contrast, of the wild and the good. Thoreau probably meant that he reverenced the wild forces in things just as much as he honored the moral differentiations which are necessary to experience. Indeed, he could not credibly mean anything else. Yet the dichotomy of wild and good is arresting, not because it is illegitimate, but because the words are a strange pair to be offered as opposites. The contrary of the wild is ordinarily the tame, not the good. The contrary of the good is ordinarily evil, not the wild. To contrast the wild and the good is, it would appear, to link the good with the tame and the wild with evil—especially when no encouragement to think otherwise is offered in the text. In the letter to Lucy Brown, quoted above, Thoreau had specifically associated the wild with "untamableness," and that fits in precisely with the pairing Thoreau offers in "Higher Laws": the opposite of the untamable, or the wild, is the tame. But the ordinary opposite of good is never mentioned, leaving a strange and striking lacuna in Thoreau's argument at the beginning of the chapter.

It is not so much that Thoreau is losing control over his language as that an ambivalence about the contrasts he is juggling creeps into his act through the language he uses to describe it. This ought not to be confused with the Blakean kind of wordplay which proves that the evaluation of contraries varies according to point of view. As the rest of the chapter shows, Thoreau is not playing with Blakean ironies, of the sort worked out in *The Marriage of Heaven and*

Hell, concerning "what the religious call Good & Evil." Nor is there any ambiguity about what the words mean: they are unusually rich, but their clarity is perfect, if not perfectly comforting. Variations of this passage appear in the "E" text of *Walden,* written in 1852-53, and they show that Thoreau was never in doubt about the import of his language or the realms of experience to which the words point.[20] However strange the pairing of wild and good, Thoreau's understanding of their denotations is quite specific and traditional. Over an early phrasing about "what is called spiritual life" he had written and then scratched out, "you may well call moral." After the remark about the spiritual life, he added, "I use this word with limitations, because though we have the idea, we have not the reality," a sentence which was dropped in the subsequent ("F") version. This sentence is followed by the section on the "primitive, rank and savage" life, exactly as it is phrased in the final text; but between that and the material on the dual reverence (which is also given as phrased in the final text) he interposes the following: "Some would say that the one impulse was directly from God, the other through nature." That too was omitted permanently by the next version, though both sentences that were left out prefigure, and conform to, the materials finally used in the remainder of the chapter. There is, in fact, no contradiction between the import of the omitted sentences and the concerns about nature and spirit that dominate the last half of "Higher Laws," but the sentences do conflict essentially with those pages in which they actually appear.

The association of the spiritual with the moral and with God, and the association of the primitive with the wild and with nature, set up a dichotomy which seems to work but in fact indicates a profound disturbance about the evaluation of the poles. This bit of slippage is neither accidental nor temporary. It points unmistakably to the contrast that will come to dominate the chapter on "Higher Laws," connecting the balancing act at the beginning of the chapter with all of the material throughout it which contradicts the overt assertions in the balancing act. In the very act of making his point about equality Thoreau shows an uncertainty about it. The first page of "Higher Laws" has one of Thoreau's most remarkable moments, and it is so not less for what it says in *sotto voce* than for his proud statements about parity of reverence.[21]

What happens in the rest of the chapter, after an interim discussion about hunting, turns into an extolling of spirit at the expense of flesh; and that adulation flatly contradicts, and is in no way reconcilable with, the equality of reverence trumpeted in the introductory pages. Thoreau places the spiritual "higher," a word he uses several times to describe it, including once at the beginning of the chapter; and he points out that his instinct for fishing, that is, for catching and eating flesh, places him among "the lower orders of creation" (214). Further, in the chapter on "Chesuncook" in *The Maine Woods* he argues that the "higher law affecting our relations to pines as well as men" involves a deep respect for that aspect of pines and men which is antithetical to their materiality: "A pine cut down, a dead pine, is no more a pine than a dead human carcass is a man" *(Maine Woods,* 121). That position is consistent with the argument he eventually develops in "Higher Laws." It is certainly possible to reverence both the wild and the good and still place one on a higher level in the overall order of human experience. It is far more difficult to place one of them higher and still give both equal love. But is it a quite different attitude from reverence to say that "there is something essentially unclean about this diet and all flesh" *(Walden,* 214), or "the repugnance to animal food is not the effect of experience, but is an instinct" (214), or

> We are conscious of an animal in us, which awakens in proportion as our higher nature slumbers. It is reptile and sensual, and perhaps cannot be wholly expelled; like the worms which, even in life and health, occupy our bodies. Possibly we may withdraw from it, but never change its nature. I fear that it may enjoy a certain health of its own; that we may be well, yet not pure. (219)

Our lower aspect is stubborn and unwelcome, part of a totality but self-contained. Its modes and interests are so different that it must be contrary in kind to the higher aspect. Thoreau then goes on to make just that point:

> The other day I picked up the lower jaw of a hog, with white and sound teeth and tusks, which suggested that there was an animal health and vigor distinct from the spiritual. This

creature succeeded by other means than temperance and
purity. (219)

And those last-named virtues are the ones which this chapter ends
by extolling. The dichotomy of flesh and spirit creates a gap which
cannot be bridged, and the hiatus exists not only between the flesh
and the spirit but between the animal and the human as well. The
beast which succeeded "by other means than temperance and
purity" can have nothing to offer to a man who wants to deal with
the best in himself, or to make the best that he can out of himself.
Nor does it seem likely that the man can find a lasting use for the
wild, the opposite of the good, since "goodness is the only
investment that never fails" (218). This whole position clashes
irreconcilably with the familiar Transcendental argument that, as
Alcott puts it, "matter is ever pervaded and agitated by the
omnipresent soul. All things are instinct with spirit." [22]

In the world of "Higher Laws" spirit does not give so freely of
itself. Thoreau mentions two instincts whose simultaneous presence
reveals a warfare within the self. One is the basis of the desire to
fish: "There is unquestionably this instinct in me which belongs to
the lower orders of creation" (214). The other, an exactly
countervailing tendency, turns up a few lines later: "The repugnance to animal food is not the effect of experience, but is an
instinct" (214). Only the latter tendency is involved with spirit. His
discomfort about fishing "is a faint intimation, yet so are the first
streaks of morning" (214). It is a hint of the dawning of the day of
the spirit, the prospective awakening referred to in the last lines of
Walden.

Clearly, the pairing of equals promulgated at the beginning of
the chapter has collapsed. What had seemed to be a confident and
compelling instance of harmonious cooperation turned out to be as
tenuous and imbalanced as any other. Though Thoreau talks
about both aspects in the same context, they are as separate and
essentially unalike as on those pages in the early journals where he
kept his desire for wildness and his repugnance for the flesh in
different compartments of his mind. By the end of the chapter
Thoreau has carried the dichotomies, and the moral imperatives
involved with them, as far as he can go: "He is blessed who is
assured that the animal is dying out in him day by day, and the

divine being established" (220). Only the most intensely sought and absolute purity can counter the animality that is in each of us, especially since one's likeness to beasts involves more than skeletal structure or even the palpability of flesh. In the "E" text of *Walden* Thoreau has the following:

> I do not know how it is with other men, but I find it very difficult to be chaste. Methinks I can be chaste in my relation to persons, and yet I do not find myself clean. I have frequent cause to be ashamed of myself. I am well but not pure.[23]

Most of these first-person comments were dropped from the final text or changed into a third-person voice; Thoreau would carry his status as an example only so far. But the issues remained in strong comments that were applicable to everyone. We have to eat, drink, cohabit, and sleep—these are all "but one appetite"—though we can accomplish these necessary duties without sensuality, if we so choose. The potential for uncleanness is always there, yet it can be overcome by a Carlylean immersion in work, "though it be at cleaning a stable" (221). All of this culminates in a sentence that is meant to clarify and summarize the movement of the whole argument which had been gathering momentum for much of the chapter: "Nature is hard to overcome, but she must be overcome" (221). This is not a sloppy use of the major substantive in Thoreau's rhetoric. "Nature," here, is all of his physical impulses as well as the material which embodies them. It is the palpable reality of his flesh and also of the bones which make up his own skeleton as well as the lower jaw of the hog. Nature is everything that spirit or the divine is not, which means, in terms of the dichotomy on the first page, that nature is the wild, the primitive, the savage, and it is most apparent in the animal aspects of natural reality. But that recognition is not nearly as pleasing at the end of the chapter as it was at the beginning.

In a curious way the facts of the dichotomy are always supported—it has these particular components for its poles—but the evaluation of the structure and components of the dichotomy has turned quite around from the beginning to the end of the chapter. The imperatives discussed at the end are of a different moral and epistemological order than those at the beginning. The ones at the end argue for separation and exclusion because of the disgusting and inherent inferiority of one of the poles. The ones at the beginning argue for inclusion of both in a well-balanced whole, and there is an insistence upon equality. It is obvious that these two sets of imperatives ought to be canceling each other out, not only because they are so different, but because only one group would be able to dominate at one time. In fact, however, "Higher Laws" is markedly schizophrenic. The order proposed at the beginning is not rejected or even referred to again after the introductory pages. Thoreau simply turns to another kind of order and goes on as though he had never mentioned the first.

His assertion about dual and equal reverence, a regard which he *still* feels for both factors, obviously cannot be sustained beyond the beginning of the chapter. Yet he does make the statement unequivocally, with the point about continuity put as clearly as that about parity. Neither one is withdrawn at any stage of the argument. It is a mistake, then, to read the movement of the chapter as in any way developmental, though that approach is taken in some of the best analyses of Thoreau's thought. Sherman Paul, for example, remarks that "[Thoreau's] instinct toward the wild has been replaced" by the higher one.[24] It would be more accurate to speak of the wild as *dis*placed, since it is not superseded but shunted aside by a different position. Thoreau's point about continuity cannot square with the concept of replacement. Joseph Wood Krutch sees the movement of ideas as progressive, arguing that one gets to the higher laws by climbing "the stepladder of nature whose first rung is 'wildness.' "[25] But Thoreau is not quite so Socratic. In the first position assumed in the chapter there is nothing said about progression. After that, as Krutch correctly notes, Thoreau talks about progressing from hunting flesh to capturing a more spiritual quarry, game which cannot be found "in this or any vegetable wilderness" (212). But then he shifts into his fiercely phrased dichotomy between repellent animality and desirable spirituality, noting specifically that they are necessarily discontinuous and can have nothing to do with each other.

The disgust, the hiatus, and the argument for equality and continuity of reverence all make it impossible to support a developmental reading of the chapter—especially one which ig-nores Thoreau's contradictory attitudes toward experience of the natural. Rather, these factors point to an ambivalence so profound and unsettling that Thoreau could get around it only by a disjunctive maneuver which avoids confrontation of the contradictory positions. It is clear that few unqualified statements can be fully valid in this swarm of inconsistencies. That is especially true when the lower elements begin to act up. Thoreau admits his weaknesses, showing that his repugnance would give way before the demands of the daily stuffing of the flesh: "But I see that if I were to live in a wilderness I should again be tempted to become a fisher and hunter in earnest" (214). And he is candid enough to admit that there might even be some pleasure involved: "for my part, I was never unusually squeamish; I could sometimes eat a fried rat with a good relish, if it were necessary" (217). No change, it seems, is dependably complete.

Thoreau's rapid turnaround in "Higher Laws" is the most dramatic version of the ambivalence he felt, and attempted to reconcile, throughout his life. Natural wildness is embodied in natural materiality, his own wildness in his own materiality, and his attraction toward the one has to live side by side (as it does in "Higher Laws") with his revulsion for the other. Whatever the changes in his attitude toward nature, Thoreau sought to establish continuity with every manifestation of wildness he ever encountered. In the broadest sense this was a way of affirming his ties to the natural world, and not at the level of a pleasant daily stroll, but through contact with the most fundamental strata of man and nature. Something essential in himself would tie in with an equally essential element in the natural world outside. This impulse was the exact parallel of Thoreau's desire to make the most private contours of his genius reach out to their counterpart in another human being. His wildness was as deep within him as his genius and his talent. Reaching out to link with other genius or other wildness, then, would be a hopeful movement from depth to depth, an act which, were it to succeed, would result in the eradication of separateness through the most intense intimacy possible. This was one of the most compelling factors in Thoreau's urge to partake of the woodchuck. Thoreau knew and stated that there were too many difficulties in bringing together genius with genius for there to be any certainty of regular success. It seemed easier to link up with nature than with men: natural wildness was always apparent and (in America) close, though often elusive, while genius was generally well hidden. Moreover, continuity with natural wildness would confirm his membership in the community of being. And of course continuity at that level would also enliven his own creative resources, a factor in anyone's desire for totemic communion.

But the revulsion he often felt for the flesh which contained the wildness demanded a sharp break, the denial or at least the rejection of continuity. Much of "Higher Laws" and all of the equivalent passages elsewhere lament that his association with the natural is only *too* continuous. All of the passages that have the ring of Ktaadn make the same point. Thoreau was fascinated by the great chain of being and its principles—plenitude, continuity, and gradation—and they affected most of his imagining in relation to nature. At times he appears to have been particularly concerned that the continuity which went along with gradation would lead to a de-gradation of the higher principles of his being, and he had to cope with that danger somehow.

At the end of "Higher Laws" Thoreau makes a small myth about John Farmer, relaxing after work and attempting "to recreate his intellectual man" (222). Farmer does not wander into a swamp, or to the equivalent wildness within himself, in order to recreate what he wants. Sitting at his door is sufficient. The sound of a flute that someone was playing drew into his consciousness the awareness of other faculties than those associated with his work; and those faculties, in turn, led him to wonder about ways of getting to a more glorious existence than the one he has now: "All that he could think of was to practice some new austerity, to let his mind descend into his body and redeem it, and treat himself with ever increasing respect" (222). All of Thoreau's old associations of "redeem" pack into this one instance. John Farmer is to reclaim a piece of man's existence from the wild, bringing it within the clearing that holds the elements won away from the natural. Thoreau's disgust with flesh has toned down, the pitch being more than was tolerable for day-to-day living; but the flesh still has burdens which can be lightened only by the redemptive imagination.

In the introduction to *Nature* Emerson distinguished the Soul from every form of externality in the world outside, with the obvious though unstated exception of spirit. His language is unambiguous and confident: "all that is separate from us, all which Philosophy distinguishes as the NOT ME, that is, both nature and art, all other men and my own body, must be ranked under this name, NATURE." [26] The centrality of Soul, both in the individual and in the universe, follows in neat logic from this position. Soul is the point outside which all the other aspects are fulfilled, even those things which men have made through a mixture of will and imagination. Soul is the unmoving center that watches while the other parts organize living into constructive and beautiful patterns. Included out there in the NOT ME is the body, the shell that houses Soul; and it shares the quality of being external with everything commonly called nature, "space, the air, the river, the leaf." They are all among the actors that the separate self watches.

Thoreau's most obvious quarrel with Emerson's *Nature* came from his awareness that the hard stubbornness of facts implies the resistance of nature to the mind. The clarification of that awareness was one of the most important processes in Thoreau's development, and it is perhaps the only pattern that shows a relatively clear and perceptible progress. His reaction to the separation of Soul from every other factor outside is far less clear, that is to say, much more ambiguous and occasionally contradictory. His joy at discovering a fragment of a handbill on a tree in the Maine woods affirms the essential unlikeness of human capacities and natural presence. On the other hand, his hunger for the woodchuck is an urge to overcome difference, not to affirm it. Yet Thoreau could also insist that the woodchuck and its wildness were as much a part of the NOT ME as his own rank flesh that had to be stuffed with pieces of the world. There was a likeness among that group of externals which he could neither ignore nor endure.

The constant which stood fast through all the varying desires was the order of consciousness. Whatever its ordeals and defeats, or its frequent and considerable victories, consciousness held to its task of making the world livable for the self. Even in his most confident days Thoreau knew that what was outside of one's private clearing could pose a considerable challenge to the activities of consciousness, particularly its persistent drive to so order the world that the self would feel at home in it. Alertness was always necessary, because consciousness could not count on easy conquests, even in the familiar surroundings in which it had learned its work. Thoreau's relations with nature came to stress its otherness, but there were stresses in other directions as well. He saw that there was an unlikeness with which it would be difficult to cope, but he also saw that the world outside was full both of likenesses that were delightful and others that could be sickening. Thus, the importance of the struggles of consciousness recorded in "Ktaadn," and their complements in the encounters with nature in "Higher Laws": in both cases he could not state unequivocally that the world outside was or was not NOT ME. No either-or answers were ever really possible for Thoreau, and as he grew older he saw more reasons why that was so. Both chapters contain situations in which there were major challenges to the essential business of consciousness, its redemptive activities.

In each of those cases an overwhelming sense of threat emerges as the dominant tone. On Ktaadn it came from nature's imperviousness to the acts of the mind and also from his consequent inability to find a place, as a man, up there where the fundamentals of nature had been reached. In "Higher Laws" the threat came from a part of himself, and it led to a challenge to another part which ought to have been impervious but was not. The chapter showed that there was no problem about finding a place in nature but, quite the reverse, in relinquishing the place that was naturally his. The ultimate threat, however, was to the coherence of Thoreau's personal wholeness. Both "Ktaadn" and "Higher Laws" show a confrontation of spirit with radical materiality (his own and nature's) which results in a fracture of the totality of self. Under the pressure of nature, which at these times is a fiercely divisive force, Thoreau loses his sense that he is a controlled, complete personality. Faust had faced the same threat, acknowledging that he had *zwei Seelen* which pulled him in opposite directions. Like Thoreau he revered nature's creative energies, aspects of which he saw within himself; yet Faust could, at times, distrust the fleshly element which bound him to the earth. Both Goethe and Thoreau were aware that natural creativity was the result of forces which were wild and potentially destructive. Goethe's poem follows Faust as he works out their relations, eventually channeling (literally) the chaos in things.

Most of Thoreau's major works show him going over similar

problems. But there were moments of tremendous rebuff to his imagination because the coherence of personality on which it depended came under such severe pressure that his wholeness began to disintegrate. (The analogous example of Coleridge is only one more instance in a vast series of similar Romantic disintegrations, whether temporary or permanent.) The challenges on Ktaadn led to the momentary collapse of private coherence and, consequently, of the ability of consciousness to face up to the wild. The threats in "Higher Laws" led to a dichotomy which is not fully crippling only because Thoreau's brief and marvelous myth about John Farmer shows, by its very existence, that the imagination can still shape elegant and veritable fictions about redemption. But nature's threat to the coherence of self was not always so fierce: indeed, it could be disguised, Lilithlike, in attractiveness. The nature which had rebuffed him on Ktaadn could be only too enticing, too easy to accept around Concord. Sometimes nature at home seemed like a Beulah land where he could relax in easy intimacy but at the price of a threat to the requirements of spirit:

> I seem to be more constantly merged in nature; my intellectual life is more obedient to nature than formerly, but perchance less obedient to spirit. I have less memorable seasons. I exact less of myself. I am getting used to my meanness, getting to accept my low estate. O if I could be discontented with myself! If I could feel anguish at each descent! (*J*, III, 66)

It might be possible to serve both nature and spirit for awhile, but nature's richness can only debilitate, asking for a partial sacrifice of the spirit. Thoreau's private state in this entry for October 12, 1851, is an uneasy mixture of guilt, disaffection, and lassitude, but not quite *acedia* because he can still feel some anxiety. Cooperation of nature and spirit, which would have to be instigated by himself, seems a hope beyond his current strength. Under certain pressures the adequacy of consciousness simply gives way, and it matters little whether the pressures are seductive or antagonistic. Whatever their tone, they led him into states whose desperation is revealed by their contradictions. On the mountain he was both awed and fearful of his body, "this matter to which I am bound." The unnerving separation from matter put him beside himself, though not in a sane or spiritually coherent sense. But elsewhere, when his own matter came through to him as both foul and famished, he coveted that same separation from matter which had so distressed him on the mountain. Such paradoxically opposed reactions indicate the struggle Thoreau's imagination was going through in finding a way to reconcile nature and spirit—in the terms applied to John Farmer, letting "his mind descend into his body and redeem it." Under these pressures his imaginative control was pushed to its limits and sometimes beyond. Its moments of triumph are a tribute to its resilience.

Sometimes Thoreau got into these difficult situations because the play of his Americanizing imagination led him in directions which were usually ignored or rejected by his more secure contemporaries. It was the importation into his experience of a day-to-day dealing with wildness that made Thoreau's combination of desires unique. Emerson, with all his probings into the ramifications of spirit, knew little about wildness directly and therefore found intimacy with spirit a less arduous and more comforting affair. Thoreau was the only one of the Concord circle whose understanding of wildness was more than verbal. Some of the Transcendentalists played parlor tricks with language, using words like "savage" as counters that could not tolerate close scrutiny. Thoreau's language, however, usually came out of felt experience, and if his words could not bear the pressure of opposing impulses, that pressure was an indication of the intensity of his interests and not of their insubstantiality. If he so eagerly wanted wildness within himself, he would have to acknowledge both the fusion of wildness with brute flesh and also the ahuman core that wildness—once he found its basis up on Ktaadn—seemed to have. But since the Romantic analogies of inner and outer had to be respected, Thoreau was faced with wondering whether he would want to bring *that* inside of himself. After all, he had once said, in clean Transcendental terms, that "whatever we see without is a symbol of something within," and if he tried to follow that dogma through in relation to wildness he could end up in a most undesirable position (*J*, III, 201). There, in its purest form, was the problem, and he saw no prefabricated way out of the difficulties.

They pursued him in Concord and also, inevitably, on every trip to Maine.

On July 26, 1857, during the excursion recorded in "The Allegash and East Branch," Thoreau and his party saw a muskrat swimming in a stream, and the Indian accompanying them decided that he wanted to eat it:

> sitting flat on the bank, he began to make a curious squeaking, wiry sound with his lips, exerting himself considerably. I was greatly surprised,—thought that I had at last got into the wilderness, and that he was a wild man indeed, to be talking to a musquash! I did not know which of the two was the strangest to me. He seemed suddenly to have quite forsaken humanity, and gone over to the musquash side. (*Maine Woods*, 206-7) [27]

Here is a continuity so intense and pure that one side (obviously the weaker) appears to have given in to the allurements of the other and given up association with its own kind. The Indian stands among the white travelers, but at this moment he seems as separate from them as they are from the muskrat. If the Indian and the animal are momentarily related through pure continuity, the visitors standing on the bank are associated with the Indian and muskrat only through proximity. The wild man and the creature are both outside the personal perimeters of these intruders into the wilderness. Once again Thoreau is aware that there is a stratum of wildness which he cannot contact. Here it has a less forbidding face than the landscape on Ktaadn, but it still forces him to a recognition that this is a world in which he has no part: "I did not know which of the two was the strangest to me." This time, however, the unreachable stratum has to do with the content of self and not with the solidity of matter. In the Indian he sees a man who shares wildness with the primitive world outside him, just as Thoreau saw himself and others doing in the woods around Concord. This instance of sharing is so extreme, and the Indian gives himself to it so thoroughly, that for a moment he seems to have slipped out of his humanity. And that, in its essence, was the risk Thoreau faced in "Ktaadn" and "Higher Laws." This episode shows a practiced, Indian-style counterpart to Thoreau's desire to partake of the woodchuck, with the important difference that the Indian is interested only in the meat of the musquash and not its wild essence.

Fifteen years before this, while he was walking over the Concord fields and meditating on past inhabitants, Thoreau spoke of the Indians as "another species of mortal men, but little less wild to me than the musquash they hunted . . . with another nature and another fate than mine" (*J,* I, 337). Here in Maine the observation is reconfirmed. To achieve such intimacy with wildness one has to go over to the side of animality. The animals cannot come up to man, and therefore man, who is more flexible and has a greater range, has to go down to them, offering his humanity as the price for perfect communion. Thoreau had found himself paying exactly the same price on Ktaadn: to get so close to nature's basis one has to give up the finest aspects of a man, leaving one's reason "dispersed and shadowy, more thin and subtle like the air." Humanity is not only incompatible with such intimacy but is destroyed by it. Nature's pure wildness is not only a threat to consciousness but is its most exacting antagonist.

A man who wanted the fullest possibilities of both consciousness and nature had to work with some severe, even brutal dilemmas. He faced a complex of intimacy and strangeness, dominance and brotherhood, desire and rebuff that required the most subtle manipulation if he were to profit by his opportunities. Thoreau knew that the consciousness whose business was to make a place for the self in the world often operated so as to create ambivalence where it wanted harmonious redemptive activities. He was always attuned to the moral ramifications of the acts of consciousness. No matter how close he came to grasping the woodchuck, Thoreau was neither Queequeg nor the cool-tempered Canadian woodchopper. With full self-awareness he realized that the order of consciousness had to be understood and managed so as somehow to accommodate all manner of conflicting claims. For the rest of this study we shall look into Thoreau's gestures toward accommodation and consider their success.

4.

The Morning Paradise

The difficulty Thoreau faced in his attempts at accommodation was in finding ways to use nature which would denigrate neither nature nor himself. His mind refused to be dragged bodily (i.e., through the body) so far into nature that he would turn over to nature all that was most precious in his own personality—his genius, his talent, and eventually his identity. Thoreau's urge to share in wildness was never an urge to personal dissolution but quite the opposite, a desire for refreshment and reaffirmation of important areas within himself. Even when the hunger for communion with wildness was most intense, Thoreau wanted to bring wildness within himself, absorb it into the sure center of self where he kept the best parts of his own being; and those parts had to remain intact because they were essential to redemption. To put it another way, the instinctive proddings of genius always led the mind to the fullest stretches of its activity, and it was never stretching further than when it was bringing over segments of the wild for the use of man. Early in "Brute Neighbors" Thoreau puts the basic Transcendental question and comes out with an unambiguous answer that must have been perfectly congenial to the Concord circle:

> Why do precisely these objects which we behold make a world? Why has man just these species of animals for his neighbors; as if nothing but a mouse could have filled this crevice? I suspect that Pilpay & Co. have put animals to their best use, for they are all beasts of burden, in a sense, made to carry some portion of our thoughts. *(Walden,* 225)

This is only a few pages after the myth of John Farmer and its moral about redeeming the body, that is, his private animal, the only piece of nature that he can truly own. The implication is that Thoreau will have to use animal nature, "made to carry some portion of our thoughts," as a vehicle through which consciousness can redeem nature. Nature will become what the Transcendentalists always wanted it to be, emblematic of human possibilities. Thus, as a source of images whose import applies to ourselves, nature will be reclaimed. But this is Thoreau's mind that is going about these activities, and he had bumped too hard against nature, felt its palpable factuality too often, to argue that nature can or ought to be fully at the service of mind. He was too sensitive to the linked economies of nature and spirit and to the law by which anything that is given to one necessarily takes something away from the other. The ratio is inverse and inexorable, and has to be watched carefully by a professional reclaimer such as Thoreau.

As a result, Thoreau concluded that consciousness, because of its business, has to impose upon nature, but that nature should still be permitted to speak in its own way and for itself. The Indian's relationship with nature, as Thoreau described it in the *Week,* was the one he usually wanted for himself as well: "The Indian's intercourse with Nature is at least such as admits of the greatest independence of each" *(Week,* 56). There must be a relationship in which nature would contribute, but not at the cost of its own extinction: though Thoreau cherished his mind he was no solipsist. And of course his own creative capacities had to be thoroughly protected from the pressures of opposing forces which could well pose a considerable threat. Further, the conquests of consciousness ought to be absolutely tangible, however respectful it was of its antagonist. Consciousness should be seen or heard working, as Thoreau learned when he scouted for spikes and pieces of handbill in the depths of the Maine woods, or when he listened, in the woods, for any sort of noise which could pass "for a sound of human industry" *(Maine Woods,* 203). He had his own stability to protect as well as nature's. But though he understandably gave precedence to his own he was a generous opponent, working over his antagonist as lightly as possible.

Such working, he discovered, was most effective out at the edge where man and his mind meet nature. As a surveyor he was used to perambulating the bounds of the town, walking the lines where the wild and the cultivated come together. His business made him familiar with the edge and with the way men pushed it farther into the area of unreclaimed wildness. It seemed inevitable, then, that if Thoreau had to establish a relationship between nature and consciousness which would give full due to each while robbing as little as possible from both, he would find his place of business out there at the edge. All the forms of perception through which he structured his world place him at or near boundaries, flexible or otherwise, and he had an extraordinary understanding of their meaning for himself as imaginative man.

Thoreau's first activities at Walden already revealed him to be in an advanced state of understanding about these issues. When he began to settle near the pond he put together the bare elements of a house, a shelter which did the job of sheltering but only *just* did it. He was definitely "settling in the world," but at this point that was no more than a gesture sufficient to protect him, though not to wall him off completely from nature *(Walden,* 85). In this instance Thoreau insisted that the boundary between himself and nature was not so firmly demarcated that one was seen to begin precisely where the other left off:

> The upright white hewn studs and freshly planed door and window casings gave it a clean and airy look, especially in the morning, when its timbers were saturated with dew, so that I fancied that by noon some sweet gum would exude from them. *(Walden,* 84-85)

The wood taken from nature is still close enough to its point of origin that it retains the tone of its home; and to the mind which wanted to make much of that closeness, all sorts of tricks of the fancy were possible. The proper stance here is timidity, perhaps even embarrassment, and this sly persona plays with images that, even as they show the mind actively at work, insist that all of this appeared to happen almost naturally, almost without his intervention. He was even willing to assert that the shelter seemed less to have been built than to have collected naturally around him from disparate pieces that fused together on their own: "this frame, so slightly clad, was a sort of crystallization around me" (85).

The self-deprecation goes further when he puts himself in a subsidiary role as the inferior envying those who have more freedom than he does: "I found myself suddenly neighbor to the birds; not by having imprisoned one, but having caged myself near them" (85). Yet though he is a prisoner of his needs he is not closed off completely, for the fuzzy edge made it possible for the world within and the world outside to live together with no competition: "I did not need to go out doors to take the air, for the atmosphere within had lost none of its freshness. It was not so much within doors as behind a door where I sat, even in the rainiest weather" (85). Though each is not part of the other—Thoreau is always well aware of what he is not—each is perfectly welcome in the territory of the other. Of course he has encroached upon nature, but, as he insists, this was done in so modest a fashion, building only what was necessary as "a defense against the rain," that he cannot be said to have won more than a place to stay. The fences are not very good, but the neighbors are excellent.

Again, this is Thoreau's extraordinarily sense-oriented imagination at work: the conquests of mind ought to be seen or heard and, if possible, known through the fingers, arms, and feet. The facts that were to blossom into truths had to be felt facts, at least gestures if not fully developed actions. Thoreau, like many of his contemporaries, could stop with the representative gesture, assuming that the point made grandly was sufficient. In that sense, the two years at Walden Pond were an extended version of his night in Concord jail. But the gestures at the pond were unusually diverse, their variety designed to come at Thoreau's two or three basic interests in as many ways as possible. *Walden* is full of these gestures. The essential tasks, clearing and exploration of the marrow (redemption and regeneration), are carried out through some patterns that are visual and static and others that are more kinetic and active. The house, in all the various shapes it takes throughout the book, stays put and is seen. In the chapter on "The Bean-Field" Thoreau shows in movement what he had been showing in the building whose walls soaked up the air and sunlight. Once again he is at the edge where consciousness meets its opposite, working with Emerson's NOT ME to make it productive without violating its integrity.

Thoreau remarks that he does not know why he kept on working at the beans, but he is being slyly ingenuous: his own answer to that question—"Heaven only knows"—is shown by several other comments in the chapter to be a plausible rejoinder. For one thing, the beans kept him attached to the earth from which, like Antaeus, he could draw further strength. It is as though heaven wants him to remember that he is partly natural and ought to have terrestrial anchors. As for his deriving strength from that contact, the parallel to his desire to partake of the woodchuck's wildness is both striking and significant, and the parallel goes further because Thoreau is less interested in the food value of the beans, though he did taste a few, than in the full context of the beans and how they manage in it: "I was determined to know beans" *(Walden,* 161). But of course it is more than beans that he wanted to know. This John Farmer is as interested in his own kind of work, and his relationship to the beans through that work, as he is in the fruits that tie him to the earth. To begin with he describes himself as an artist working on materials, and not just as a husbandman. More comprehensively, he is a cultivator, cultivating a long acquaintance with beans (the puns are Thoreau's); thus, he is a friend of the wild who brings the cultivated and civil up to the edge where the wild begins. Here, though, Thoreau is not the Blakean artist who has to build a Golgonooza in opposition to the natural but, instead, one who wants to cooperate with nature so as to make it work for man without ceasing to be fully itself. The operation is delicate, but Thoreau manages it as skillfully in "The Bean-Field" as anywhere else in his work. That chapter is one of the more remarkable documents in the history of his mind at the edge. Among other things, it reveals that if his work gave him the strength of Antaeus he channeled that strength back into the work itself, in a self-perpetuating activity that exemplifies the mutual enrichment of the artist and his material.

Thoreau's making is interestingly mixed, since his shaping spirit performs simultaneously in both tactile and verbal media: barefooted in the morning, he dabbles "like a plastic artist in the dewy and crumbling sand," but what he does is to make "the yellow soil express its summer thought in bean leaves and blossoms ... making the earth say beans instead of grass" (156-57). The idea of plastic shaping is an obvious leap from Thoreau's work with the hoe; but the switch to a verbal context not only brings him back to the modes with which he is most at home but makes possible a further clarification of the full import of his work. As a verbalist he can give one more reason for hoeing in the fields: "some must work in fields if only for the sake of tropes and expression, to serve a parable-maker one day" (162). Thoreau is (probably deliberately) unclear as to whether he is himself the parable-maker, storing up materials for his own imagination to work on, or whether he is working to supply a great Parable-Maker with materials for ultimate expression. The passage takes in both possibilities at once. He shapes the yellow soil so that it can express itself, but he allows it to do its own speaking in a way that is also useful for him. Thoreau's skill is particularly impressive here because he can combine what he wants to do and what the earth naturally performs in a scheme which does justice to all of its components. In a journal entry for May, 1853, he echoes the materials of this passage but with the emphasis entirely on the earth's usefulness for man: "He is the richest who has most use for nature as raw material of tropes and symbols with which to describe his life.... If I am overflowing with life, am rich in experience for which I lack expression, then nature will be my language" (*J,* V, 135).

In the pages in "Spring" on the sand foliage produced by the thawing sand bank, Thoreau remarks on the contrary of man's desire, the earth's own needs: "No wonder that the earth expresses itself outwardly in leaves, it so labors with the idea inwardly" (306). Thoreau's work in "The Bean-Field" respects both the earth's instinct for self-expression and man's desire to use its elements to image his own kind of experience. As a parable-maker Thoreau does not force himself upon the soil but simply gives it an alternate possibility for expression, beans instead of grass—that is, different tropes. And that is what a great Parable-Maker would do with Thoreau as well. Out at the margins Thoreau could express himself with beans and soil rather than with words. Both he and the soil, then, would be utilizing modes other than their usual ones: hoeing instead of language for the one, beans instead of grass for the other. Each would supply parables for a being who is higher on the great chain, which means that there is creative parable-making, a multiplicity of the same kind of expression, all the way up the chain of being. Indeed, the chain of being is also a ladder of creativity as well, as it was in a persistent pattern throughout Romanticism.[1] This also means that (1) the material world is tied to the spiritual through the transitional figure or mediator; and (2) Thoreau's role as both artist and material puts him in a crucial midway position shared by no other being on the chain from bean to Parable-Maker. He does more than stand at the border between flesh and spirit: he *is* the border, and as he hoes he fulfills his roles in both worlds. He is both cultivator and (in Thoreau's multi-leveled pun) cultivated as well.

Not all mediators are redeemers. The biblical prophets stood between God and man, talking to each for the sake of the other, but they were only agents. They could lead men to redemption, but the saving activity had to come from within the men themselves, and also from outside, from the One Who redeemed. In its Transcendental forms the Romantic imagination was under an obligation to redeem nature, which could not help itself in that way. It also wanted to redeem man, who certainly could do it on his own but needed the impetus of an example. Thoreau stood not only between bean and God but at the dividing point between natural wildness and the fully cultivated world of Concord and Emerson's parlor. While he was working the beans the town came to Thoreau only through the sounds of distant music and military turnouts. These were not, however, his primary focus of interest at that time, but merely a reminder of other forms of struggle. He was not concerned, at that point, with the destructiveness of military affairs, but with the flexible creativity possible to the man at the edge. He wanted to keep all analogies within the context of farming (omitting the kind of cultivation that created Transcendental circles), and he wanted to show that there was a useful distinction between man's full takeover of nature, in which it is treated as an object to be "carefully weighed, the moisture calculated," and the Thoreauvian approach (158). The latter is more of a coaxing ("encouraging this weed which I had sown") or a rechanneling of natural effort (157).

Ultimately the activities ought to be sacramental rather than merely instrumental. As for himself, the man at the edge wanted open options which would grant him a foot in both worlds, offering due respect to each without a final commitment to either. Given all these conditions, the imagination has to work as it did in the house that barely managed to shelter him. The lines of demarcation were to be slightly fuzzed, more so even than in the new house which still exuded the freshness of nature but had to keep on being a house. But there was far more activity at the margin of the bean field than at the edge of the house. This mediator's crops were more aggressive than the wood that still partook of nature because the crops were always pushing back to the state out of which they came. In the *Week* he had mentioned nature's tendency to "recover and indemnify herself," and nature follows that inclination in his bean field *(Week,* 63). Though it never quite returns to the original state of things (Thoreau does, after all, want beans), nature is always pushing back toward a situation where the beans would not be his anymore:

> Mine was, as it were, the connecting link between wild and cultivated fields; as some states are civilized, and others half-civilized, and others savage or barbarous, so my field was, though not in a bad sense, a half-cultivated field. They were beans cheerfully returning to their wild and primitive state that I cultivated, and my hoe played the *Ranz des Vaches* for them. (158)

(The *Ranz des Vaches* is a Swiss cowherd's song for calling cattle.) Thoreau holds on to the beans carefully but barely, redeeming nature for man but only half so, permitting each to be itself as far as that is compatible with the need to do some cultivating. And thus the edge between the wild and the partly tamed is calculatedly imprecise. When the respectful connector does his job well, he makes distinctions which can never finally hold because the half-redeemed is always slipping back to its original state. He learns that the crops he has won can never be more than partly his own.

The experience with the bean field was an advanced problem for Thoreau, perhaps the most subtle practical calculation he ever made. He did this intricate job of edging only for awhile, but he did it very well while it lasted. Of course, since this was merely an experiment, there was no need for him to continue once he had made his point. And of course he had worked at another delicate job of multifaceted respect when he tried to balance the wild and the good; but in *Walden* that attempt at equilibrium lasted little longer than the statement of its conditions. With that temporary success in mind we are entitled to wonder about the sustaining capacities of such half-cultivation, however impressive Thoreau's skill in handling it in "The Bean-Field." It is well to remember that Thoreau was the middle figure between bean and God as well as between wildness and Concord. For that reason there may have been a question whether the compromise of half-cultivation would suffice for the considerable demands of the spirit. And in fact several indications that it could not fully suffice surface toward the end of the chapter when Thoreau, in his predictable emblematic manner, begins to talk about planting the seeds of virtue rather than beans and corn (cf. *Paradise Lost,* XI, 22 ff.). The men he usually encounters are stooped over the economy of the earth, "busy about their beans . . . plodding ever, leaning on a hoe or a spade as a staff between [their] work" (165). He would prefer the sort who are "partially risen out of the earth, something more than erect": that is, more than just animals standing on their hind legs. He wants them to be "like swallows alighted and walking on the ground," those who have come down to earth rather than those who have stood up from it.

All of this indicates that the rhythm of ideas in "The Bean-Field" is much like that at the end of "Higher Laws"; in the *Week;* in the essay on "Walking"; and, indeed, in the whole of *Walden.* It is a recurrent cadence of thought in which his consciousness plays at the edge of experience, demonstrating something there which is superior to what he has rejected, and then ends by hedging somewhat on the value of what it has just demonstrated. In each of these examples Thoreau argues with fierceness and wit for a way of being that is economically sounder (more satisfying to all sorts of human economy) than the usual ways of the townspeople and the farmers; and whatever the permanent success of his demonstration he does make it work for awhile. John Farmer is surely more than an erect creature; he is something more like the swallow. He makes an effective compromise, learning how to live in the world so as to redeem the body and grow bread for it. But, though his compromise is better than the usual ways of men, who do not understand what he knows about the need to redeem the body, it is not nearly as good as the glorious existence he heard of through the flute sounds "coming out of a different sphere from that he worked in." In terms of the highest standards, his solution is better but necessarily imperfect.

At the end of "The Bean-Field" Thoreau makes the same kind of point about limitations. After he has proven his theory about the best modes of cultivation by giving a fine example of fuzzy edging, Thoreau qualifies his own example by showing that it is good but insufficient. It is better than the voracious practices he has rejected, but it is still not as good as the best; and the best is not a way that is at all profitable or, perhaps, even possible now in this state. Finally, after he makes the point about the swallow-men, Thoreau comes back to the question of the value of cröps. In keeping with his duties at the edge, which require him to talk about the limitations of his work as well as the fruits of it, this cultivator of clearings shows the proper, qualified respect for his enchanting antagonist:

> Bread may not always nourish us; but it always does us good, it even takes stiffness out of our joints, and makes us supple and buoyant, when we knew not what ailed us, to recognize any generosity in man or Nature, to share any unmixed and heroic joy. (165)

This consummates the rhythm of "The Bean-Field." In the end, through an irony which follows Thoreau everywhere, the model he has set up is shown, by himself, to be worth a qualified, if definite, acceptance. It is better but not perfect. He can show men how to get bread a better way without doing severe injustice to the source of supply, modestly permitting the source to be a co-worker and not just the victim of a predator. But the result is still only bread, not a fully satisfying sort of nourishment.

This tempo of ideas, a rhythm of advance and sidestep, is a basic cadence in Thoreau's thought, a pattern which, as I shall argue in the next chapter, informs most of his major works. Since it is always involved with the exploration of new possibilities, and the adjustment of the new to the old desires of man, the cadence is the working rhythm of the mind at the edge of experience. As such it is often discernible in those journal entries where Thoreau's perceptions take their first firm shape. In one long series, written no later than early February 1851, Thoreau considers several foreign comments about American flora and fauna, quoting from Michaux and Guyot. It is in this series, part of which went into "Walking," that he first talks about the English forest as "a greenwood, her wild man a Robin Hood," and ends by remarking that "there was need of America" (*J*, II, 142 ff.). The old and eastern is rejected for fresh western possibilities: "the West is preparing to add its fables to those of the East" (145). Thoreau speaks warmly of a panorama of the Rhine which he had gone to see and compares it to a panorama of the Mississippi which he visited shortly thereafter. The remarks are predictable, dealing with the landscape and places associated with both rivers, ending with Thoreau "still thinking more of the future than of the past or present" (147). But Thoreau cannot go this far, even into such mild chauvinism, without drawing back and growing somewhat nervous about the alternative he has just proposed. He has clearly reached that point in the sequence at which qualifications are drawn into the cadences of his thought:

> The Old World, with its vast deserts and its arid and elevated steppes and table-lands, contrasted with the New World with its humid and fertile valleys and savannas and prairies and its boundless primitive forests, is like the exhausted Indian corn lands contrasted with the peat meadows. America requires some of the sand of the Old World to be carted on to her rich but as yet unassimilated meadows. (147)

The beginning is phrased in the rhetoric we would expect from a series of passages, many of which went into the early lecture versions of "Walking." (Thoreau was starting to deliver those lectures at about this time.) But the last sentence is unexpected, even startling, since it is out of tone with all the comments preceding it. Westering had just been referred to in the previous entry: moved by the panorama of the Mississippi, he "saw the Indians removing west across the stream, and heard the legends of Dubuque and of Wenona's cliff" (147). That vision becomes the inevitable transition to the comparison of the Old World and the New.

Westering is the national business of the man at the margin because the farthest west is the newest and wildest, and he always wants to stand at the wildest point. Yet even in the New World one has to compromise, it seems, bringing in the sand of Europe to give the necessary variety to the raw peat of America. The "unassimilated meadows" would become half-cultivated, then, as the leaven is mixed in and absorbed. To complete the cadence Thoreau inserts a comment of his own into a group of quotations from Guyot on American flora:

> The white man derives his nourishment from the earth,—from the roots and grains, the potato and wheat and corn and rice and sugar, which often grow in fertile and pestilential river bottoms fatal to the life of the cultivator. The Indian has but a slender hold on the earth. He derives his nourishment in great part but indirectly from her, through the animals he hunts. (148)

This remark is not quite neutral, for there is clearly a price that the highest fertility will sometimes exact, something more than the Indian would ever have to pay. The qualifications about the usefulness of unassimilated American peat have thus been followed by some further hedging on the cost of fertility, hinting that redeemers may not go quite unscathed. Even with this deep tinge of ambivalence it is clear that only the cultivator carting some of the dryness of old Europe into the savannas and prairies of America can bring about such productive assimilation. At the end of the cadence Thoreau has come to say both more and less than in the brash assertions at the beginning. Europe is tame and America is necessary; but the raw wildness of the unassimilated continent could remain unrealized unless the redeemer brings it halfway toward the old. Of course when he does so the land that he has. made so productive may also become pestilential as well, "fatal to the life of the cultivator." The cost of one's ties to the earth could be high, and it is his realization of that cost that forced Thoreau, here and very often elsewhere, to qualify his eager positiveness about man in American nature.

The patterns in this long entry from the notebook are somewhat starker than their counterparts in "The Bean-Field," "Walking," the *Week,* and the whole of *Walden,* but they make the same kind of total statement. Sometimes the rhythms are less complex and therefore easier—perhaps too easy—to manage. They turn up often in relation to the idea of half-cultivation, which is an obvious (though potentially facile and sentimental) compromise, one which mitigates the inhospitability of full wildness by associating it fruitfully with cultivation. One possible result of the attempt to extol half-wildness is a blend like oil and water, with each component remaining distinct though a part of the whole. Thoreau ends "Chesuncook" with another version of the dominant cadences we have been examining, and praises a form of association in which all the parts stay separate and identifiable. He rejects full wildness (the inhabitants of the wilderness are *salvages)* and praises the situation around home where the woods and fields have occasional "primitive swamps scattered here and there in their midst, but not prevailing over them" *(Maine Woods,* 155). He then goes on to say, in the expected· partial disclaimer, that "the poet must, from time to time, travel the logger's path and the Indian's trail" (156). In other words, Thoreau needs what he called in the penultimate chapter of *Walden,* "the tonic of wildness." Here, the compromise works in form but not in tone. The sentimentalism which Thoreau's irony could not always fight off ends, jarringly, the second of his extraordinary tests of the limits of consciousness in the Maine woods. All the materials of the compromise are there in the last pages of the essay: the acknowledgment of the otherness of the wilderness and its inhabitants; the contrast of the *salvage* and the half-cultivated; the images of the logger and the pioneer (the men at the edge), who have "built hearths and humanized nature" for the poet; and finally the capacity of wildness to regenerate men.

But if there is nothing in his comments about the tougher issues of "Ktaadn," Thoreau also passes over the paradox which lies open on these pages, that is, the need to both humanize the wild, as the loggers and pioneers do, and yet use it as a source of regeneration, which is what the poets want. If the latter find redemption *in* the wild, the former practice the redemption *of* it. These blatantly contradictory impulses pursued Thoreau throughout his life, but he passes up the chance to work on them here. The final pages of "Chesuncook" are as remarkable for their evasiveness as for their understanding of the components that go into the most difficult issues. Thoreau does bring in some hints of the unease fostered by the unbroken wilderness, but not enough of the transforming capacities of consciousness to make the poet's necessary forays something more than a delicate refreshment. Thoreau's view of his role is unusually saccharine: "there are not only stately pines, but fragile flowers, like the orchises, commonly described as too delicate for cultivation, which derive their nutriment from the crudest mass of peat" (156). It is these flowers, he indicates, which are to remind us of the poet. Consciousness can be very excited when it is at the edge of things, and when Thoreau is writing well he brings out all the felt life in the activities of the exploratory, creative, reclaiming, aspects of the self. Unfortunately, there is none of that life at the end of "Chesuncook."

On March 4, 1852, a year and a half before he went on the trip recorded in "Chesuncook," Thoreau entered a passage in his journal which is concerned with the humanizing of nature mentioned at the end of "Chesuncook" but treats it with all the reach of implication in "The Bean-Field":

> I love that the rocks should appear to have some spots of blood on them, Indian blood at least; to be convinced that the earth has been crowded with men, living, enjoying, suffering, that races passed away have stained the rocks with their blood, that the mould I tread on has been animated, aye, humanized. I am the more at home. I farm the dust of my ancestors, though the chemist's analysis may not detect it. I go forth to redeem the meadows they have become. I compel them to take refuge in turnips. (*J*, III, 334)

Redeeming at the margin of the clearing can involve the dust of men as well as the stalks of plants. The imprint of men's lives is visible in the blood which gives evidence of their deaths, and the product of those deaths is a richness which the earth by itself could never have: "the mould I tread on has been animated, aye, humanized." This is an extravagantly ironic extension of the Blakean-Thoreauvian insistence that "where man is not, nature is barren." Thus the spots of blood, "Indian blood at least," do the same as the fragments of handbill in the Maine wilderness: men have been here and, in a special way, have subjugated the earth by dying into it. Even when minds are extinguished, their dust can continue the business of humanizing, bringing ordinary earth closer to the men working on it because there are men mixed into it. Though the price is exceedingly high (compare the river bottoms that are "fertile and pestilential"), this is a fine way of combining the wild and the cultivated to achieve a blend that has a good bit of both. That, of course, is the kind of amalgam that Thoreau, the coaxer of bean fields, would appreciate: men and the earth are compounded so perfectly that there is no longer a definite, discernible line where one begins and the other ends. The distinctions are as fuzzy as those he wanted at the fringes of the bean field. This is therefore no ordinary mold that Thoreau walks on but humanized dirt. With real blood spots, or even with a similitude of them, the earth will not be so strange and other: "I am the more at home." Now he can dig into this semiredeemed mold and bring the men mixed into it part way back to the clearings from which they came. The man at the edge works with the men in the earth, and all cooperate in making the earth express itself in turnips.

Thoreau's sense of the ground that he stood on always included an awareness of those who had lived on it before him. He was more an existential historian than a factual one, that is, he was less interested in the particulars of the history of a spot of ground than he was awed by the fact of a previous *presence:* men had actually been here, lived and farmed and turned to mold themselves. The varied historical passages in the *Week* not only give a context to the places he visits but confirm that other men had once had their being in those places. What Thoreau was responding to was a set of associated facts but, even more, the personal immediacy that had realized its existence through those facts. The arrowheads Thoreau was forever turning up were pieces of a life that had been, chunks of palpable presence, and when he touched them he was touching a man.

In a long, late journal passage (March 28, 1859) Thoreau explains the meaning of his perpetual hunt for arrowheads. As he wanders over the fields looking for them he is attached to the earth, "getting strength to all [his] senses, like Antaeus" (*J*, XII, 89). His work in the bean field had also turned him into Antaeus, drawing spiritual strength from harvesting a physical crop. In the case of the arrowheads, his strength begins with the recognition that "my eyes rest on the evidences of an aboriginal life which passed here a thousand years ago perchance" (88). But these finds offer more than general cultural data. Each arrowhead reveals the essence of a life—not the life of the body, which left no more than the remnants of bones—but the life of the mind, the wit of the arrowhead's maker:

> Each one yields me a thought. I come nearer to the maker of it than if I found his bones. His bones would not prove any wit that wielded them, such as this work of his bones does. It is humanity inscribed on the face of the earth. (90-91)

One gets closer to the essence of a man by examining his artifacts, "this work of his bones," than by poring over the bones themselves. The latter have little part in the most important business of a man, his task of humanizing the face of the earth. These results of the work of consciousness are more comfortably at home in nature than are the more elaborate artifacts stored in the British Museum. The arrowheads are closer to natural forms, still stonelike, yet they afford all the evidence needed to establish the effect of mind on the world. Each arrowhead is a "mind-print." They are all "fossil thoughts, forever reminding me of the mind that shaped them. I would fain know that I am treading in the tracks of human game,—that I am on the trail of mind" (91). Ultimately he is after what the stones reveal of the work of consciousness upon nature, the inscription of humanity on the surface of the earth. These are the oldest crops of the mind.

Thoreau, the inveterate humanist, could not take part in such

cultivation (whether of turnips or arrowheads) as though he were
the first man in that place to do so. He knows that when he is
disturbing the earth he is stirring up other men as well: "Wherever
I go I tread in the tracks of the Indian. . . . In planting my corn in
the same furrow which yielded its increase to his support so long, I
displace some memorial of him" (*J*, I, 337). These remarks in the
journal were written in March 1842, exactly ten years previous to
the passage about the humanized mold that helped Thoreau to
make turnips. After his earliest abstract thinking, which occurred
during those days in the thirties when he was closest to Emerson's
principles, Thoreau's conception of time and history took on a
permanent ambivalence caused by his awe at the tangible
immediacy of the past. When he broke into the earth to make it
speak beans or turnips, he was literally dipping into the past,
making the present into a serviceable bed for the future, an
eminently American act of the sort that Whitman extolled; but
Thoreau had touched at Indian artifacts too often to be perfectly
at ease with the earth he was turning over.

Some of the temporal complexities in Thoreau's occupation as
redeemer are now beginning to emerge. Though he was moved
deeply by the pastness of old times, especially Indian life, Thoreau
knew that the imaginative potential of his (and John Farmer's)
work at the margin included the capacity for redeeming the shards
of the past. Redemption in this context could also mean completing the past, bringing to fruition what it could not accomplish by
itself. At the beginning of "The Bean-Field" Thoreau mentions
that when he was four years old he had been brought "through
these very woods and this field, to the pond. It is one of the oldest
scenes stamped on my memory" (*Walden*, 155). Now, in his
maturity, he has worked over these wild lands, "help[ing] to clothe
that fabulous landscape of my infant dreams," showing his
"presence and influence . . . in these bean leaves, corn blades, and
potato vines" (156). His own past has been completed and made
part of the fruitful present. From such personal fulfillment it was
easy to move, as Thoreau often did, to the realization in
contemporary America of the fabulous potential in the old dreams
of other civilizations. When Whitman or Thoreau talks of realizing
those public fantasies, it is viewed as what one has to do, as an
American or simply as a mature person. But such relatively

unqualified, chauvinistic fulfillment tended to ignore the complex responses which Thoreau experienced in farming the dust of ancestral men. A fragment of Indian hearthstone may remind him that while he meditates on "the unexhausted energies of this new country, I forget that this which is now Concord was once Musketaquid, and that the *American race* has had its destiny also" (*J*, I, 337).

As he works on his bean field he keeps bringing up into the contemporary world all manner of Indian hunting materials as well as pottery and glass which were left by more recent cultivators. The sound of his hoe hitting against these relics and the natural stones among which they were mingled was a kind of music, perhaps in a strain similar to the notes John Farmer heard. When this occurred Thoreau's work in redeeming the land had more than beans for result: "that music echoed to the woods and the sky, and was an accompaniment to my labor which yielded an instant and immeasurable crop. It was no longer beans that I hoed, nor I that hoed beans" (*Walden*, 159). He and the past have become one, and he harvests the crops of memory. This experience has exactly the same form as the one we looked at earlier in which Thoreau shows his awareness of a community of thought that acknowledges no temporal boundaries: "Sadi entertained once identically the same thought that I do, and thereafter I can find no essential difference between Sadi and myself. . . . By the identity of his thoughts with mine he still survives" (*J*, IV, 290).

In *Walden*, this community within consciousness reappears, its conquering of time allying Thoreau with the ancients in a perennial newness:

> The oldest Egyptian or Hindoo philosopher raised a corner of the veil from the statue of the divinity; and still the trembling robe remains raised, and I gaze upon as fresh a glory as he did, since it was I in him that was then so bold, and it is he in me that now reviews the vision. (99)

In each case all separateness in time has collapsed into a union of selves. With Sadi and the Egyptian philosopher it was Thoreau's thinking that dissolved the boundaries, while with the American Indians and the more recent cultivators of the soil it was the activity of his hoeing. From this and every other related instance it is apparent that Thoreau saw mind work and hoe work as closely analogous activities. Once again the pun on cultivation fuses Thoreau's various occupations: working in the fields of the mind does the same for him as working at the edge where the wild learns to speak in beans. Each serves to bring the past into the present and, ultimately, to make presentness (which is sometimes seen as an eternal present) the field in which one does the most fruitful work. Of course the hunt for arrowheads, which he thought of as the harvesting of one of the earth's most special crops, has exactly the same structure and effect:

> There is scarcely a square rod of sand exposed, in this neighborhood, but you may find on it the stone arrowheads of an extinct race. . . . Such are our antiquities. . . . Men should not go to New Zealand or write or think of Greece and Rome, nor more to New England. New earths, new themes expect us. Celebrate not the Garden of Eden, but your own. (*J,* X, 118)

The touch of chauvinism is excellent: bringing the past into the present in this way leads him to argue for the ultimate temporal redemption, the recovery of Eden. But Thoreau is not always so grand. If it is not Sadi or an Indian or one's youthful self who is contacted it could be a more grotesque immortal: "from under a rotten stump my hoe turned up a sluggish portentous and outlandish spotted salamander, a trace of Egypt and the Nile, yet our contemporary" *(Walden,* 159). In the *Week* it is a smaller bittern that has survived, enfolding the past and present in a harmonious unity simply by its enduring presence: "It is a bird of the oldest Thalesian school, and no doubt believes in the priority of water to the other elements; the relic of a twilight antediluvian age which yet inhabits these bright American rivers with us Yankees" (249-50).

The form through which Thoreau's consciousness and his tools deal with time and the land is essentially ritualistic. When he brings the dead into the present, through their relics if not through memory, the activities he performs in order to do so are the same activities performed by his forebears. He farms (on the land and in the mind) as they did, reliving their deeds through repetition. This is the same unifying repetitiveness through which the process of ritual not only bridges disparate moments in time but effectually collapses the gap between those moments. The past is no longer unreachable but—because it is doing its work again—it is immediate and functional. Thoreau's experience in reliving Sadi's identity is homologous with his work on the land, because in the case of Sadi he also repeats the actions of the past: it is the fact that he has had the same thought as Sadi or the Egyptian philosopher that fuses the identity of the dead and the living. Ritual performances, and those allied to them, are refutations of temporal distance. As a ritualist who redeems the time, Thoreau absorbs and uses the past to give a fuller dimension of meaning to the present. When he repeats those old actions, he is not only performing his own acts but those of others as well. In doing so, he is working in one of redemption's most traditional modes.

In one way or another the man at the edge is always refuting time because his position necessarily involves him in pure presentness. Ritual, of course, puts its participants into touch with the eternally present; that is, with timelessness. Yet even when Thoreau is not concerned with echoing the past but with facing the new and the wild he can find himself in a state of absolute immediacy. In "Walking" Thoreau pushed the meaning of his perambulations in various directions, one of which, a version of the "fronting" he encouraged in all of his books, kept him in a place that was forever new: "one who pressed forward incessantly . . . would always find himself in a new country or wilderness, and surrounded by the raw material of life" *(Excursions,* 226). Compulsive walking, with its energetic exploratory drive into the wild, is a perpetual refashioning of perimeters, an activity in which one is neither in the future, which one is always just breaking into, nor in the past, which one is always just putting behind oneself. There is no question of bringing the past into the present, as Thoreau does with his ritualistic gestures, but of staying between the past and the future.

In a more static version of this positioning of self Thoreau talks, in *Walden,* of being anxious "to stand on the meeting of two eternities, the past and future, which is precisely the present moment; to toe that line" *(Walden,* 17). The line is the edge where the developed or redeemed ends and the "raw material of life," the wild, begins. He wants to stand continually in "the foremost rank of time" and only there *(Excursions,* 246). After all, "God himself culminates in the present moment, and will never be more divine in the lapse of all the ages" *(Walden,* 97). As for man, "you must live in the present, launch yourself on every wave, find your eternity in each moment" *(J,* XII, 159). To stay precisely on the line of the present is a telling refutation of time.

This attitude has ramifications which are both public and private: the former is peculiarly associated with the contemporary Americans' sense of themselves, and the latter with one of Thoreau's major modes of understanding the self's relation to experience. In *The American Adam* R. W. B. Lewis examines the early nineteenth-century view of America as the place of the clean start where a new history commences that owes nothing to the old.[2] The hero of this new birth is (or begins as) an unfallen Adam with no commitment to the past. He is unlike the Byronic versions of the European Romantic hero because the American Adam is freed from the past, whereas the Byronic hero is burdened by it. No *mal du siècle* was possible for the hero of the New World. A creature of the immediate present and of any future that may derive from it, he owes allegiance only to his contemporaries and peers. In their most extreme form these views developed into "the principle of the sovereign present," which argued for an absolute disjunction between generations, including not only the question of the inheritance of property but the transmission of institutions and ideas as well.[3] To put it in Thoreau's image, America as a whole toed the line of the present while the country prepared for its extraordinary future. The entire construct was mythic because it explained to the American people how they, as a group, related to the forces in their environment that determined their existence.

The embodiment of this myth in literature took the form of the Adamic figure whose history Lewis charts, but the attitudes also turn up in Transcendentalist prose, whose derivation from European idealism combines surprisingly well with an often strident chauvinism. Emerson personalized the myth frequently; for example, in *Self-Reliance,* where he argues that the mind which is "simple and receives a divine wisdom . . . lives now, and absorbs past and future into the present hour." [4] Men ought to be like roses who exist for themselves and God, unconcerned with former roses or better ones, oblivious to time. Contemporary man ought to be more natural, less concerned with the prop of past thoughts. "He cannot be happy and strong until he too lives with nature in the present, above time." [5] He too must live in a condition of timelessness. Only then will he be fully self-reliant as befits an American intellectual whose work is part of the current transactions in and with the present.

Thoreau's search for flexible modes of expression, as well as his sensitivity to contemporary idiom and rhetoric, guaranteed that he could, at times, be as Adamic as anyone. His versatility of tone is remarkable. In the *Week,* for example, he argued that the obstacles to life "have not been living men but the institutions of the dead. . . . I love man—kind, but I hate the institutions of the dead unkind" *(Week,* 134-35). Later, rejecting tales about the ruins of Egypt, he adds, "are we so sick or idle that we must sacrifice our America and today to some man's ill-remembered and indolent story?" *(Week,* 266-67). In "Walking" Thoreau proved that he could compete in stridency with anyone. That essay in particular showed how the spectrum of his reactions to his world included some of the voices that could be heard in contemporary journalism and exhortatory prose: "It is too late to be studying Hebrew; it is more important to understand even the slang of to-day" *(Excursions,* 223). But the same essay shows how the patriotic view of temporality slides easily into a more personal view: "Above all, we cannot afford not to live in the present. He is blessed over all mortals who loses no moment of the passing life in remembering the past" *(Excursions,* 245-46).

The Adamic is thus seen to be the public-spirited version of a concern with presentness and immediacy that took a variety of forms. Early into *Walden,* in another instance of extra-vagance, Thoreau insists that in all his thirty years none of his seniors has given him "the first syllable of valuable or even earnest advice"—a remark which must have left Emerson feeling somewhat ambivalent *(Walden,* 9). Thoreau's irony can sometimes save him from the dangers inherent in such extreme positions. Among a series of undated journal entries for 1845-47 he records a dry poem on presentness ("I seek the present time,/No other clime,/Life in to-day") and follows it with some exuberant prose on the didactic value of exaggeration and its contribution to our understanding of our culture and ourselves (*J*, I, 409-11). At the end of the passage, in a rich bit of self-mockery but with no direct reference to his poem, he lists among his many examples of profitable exaggeration the way in which "we give importance to this hour over all hours" (412). In effect, he has completed a circle in which he qualifies but does not repudiate his poem. The rhythm of ideas in this passage is that same pattern of advance and sidestep which informed so many other cadences of his imagination. Though the poem and the prose can stand separately, they make, together, the sort of exhortatory statement whose built-in ironies show Thoreau in his better form. But the qualifying potential of the passage on exaggeration disappeared completely when Thoreau used it, with no poem to refer back to, in his essay on Carlyle. He gained an insight on Carlyle but lost another, wilfully so, on one of the best of his own working modes.

Obviously we ought to be cautious about Thoreau's Adamic stance on temporality, more cautious than he usually was himself. The patriotic voice in which he announced that he too was in the van of time spoke for his public position; and as a rule Thoreau did not qualify that, at least not blatantly. (The interplay between presentness and exaggeration in the passages we have been examining is lost without a slow retentive reading and an awareness of the way Thoreau manipulates juxtaposition.) The official position was simply one among many that could be taken in relation to temporality, and Thoreau was far too lucid about complexities to keep the various positions permanently divorced. He saw that to front the new and wild by being at the most forward point of experience was a very private (and often very difficult) affair as well as a public issue.

This combination of open and secluded facets can be found elsewhere as well, in a context which is closely related to Thoreau's Adamic stance. The map which organized Thoreau's image of the American consciousness in the American landscape pictured an enormous expanse of the wild illuminated by scattered dots of man-made clearing. From one perspective this was a depiction of contemporary American society in its redemptive role as a clearer of the wilderness, its agents a myriad of Adams making places for future paradises in the unexplored world. Yet this was also the state of each private consciousness in which "each man's world is but a clearing in the forest." These readings of the map are complementary, not mutually exclusive. If one is always positive and optimistic, the other can sometimes be troubled, less at ease with some of the possibilities in that landscape. Thoreau knew this better than most of his contemporaries, and that sometimes dark knowledge troubled him to the point where, like the grit in the oyster, it built up some lovely work of the imagination.

In a passage from the journal for February 3, 1841, Thoreau complains that "the present seems never to get its due; it is the least obvious,—neither before, nor behind, but within us" (*J,* I, 190). The sentence obviously echoes the observation from Luke: "Neither shall they say, Lo here! or, lo there! for, behold, the kingdom of God is within you." And in fact Thoreau does say that "God himself culminates in the present moment" (*Walden,* 97). The kingdom of God is here, now, and subjective, an assertion which offers something more than the insights of contemporary chauvinism or Transcendentalism, though it has close relations to both. To apprehend the kingdom of God we have to "live above all in the present," as Thoreau encouraged himself to do, and we also have to be aware of all that goes on within ourselves (*J,* II, 138). So far Thoreau's thought on this issue seems relatively straightforward; but subjectivity, at the center of which stands the locale of private genius, had its areas of uneasiness for Thoreau, and he was particularly aware of them when he stood on the line of the present at the edge of the new. For the subjective is also the secluded world within, and Thoreau had tried too many times without success to make that world available to others. The kingdom within is the point of absolute presentness, as Thoreau's reworking of the sentence from Luke makes clear; but it is also a hidden kingdom, and that is what causes the uneasiness. Floating on the periphery of Thoreau's concern with subjective presentness were some perennial discomforts that could emerge, under the right pressures, into consciousness. When they did so they were often clothed in deceptive language. On August 9, 1841, seven months after he wrote the passage echoing Luke, Thoreau recorded some materials which went, nearly verbatim, into the *Week.* He begins with several commonplaces about historical fact ("Of what moment are facts that can be lost,—which need to be commemorated?") and turns them into a succinct and precise imagining of the men involved in the recovery of fact:

> The researcher is more memorable than the researched. The crowd stood admiring the mist and the dim outline of the trees seen through it, and when one of their number advanced to explore the phenomenon, with fresh admiration all eyes were turned on his dimly retreating figure. (*J*, I, 269)

The historian, admired because he is himself a present fact, goes off alone but as it turns out his work will be in vain if he plans not just to walk over and explore the phenomenon but to bring it back to his contemporaries as well: "the *past* cannot be *presented;* we cannot know what we are not." That is the voice of the Adamic consciousness speaking extravagantly, as it often did. But if extravagance is a wandering beyond the usual boundaries in search of truth, what it finds here, revealed through his public voice, is an exact echo of some of Thoreau's most private sounds. He has put into the Adamic vocabulary much of his own persistent uneasiness about the possibility of the deepest communion with other men. We are confined to the immediacy of the moment, but we are too often confined to the immediacy of our selves as well. We cannot know the past because it is not ourselves, but for exactly the same reason we are as distant from other men who surround us now as we are from the men who were here before. That too was incorporated into the *Week:* "How can we *know* what we are *told* merely? Each man can interpret another's experience only by his own" (*Week,* 389); or, as he put it in a letter of March 27, 1848, to H. G. O. Blake, "if any should succeed to live a higher life, others would not know of it ... difference and distance are one" (*Correspondence,* 214).

Of course in certain conditions this gap is of no moment. Once again we have to refer to the paradigm of pure presentness offered in Rousseau's *Cinquième Promenade,* where there is only the immediacy of consciousness to be celebrated and only the sound of the waves to confirm another presence. At such times (which are actually an absence of times) there are no connections to the past or to any other person but only to the reality of our radical selves and, perhaps, to the deepest life in things. We need to hedge on that second point because in the experience presented in the *Cinquième Promenade* there is no temptation to gaze at the pure immediacy of anything else but one's own self as it *is* in this timeless moment. There, Rousseau contacts only so much of the world's noise as is necessary to keep him from the stillness that is too much like death. Because of this focus within, one runs the danger of losing the sense of context, of a total structure in which one's own deep center reflects and is part of the whole—that is, the pattern found in Coleridge's "One Life within us and abroad" or Wordsworth's "something far more deeply interfused." There can be no possibility of attaining a Keatsian "fellowship with essence" in these circumstances. Thus, since the relations of macrocosm and microcosm cannot be explored, a potent source of imagery has to remain dormant. If that restriction were to exist for Thoreau it would mean the loss of the multiple reference which characterizes so many of his moves and makes it possible for the acts of his imagination to have both public and private facets at once. Finally, self-absorption of the nearly total sort that Rousseau shows in his reverie would prevent the imagination from indulging in those continual searches of the world which are necessary to its redemptive activities.

Ordinarily Thoreau can stay in a condition of absolute presentness and still find primal meaning in the world outside himself. On the first page of "Solitude" in *Walden* he records an experience which includes many of the characteristics Rousseau outlines, including the waves which ripple outside. But he also stresses sympathy, congeniality, and other effects that denote the association of the inner and outer worlds. There is no penetration to the depths of natural experience, but there is also no deep stare which is limited only to the immediacy of consciousness. In this passage the primary impression is of a moment from which there are no exclusions: everything around and within him is experienced as part of the felt present. A more complicated instance occurs in the *Week*, only a handful of pages before the lament about the impossibility of really knowing another's experience:

> Sometimes we see objects as through a thin haze, in their eternal relations, and they stand like Palenque and the

Pyramids, and we wonder who set them up, and for what purpose. If we see the reality in things, of what moment is the superficial and apparent longer? What are the earth and all its interests beside the deep surmise which pierces and scatters them? While I sit here listening to the waves which ripple and break on this shore, I am absolved from all obligation to the past, and the council of nations may reconsider its votes. The grating of a pebble annuls them. Still occasionally in my dreams I remember that rippling water. *(Week,* 383; cf. *J,* I, 131)

Most of the usual components are here, especially the presentness and the sound of the waves that appear in Rousseau and elsewhere in Thoreau; but they all add up to an unusually rich combination which includes both immediacy *and* a penetration to the deep center, "the reality in things." The combination puts Thoreau at a single point in time, yet it also involves him in the largest possible context. He is not only at the absolute frontier between past and future in a sort of timeless or eternal moment, but he also sees as deeply within things as is possible to go. And the reality he sees is as much within himself as it is outside: in the previous paragraph he had spoken of "an always unexplored and infinite region [which] makes off on every side of the mind," and that too is the object of his exploratory seeings. A similar moment of vision appears in "Tintern Abbey." There, Wordsworth uses "the breath of this corporeal frame/And even the motion of our human blood" for the same purposes that Rousseau and Thoreau had used the sound of the waves: they give a minimal but definite tie to active experience. With his own version of Thoreau's "deep surmise" Wordsworth is then able to "see into the life of things," presumably the same elemental source that Thoreau calls "the reality in things."

Whatever the differences among these experiences of immediacy and context, the presence of another personality in any one of them would obviously be an encumbrance; and Rousseau, Wordsworth, and Thoreau can attain to such states only by the diligent lifting of encumbrances. The presence of other times is equally objectionable because the seeing has to be done here and now, and anything not in those categories is an impediment. One has to be "absolved from obligation to the past," which could, however, mean seeing objects "in their eternal relations," a complex combination which Thoreau brings off successfully in the passage just quoted. For Thoreau the reduction to essence is one of the private versions of his overt, public attempt, by living near Walden, to "suck out all the marrow of life . . . to drive life into a corner, to reduce it to its lowest terms" *(Walden,* 91). One has to dig profoundly to make a deep surmise about marrow, and that can be managed only with the most stringent public and private economy. When he states that his purpose at Walden is "to front only the essential facts about life" (i.e., the facts about essence), it is the present (and eternal) life within himself as well as in things that he wants to face *(Walden,* 90). Fronting, it appears, is the activity that makes possible all the deep surmises.

There are a number of other ways in which temporality functions as an efficient connective among various patterns in Thoreau's consciousness. Many of the ways turn up in relation to the wood thrush, a bird which he always associated with the purest wildness available in the Concord woods. He seems to have been fascinated by the song of that bird, which is referred to repeatedly throughout the journal, and he tried at various times to work out exactly what the bird meant to him. One of his earliest attempts, recorded in the journal for July 17, 1840, has Thoreau sounding conventionally American Adamic: "The wood thrush is a more modern philosopher than Plato and Aristotle. They are now a dogma, but he preaches the doctrine of this hour" *(J,* I, 171). This remark is all assertion and no exploration, with no hint given as to how the thrush comes to have any sort of meaning for Thoreau. All we have of the bird here is its identification with presentness and immediacy. The remark itself is one of that day's series of ponderous observations, some of which are couched in the tones of his early mannerisms.

Twelve years later, with all kinds of experience of objective nature behind him, Thoreau has come to identify the song of the thrush with freshness and permanence:

> . . . cool bars of melody from the atmosphere of everlasting morning and evening. . . . The thrush alone declares the immortal wealth and vigor that is in the forest. . . . Whenever

a man hears it, he is young, and Nature is in her spring. Wherever he hears it, it is a new world and a free country, and the gates of heaven are not shut against him. (*J*, IV, 190)

To the degree that it is associated with immortality, Thoreau's maturer thrush is the counterpart of Keats's nightingale, singing viewless out of the depths of the wood. Both birds are associated with unseen sources of melody, which may explain much of the richness in Thoreau's sense of the bird. (In only a few of his many passages on the thrush does Thoreau speak of actually seeing the wood thrush.) Because his experience of the bird does not, for the most part, include one of the terrestrial senses, its song seems several steps closer to eternity than the song of a bird whom one actually sees singing (though his experience is still several steps away from the unheard melodies which to Keats were the sweetest of all). There is one less sense to tie the bird's song to the earth. He seems all the more disembodied because we do not see him. Thoreau's thrush is therefore an interesting local version of a commonplace Romantic phenomenon. But in fact Thoreau manages to combine the eternality of the Romantic bird with the immediacy of the American thrush he had evoked in 1840. That is, his thrush of 1852 is both immortal and immediate, which means that it is located in an eternal present. As such it takes part in what Rousseau wanted to achieve in the *Cinquième Promenade,* a moment of pure immediacy that lasts forever. And, though the effect of the bird is far lovelier than that of the "portentous and outlandish spotted salamander" which Thoreau unearthed in his bean field, the bird's permanence impresses him as much as that of the sluggish animal who was "a trace of Egypt and the Nile, yet our contemporary."

In the passage from 1852 Thoreau uses Adamic language to describe the song of the bird; but because he is concerned, most of all, with modes of temporality, he avoids the usual oppressive chauvinism. The bird sings out of the heart of newness, "a new world and a free country." To approach it, to break through to the point from which it sings, is to touch at the arena of the eternally new, something which has, simultaneously, both permanence and Adamic freshness. The thrush, then, sings of something more than its own concerns: "this bird never fails to speak to me out of an

ether purer than that I breathe, of immortal beauty and vigor."
The song of the invisible thrush is yet another version of the music
John Farmer heard, the sounds which made him aware of a more
glorious existence.

Though he does not work out all the possible relations of time
and immediacy which are glanced at in this passage, Thoreau was
beginning to develop the association (which was almost an
equation) of the wild and the new. Nearly a year later the thrush's
song comes up once again in the journal, but with the implications
of the previous July's entry now drawn out to their fullest reach.
Not all of the implications are quite as comforting as those in the
earlier entries on the thrush. Thoreau extols the bird's song as he
had done before, but what he praises most is the thrush's ability to
transform the world and bring it closer to the perfection of desire:
"As I come over the hill, I hear the wood thrush singing his evening
lay" (*J,* V, 292). What the lay does is to "[change] all hours to an
eternal morning," that stage of the day when it is still new and
unproved, still in its purest freshness. Thus, the bird redeems the
day by translating natural time into ideal time.[6] Thoreau was so
accustomed to associating redemption with the morning that the
paradoxical play with "evening lay" and "eternal morning" came
effortlessly. Morning was the time of terrestrial renewal, a guarantee of temporary freshness, a period when "for an hour, at least,
some part of us awakes which slumbers all the rest of the day and
night" (*Walden,* 89). These lines from "Where I Lived and What I
Lived For" are part of a paean to morning. It is not simply a time
of promise but of an unparalleled purity and intensity of response,
an intensity which, if it could be sustained, would make living
forever fresh: "To him whose elastic and vigorous thought keeps
pace with the sun, the day is a perpetual morning" (89). If these
are still earthly affairs, the shift to the possibility of redemption
into an eternal morning would be predictable in the proper
context. There would be no change in the basic figure but merely a
transformation of the time scheme from diurnal to enduring
mornings. In "Higher Laws" Thoreau foresees the shift when he
points out that his discomfort with fishing "is a faint intimation,
yet so are the first streaks of morning" (214). The hegemony of the
higher instincts precedes redemption into the situation of eternal
purity, which is the state of men in the thrush's "perpetual

morning." As Thoreau puts it in the *Week:* "At rare intervals we rise above the necessity of virtue into an unchangeable morning light, in which we have only to live right on and breathe the ambrosial air" (394).[7]

With these suggestions of a morning that is more than a prelude to the day's work, Thoreau points to the same transcendent state that the thrush announces; but when he does so his activities differ from the redemption of time that is accomplished by his ritual gestures. The latter form of redemption stays within the confines of terrestrial business, while the bird's act of redemption into an eternal morning (and Thoreau's own hints at that possibility) transcends the borders of Thoreau's usual world. Further, Thoreau's ritualistic redemption of time reconciles the past and the present, bringing them productively together, while the bird's song rejects one kind of time for another. Each breaks the boundaries that surround present time, but they break them in very different ways and with different effects upon time. The meaning of those differences becomes starkly apparent as the passage about the thrush and his song moves on. Thoreau begins in a genial tone, but he develops the potential of the passage very quickly. For the first time in his many meditations on the song of the thrush Thoreau speaks of a radical, irreducible division between the bird's world and his own. The business of the village takes place in a time frame different from that of the bird: "How can they be contemporary when only [the village] is temporary at all? How can the infinite and eternal be contemporary with the finite and temporal?" (292-93). They cannot, obviously, and any transformation of the day that is accomplished by the bird's song can itself only be temporary. The cycles of change will continue, and the bird's work will have to be renewed again and again. The division between the world of the bird and the world of the village is as unbridgeable as the closely related gulf between flesh and spirit. By now Thoreau has completely reversed his identification of the thrush with American Adamism, probably because the latter, cherishing the present and palpable, is tied down irrevocably to the bourgeoning life of the village.

The alternative to the village is a world that looks like the order of nature but is forever involved with potentiality. As it turns out, the perfection of desire does not demand a rejection of wildness (which cannot, especially in an eternal morning, be separated from newness) but a purification of wildness that results in its apotheosis. This wildness wears the image of nature but is in fact beyond it:

> I long for wildness, a nature which I cannot put my foot through, woods where the wood thrush forever sings, where the hours are early morning ones, and there is dew on the grass, and the day is forever unproved, where I might have a fertile unknown for a soil about me. (293)

Thoreau wants everything all at once, that is, to hold on to wildness but to clean up its compulsions and unpleasantness by removing it from the transience of the physical world into the thrush's perpetual morning. In this version of wildness there are no hints of any hunger for woodchuck meat, and of course his alternative does not respond directly to the bleak facts of Ktaadn or its related experiences. One removes the discomfitures of wildness—pure matter and pure appetite—by removing oneself from the place where they are located. A world in which there are no cycles of time, where it is always early morning, will have none of the hungers that are associated with those cycles. There can be no evils in such a world because it is too fresh to have been tainted; and since this is perennial freshness ("the day is forever unproved") no spoilage can ever occur. Finally, Thoreau completes the paradigm by pointing out the fertility that any respectable vision of paradise will associate with its untried potential. His tiny myth, the vision of "a New Hampshire everlasting and unfallen," is an early harbinger of the brilliant ending of "Walking."

Yet Thoreau is not quite ready to go all the way with his myth and give up the world. For one thing, he is still part of the village, not so much as an active citizen, but as a busy participant in his own terrestrial affairs—watching the seasons, hoeing and surveying, all the work of a cartographer of the American consciousness. He follows the passage containing the myth with some strained wit about goodness as "the only investment that never fails" and then returns to the thrush for some final comments. Perhaps because the apotheosis of wildness tempered his disgust with the village's temporary world, Thoreau comes to a more familiar kind of balance. Now he can acknowledge implicitly that the split he proposed was, for the moment at least, too radical, or perhaps just too difficult to live with. Both worlds, properly purified of course, deserve their due. The thrush, he now sees, is the great mediator (another one of the redeemer's functions) who purges the barbaric potential of wildness and makes the wild fit to be used by the civilized: "All that was ripest and fairest in the wilderness and the wild man is preserved and transmitted to us in the strain of the wood thrush. It is the mediator between barbarism and civilization. It is unrepentant as Greece" (293). The civilized can get all the energy it needs, "all that was ripest and fairest," out of wildness, but it can reject the attendant horrors. Once again the half-wild is a useful solution, one that keeps us in the world (where we have to stay anyway) through an effective compromise. The myth of the wildness beyond nature was a good guess, but it was obviously unworkable, at this stage, for a maker of clearings in the forest. Yet if it had to be put aside for now, Thoreau knew that he could bring it out frequently and allow his imagination to play at futures with it.

At this juncture it will be useful to look at some earlier material in which Thoreau appears to be speaking about a wildness beyond the immediate but is actually doing something very different. In the *Week*, just after the passage about the Indian's respect for nature's independence, Thoreau referred to owl sounds which seemed to come from a strange world out beyond the confines of immediate experience: "After sitting in my chamber many days, reading the poets, I have been out early on a foggy morning and heard the cry of an owl in a neighboring wood as from a nature beyond the common, unexplored by science or by literature" (56). At one time Thoreau had speculated that out in such unorthodox nature there could be red Election-birds whose plumage "would assume stranger and more dazzling colors, like the tints of evening, in proportion as I advanced farther into the darkness and solitude of the forest" (57). But if there were any such birds, nature had never come up with them: "None of the feathered race has yet realized my youthful conceptions of the woodland depths" (56). His mind, it seems, can guess at grander possibilities in nature than his actual experience of nature has been able to confirm. Whether the fault is his own or nature's is not specified. Further, Thoreau has never found those finer colors in the offspring of any other creative imagination: "Still less have I seen such strong and wilderness tints on any poet's string" (57). This final gibe complements a remark in the previous paragraph which was to appear again in the summary essay on "Walking": our poets have ignored the "savager and more primeval" aspects of nature and have given us weaker stuff, "white man's poetry." It is obvious that the relations of consciousness and nature suffer from various forms of inadequacy and insufficient realization. The poets play only with tame surfaces, and there is a deficiency in either Thoreau or nature when it comes to matching up the facts of reality with the speculative reach of his imagination. But in any case Thoreau is not looking for a nature beyond nature but for more profound and denser strata within the nature around him. His imagination is still naturalized, though unsatisfied. He does not want to transcend what he sees but to penetrate it more deeply than anyone else has done.

The effects of the owl's sounds had set Thoreau meditating on these matters long before the *Week,* and he continued to do so long after the book was published. In August 1845 he wrote that owls "give me a new sense of the vastness and mystery of that nature which is the common dwelling of us both" (*J,* I, 378); and on November 18, 1851, two years after the appearance of the *Week,* Thoreau developed the relation of owl sounds and natural mystery into a remarkable passage, parts of which were to appear in *Walden:*

> It is a sound admirably suited [to] the swamp and to the twilight woods, suggesting a vast undeveloped nature which men have not recognized nor satisfied. . . . This sound faintly suggests the infinite roominess of nature, that there is a world in which owls live. Yet how few are seen, even by the hunters! (*J,* III, 122-23)

Once again it is the unplumbed vastness within nature that is at issue. All the mysteries are still terrestrial. Thoreau's complaint about men's insufficient comprehension of nature is partly an attack upon superficial readings of the natural world, partly the result of his own awe at what can only be surmised.[8] But the earlier material from the *Week* has a tendency which this passage does not show, a potential for dissatisfaction with nature itself as well as with the men who look at it. Thoreau's boldness in that passage goes beyond any Transcendental veneration of the mind, and the implications of his speculations could take him into some heady areas. For example, if nature, after all his intense guesswork, still cannot match up with the conjectures of consciousness, then the fault is surely not in the speculator—after all, he has brought imagination to its fullest stretch—but in the materials in nature which ought to equal the subjective models he has imagined. Nature cannot satisfy him because it is more limited than consciousness.

None of these drastic positions was brought out overtly in the passage from the *Week,* but the possibility was there, as evidenced by what followed. Between 1849, when the *Week* was published, and 1854, the year of the publication of *Walden,* Thoreau learned how far he could go. On May 22, 1854, for example, he ponders the song of crickets, one of whom suggests a wisdom and maturity "above all temporal considerations" (*J,* VI, 290). Birds remain creatures of impulse through whom nature speaks, but the crickets "sit aside from the revolution of the seasons" and sing in a strain "unvaried as Truth" (291). To hear their voices one has to be eminently sane, for the crickets "dwell forever in a temperate latitude ... forever the same in May or in November" (291). Thoreau calls that place heaven, but it is also the morning paradise he had fashioned eleven months earlier when he wanted to go to the locale of unchanging wildness where the wood thrush unceasingly sings. There is no pain in that earlier entry or in this, only the awareness that immediate nature cannot hold the full knowledge that he wants. On the next day, May 22, Thoreau carried this awareness to an extraordinary pitch of imagination in one of the richest and most subtle entries in all the vastness of the journals. He begins it with the startling but calmly voiced statement that "we soon get through with Nature" (293). The extent of the whole entry requires some background and examination.

In the *Week* Thoreau had established at least the possibility that consciousness could find nature insufficient. Later hints of that possibility appear even on the ambiguous first page of "Higher Laws," the most impassioned paean to wildness in all of *Walden.*

Under the pressure of "a strange abandonment" he sometimes ranged the woods looking for "some kind of venison which I might devour, and no morsel could have been too savage for me" (210). Thoreau is willing to go into the world of wildness as deeply as he is allowed. (In the original passage he says, "I am permitted to see the woodchuck stealing across my path" [*J*, I, 385].) And that hunger compels him with particular urgency because "the wildest scenes had become unaccountably familiar," losing the necessary newness which is basic to their character. He has already used up the full range of wildness around him; yet he continues to want more. On this page there is no evidence that he ever found more in nature, or that he could do anything other than look for it. Indeed, some of the ambivalence and unresolved dichotomies of the chapter on "Higher Laws" may come out of this unexamined stalemate.

At any rate, it is apparent that what Thoreau can find in the nature around him is not, at the beginning of "Higher Laws," sufficient to satisfy so compulsive a craving. But in the journal passage contrasting the wild world of the thrush with the temporary life of the village Thoreau showed that what holds us back from the perfection of desire is our own engagement with nature itself, the temporality of our lives and their commitment to natural cycles. That is, nature has its insufficiencies, but our diurnal obligations and inclinations create insufficiencies in us as well. When both of these tendencies come into play at once, the potential for frustration is considerable. We can attempt to put nature behind us, but the weight of our natural concerns (as well as our compelling hungers for the marrow of nature) make such a move very difficult. The myth of the morning paradise—the nature beyond nature which has all of the contours but none of the frustration—had been fashioned in order to alleviate the pressures of these tendencies; but Thoreau never tells us how one finds access to his paradise of potential. Still, his insights into the way time and redemption work together had led him to envision a permanent, preternatural wildness that sits on the summit of Ktaadn. Whatever inadequacies this state of the myth may have hidden, its expression was a satisfactory achievement, and Thoreau seemed pleased with it.

Echoes and transformations of the myth of the morning

paradise appear in the later journals and in much of Thoreau's most mature work. Some of its aspects seemed to create a special uneasiness. For example, his contrast of the wood thrush's temporal context with that of the village had led, in the radical version of the myth, to both a painless transcending of natural boundaries and a longing for their permanent dissolution. But such shattering was not so easily accomplished, and there were moments when Thoreau stood immovably on one side of the boundary and could only stare at the dark areas where the other must begin. Most of the qualities of those discomforting moments appear in the important entry for May 23, 1854, which begins with a rejection: "We soon get through with Nature. She excites an expectation which she cannot satisfy. The merest child which has rambled into a copsewood dreams of a wilderness so wild and strange and inexhaustible as Nature can never show him" (*J,* VI, 293). Once again Thoreau has seen that nature can lead beyond itself. He soon exhausts the finite order of the woods and finds his desires still unappeased. Yet the transcendent wilderness that Thoreau envisions as a result of his frustrations is not known directly but, at best, peripherally. In Thoreau's rendering of the scene we can guess that there is a deep center of wildness, but we have to do so from a position beyond the edge of the area in which the center is located:

> The red-bird which I saw on my companion's string on election days I thought but the outmost sentinel of the wild, immortal camp,—of the wild and dazzling infantry of the wilderness—that the deeper woods abounded with redder birds still; but, now that I have threaded all our woods and waded the swamps, I have never yet met with his compeer, still less his wilder kindred. The red-bird which is the last of Nature is but the first of God. (293-94)

This is Thoreau's answer to the challenge he had directed at nature in the passage from the *Week;* and the answer is framed, inevitably, in terms of the same birds he had spoken of before. The colors in his imagination can never be matched in reality, and therefore "we soon get through with Nature" and look for those places where all hues are as deep as the deep places where they are found. By this time the Election-bird has become more than a model of grand color. He is a boundary figure, a red-coated sentinel at the margin between the "wild, immortal camp" and this world's nature: "That forest on whose skirts the red-bird flits is not of earth" (294). The bird is like one of the angels placed at the gates of Eden, except that he is not so much protecting it as showing that it is still there. From another point of view, he is a mediating figure, as was the thrush of June 22, 1853: this bird combines heaven and earth within himself, since he is "the last of Nature [and] the first of God" (294).

The myth of the morning paradise has obviously taken on some new and unsettling dimensions, derived in part from Thoreau's perception of the forms through which redemption occurs. On our side of the margin is the clearing we have redeemed through exploration ("I have threaded all our woods and waded the swamps"), but Thoreau adds a blunt suggestion that we are not yet able to get out of it ("I have never yet met with his compeer, still less his wilder kindred"). His challenge to nature in the *Week* has been answered, but the result is irony and more frustration. If terrestrial nature is incapable of meeting the needs of the mind, he is himself not sufficiently skillful to get beyond nature's control and into the pure center which intuition tells him is there. He cannot even do it in fancy, as Keats did in the "Ode to a Nightingale." We know how Thoreau was sometimes oppressed by the feeling that the best part of himself, his genius, could not be communicated beyond the deep confines of the individual self. Here the difficulty is the same, but the field of exploration has been enlarged, as befits the sublimer problem of transcending the merely temporary. The best part remains within the clearing that is the world, and there seems no way to redeem it into that inexhaustible wildness where the best part could be fully itself.

The entry as a whole is designed to spell out with absolute clarity the problem of mutual insufficiencies, his own and nature's. Thus, he shows that if the area beyond the bird remains murky and inaccessible, all movement heading toward him from the other side seems also to have ceased; and the failure of that movement is attributable to another inadequacy in Thoreau's own capacities, in this case his inability to hear the music of redemption. After the section about the redbird and the exhaustibility of nature,

Thoreau begins a transitional section in which he manages to unify mind and nature by bringing objective and subjective inadequacies together. He does so in terms of the tradition of transcendental idealism. By arguing that the landscape outside is only an extension of the landscape within, Thoreau implies that his own and nature's insufficiencies are essentially the same: "This earth which is spread out like a map around me is but the lining of my inmost soul exposed. In me is the sucker that I see. No wholly extraneous object can compel me to recognize it. I am guilty of suckers" (294).

All of the rebuffs which nature has given Thoreau, all of nature's hard evidence that it has a life independent of his own, cannot quite drive out of his consciousness the occasional penchant for an idealist reading of experience. Here, though, the reading is as much a tool of rhetoric as it is a statement about reality. It permits Thoreau his usual extravagance, which is always a method of argument as well as a comment on men's lives. Part of the statement is a serious mockery of nature's tired vulgarity, as evidenced in its most ignoble models: "How many springs shall I continue to see the common sucker *(Catostomus Bostoniensis)* floating dead on our river! Will not Nature select her types from a new fount?" (294). Part of it is a sad reprimand of himself, his own inability to come up with better models than the ones in the nature around him. Thoreau is, as he says, guilty of suckers, but he has other failings too, as he goes on to point out. Using the language of subjective idealism as a transition, Thoreau turns from nature to himself. After the extreme subjectivity of his remark on nature as an extension of consciousness he offers a less daring assertion, the argument that the mind is a conduit for the eternal music of redemption, the song John Farmer heard. In making this next point Thoreau draws on imagery and voices set forth by English Romanticism a half-century earlier:

> There was a time when the beauty and the music were all within, and I sat and listened to my thoughts, and there was a song in them. . . . I sat and listened by the hour to a positive though faint and distant music, not sung by any bird, nor vibrating any earthly harp. (294)

This is the tone and language established in Wordsworth's "Immortality" ode, whose introductory stanzas tell of the falling-off of light:

> There was a time when meadow, grove, and stream,
> The earth, and every common sight,
>   To me did seem
>   Apparelled in celestial light,
> The glory and the freshness of a dream.

It is also the language of Coleridge's echo of Wordsworth in his ode to "Dejection" of 1802:

> There was a time when, though my path was rough,
>   This joy within me dallied with distress,
> And all misfortunes were but as the stuff
>   Whence fancy made me dreams of happiness.

For Coleridge, whose loss was more drastic and dramatic than Wordsworth's, both sound and light have fallen away. Later, rewriting "The Eolian Harp," a poem of 1795, he would identify that combination of sound and light with the creative energy of the One Life. The "Harp," in all its versions, shows Coleridge working his way toward a rapprochement with nature, and he ends his quest in the poem by turning his consciousness into a wind harp, totally receptive to the music-making impulses raised up in him by nature's breezes. But his success was no more than tentative. By the time of "Dejection" Coleridge was pleading for those same breezes to roar into a pitch of intensity which might waken his sluggish soul. No longer attuned to nature's harmonies, he could only stare helplessly and unfeelingly at "that green light that lingers in the west." These odes by Wordsworth and Coleridge are magnificent images of failure—in Wordsworth's case, overtly ambivalent, juggling the balance of loss and gain; in Coleridge, with a more direct awareness that no real compensation is possible. Powers have been lost which, at their fullest, led the poets out beyond the immediacy of their routine lives.

The odes made their authors fit models for Thoreau, who chose his predecessors well. In the introspection recorded on May

23, 1854, Thoreau reveals that he too had been an instrument receptive to distant music, though with him the state had been more of a habit than it was with his sometime double, John Farmer. Thoreau turns the transcendental language of his sentences on the sucker, with their sense of the mind's dominance over experience, into a passiveness drawn from some of the voices of early Romanticism: "You sat on the earth as on a raft, listening to music that was not of the earth but which ruled and arranged it. Man *should be* the harp articulate" (294). Man should receive and sound forth, and what he articulates should be a musical version of the tropes and parables Thoreau was cultivating in the bean field. But Thoreau's tense, like that of Wordsworth and Coleridge, was of the past: "there was a time" when his capacities were fresh and alive. Just as his predecessors, Thoreau knows what he can no longer do, and he knows also that the fault is his own. There is no use in "going abroad out of one's self to hear music,—to Europe or Africa," since the finest sounds will come to us only when we so live "as to be the lyre which the breath of the morning causes to vibrate with that melody which creates worlds" (295). That morning breath, of course, comes from Thoreau's morning paradise, his best guess about the source of permanent potential and unearthly music. The moods recorded on this day had their long and persistent history in Thoreau's consciousness. Their occurrence at the time of the publication of *Walden* reveals a stubborn, radical ambivalence in his sense of the world and himself.

His mixed feelings grew even more intense. Thoreau's ties to nature appeared to be loosening, and with good reason; yet they remained, though somewhat slackened, because his fascination with nature's density and self-subsistent intensity never left him, even when the nature immediately around him was not enough. If there were many moments when the inadequacies of nature were offset by the vision of a superterrestrial wildness, there were others when the old desire for more of the wildness within nature reemerged. In other words, there is no pure, simply described movement in Thoreau from the natural to the supernatural, from an exaltation of nature to a rejection of it. What we do see is a progressively increasing uneasiness with what the natural world has to offer. Thoreau's dissatisfaction with what was available is plain enough, and the evidence of his inclination to move away from immediate nature is massive and convincing. To ignore that inclination is to sentimentalize a complex mind which found few if any equals in its time.

On the other hand, concomitant with Thoreau's growing discontent with nature's capacity for complete fulfillment is his extraordinary immersion in natural fact and details, a practice revealed conspicuously in the later journals. If there were no other indication that Thoreau's discomfort with nature was balanced by a constant engagement with it, these volumes would suffice to make the point. They show that he could still turn to nature as a source of meaning for his spirit. But there are ambiguities even here. The volumes are replete with untransmuted minutiae, as though Thoreau were bathing himself in the concrete, hoping that the pressure of all these facts would somehow, by their quantity if nothing else, make them light up into truths. They rarely did so, though he kept on trying. His disappointment (or rather, ours) may come from the recognition that, even for Thoreau, nature was a means as well as an end, and nature alone could never do for him what he could no longer do for himself. One can argue further that Thoreau was urgently hunting for enlightenment in the way he knew best, through an absorption in the familiar repletion of the physical world. Certainly there are hints of desperation in his immersion in natural fact. But despite these ambiguities physical nature could never become merely a *pis aller* for Thoreau, however persistent his uneasiness with it. Nor was he a caricature of a solipsistic Transcendentalist at home only in the spirit. True, *Walden* does show how the things of this world had become more and more resistant and independent as he grew older. Perhaps that was one reason why facts became harder to transmute. Yet, stubborn as they were, he had had too much pleasure *and* enlightenment from them to permit his disappointment with nature to gain permanent sway over his spirit. What grew most of all was Thoreau's ambivalence about the content of this dilemma.

Some two years after the rich entry linking his own and nature's inadequacies Thoreau worried, in the journal, about the decline of wildness in his American surroundings. On March 22, 1856, he pondered the present lack of nobler animals such as the cougar and the moose, asserted that his predecessors had damaged the complete poem of nature ("my ancestors have torn out many of the first leaves and grandest passages"), and lamented the resultant state of incompleteness in which he was compelled to live: "All the great trees and beasts, fishes and fowl are gone. The streams, perchance, are somewhat shrunk" (*J*, VIII, 221-22). Here the fault is in the world and not in himself. There is no question of his inability to respond but of a paucity of stimuli to which he can respond. The forms of idealism through which Thoreau had asserted the continuity of consciousness and landscape are put away for a set of remarks on their inequality. This is a variant of the first part of the entry of May 23, 1854, the one which Thoreau began by stating calmly that "we soon get through with Nature." Now we know one reason why he could say that. The nature with which he is conversant is "maimed and imperfect. . . . I listen to [a] concert in which so many parts are wanting" (221). Consciousness is inhibited, most of all in its compulsive desire to drive further into the wild reaches beyond the perimeters of the explored world: "I seek acquaintance with Nature—to know her moods and manners. Primitive Nature is the most interesting to me" (221). Thoreau is trapped within a region which has lost its creative impulse, that thrust toward elemental wildness which enlivens imagination and provides fertility from the deep, savage source of things: "I cannot but feel as if I lived in a tamed, and, as it were, emasculated country" (220). This is a severely imbalanced situation and therefore a limited one, not a morning paradise of potential but an older world showing all the signs of approaching exhaustion. In "Walking," which he was reading as a lecture throughout the fifties, Thoreau reserved such language for the landscape and poets of Europe. Here, speaking quietly to himself, he holds the mirror up to America.

Thoreau does not suggest alternatives that he could have taken, the most obvious being a return to those areas in Maine where the grander sorts of wild animals could still be found. As an explorer in place, he has to find his permanent satisfactions at home or not at all. Other places are relevant only for instruction or diversion. (Thoreau took his final trip to the Maine woods during the following summer. It was to be his last opportunity to confirm the feel of the truly primitive, but of course without a replay of the shattering experience on Ktaadn.) Still, though it is clear in this entry that his dissatisfaction can never be appeased by the incomplete landscape at Concord, Thoreau does not go so far as to propose a rejection of immediate nature, as he had done two years earlier. In fact, he proposes nothing directly. The passage constitutes his examination of an impasse in which he says that he is still committed to the natural world ("I seek acquaintance with Nature—to know her moods and manners"), but he has found no way to keep up the commitment and still continue to push at the margins where the truly wild begins (221).

Yet there are some odd reverberations in this entry which ultimately expose Thoreau's unwitting ambivalence about his commitments. First, the incompleteness he complains of was there as long as he was. He never knew a Concord where he could find panthers or bear because those animals had long since been exterminated or driven out by his ancestors. The model of such raw local wildness exists only in his own speculations or in secondhand memories. It is not so much a decline that Thoreau ponders but a deficiency, recently recognized, in the nature that he has always experienced around Concord. His echo of a chapter title in *Walden*—"brute neighbors"—underscores his awareness that it is the natural world at home which no longer suffices, although he had once been convinced that it was more than enough. At one time Thoreau could shape "tropes and expression" out of the bean fields, but he has come to feel that "the forests and meadows now lack expression" because they no longer contain the moose and bear which had roamed in them long before. Thoreau's unhappiness over changes he could not have experienced directly is the signal of a profound, complex disturbance. His ties are still terrestrial because his model, old Concord, is not supernatural but part of a nature that once was there. Yet his loyalty now is to a mode of wildness that he, personally, has never known in Concord. Though his affections are still tied to nature, his present desires have placed him at one remove from any forms of Concordian nature he could ever have encountered. He can now contact what he admires most only in consciousness, that is, in a world beyond immediate nature. The grounds for ambivalence have been well established.

Further, Thoreau begins the entry by associating his brute neighbors with seasonal changes: "By their various movements and migrations they fetch the year about to me" (220). The animals make him conscious of the regularity of cyclical rhythm in the world he shares with them, the same rhythm of decline and regeneration which Thoreau had used to give *Walden* its major form. The orderly cadence of nature's changes made possible the book's assertions about the association of man's life with natural life: because man was natural, Thoreau could draw analogies from nature, equating dominant rhythms of his spirit with the patterns that brought spring back to the world and a beautiful bug out of an old wooden table. There are, after all, guarantees of a most dependable sort. But several unexpected ironies emerge from Thoreau's association of migration and natural cycles in the journal entry, because he sees that a large group of the animals who had lived by those cycles are no longer around to take part in them. He is as impressed by the size of the list, which he turns into a litany, as he is by the animals' absence: "the cougar, panther, lynx, wolverene, wolf, bear, moose, deer, the beaver, the turkey, etc., etc." (220). The guarantees of return, then, apply to the cyclical patterns themselves but not to the participants in them. The latter eventually go in a direction which does not turn back to another beginning. The cyclical and the linear, though opposites, are linked but separate rhythms, and every participant in nature has a share in each one of them. At the least, this means that our life in nature is an ambiguous affair, with simultaneous tugs in various directions. What is more, the fact of the participants' decline means that a later version of nature cannot be as replete or impressive as its earlier forms:

> When I think what were the various sounds and notes, the migrations and works, and changes of fur and plumage which ushered in the spring and marked the other seasons of the year, I am reminded that this my life in nature, this particular round of natural phenomena which I call a year, is lamentably incomplete. (221)

Thoreau's disappointment is obviously connected with cycles, which from one point of view are the best news that nature has to offer. His ambivalence about the cyclical is as evident in what he does not say, what he cannot bring himself to say, as in all of the insufficiencies that he spells out. He cannot reject the earthly, but he can lament its imperfection; and though he does not say outright that he shall never find in nature the completeness that he wants—the seasons still hold him too tightly for such a harsh declaration—he is far too aware of the inevitability of decline to expect to find fullness in Concordian nature. What he does say about all of this is precise and poignant: "I wish to know an entire heaven and an entire earth" (221). He wants completeness in everything, finally, not only in nature but also in the supernatural, and not with each realm separately but with both in a totality together. He still holds on to the Transcendentalist idea of the sphere as the symbol of completeness and perfection, yet the fullness of desire evident in his statement betrays the painful gap between what the seasons can show him and the possibilities in his mind.

Thoreau, no existential man, could not for long endure such a state of uncertainty. The entry for this day is in two parts, the second entitled "P.M.—To Walden" (222). Early signs of spring are beginning to show, and Thoreau goes to look for them around the railroad and the sandy slopes near Walden. Though no spring life has yet come forth, he finds warmth and melting snow there, and he can see "the yellow sand and the reddish subsoil." In itself this is very little, but it is quite enough for the reassurance that Thoreau needs: "The eternity which I detect in Nature I predicate of myself also. How many springs I have had this same experience! I am encouraged, for I recognize this steady persistency and recovery of Nature as a quality of myself" (222-23). Under the pressure of his uncertainties on that day in 1856 Thoreau had to come down on the side of some affirmation, and he inevitably chose the one which offered present security, standing firm on the value of his current experience. It was also the affirmation whose lineaments had already been fully developed as the dominant structuring image in *Walden.*

Not only does Thoreau discover the reassurance at Walden, the locale where it originally had been worked out and grounded; he also returns to the very materials around Walden from which, in the book, he had created a stunning symbol of the resurgence of natural life in the spring. In the chapter on "Spring" Thoreau drew out all the imagery of regeneration inherent in "the forms which thawing sand and clay assume in flowing down the sides of a deep cut on the railroad" *(Walden,* 304). Winter is purged, Thoreau sees that "there is nothing inorganic," and the earth is recognized as "a living earth; compared with whose great central life all animal and vegetable life is merely parasitic" *(Walden,* 308-9). This had been a moment of triumph for Thoreau's imagination, when the forms in his mind and the potential in nature came together in lovely coalescence. Later, on that day in March 1856 when Thoreau was depressed over nature's inability to match up with his mind, his instincts drew him back to the locale and materials which had once offered both insight and resolution. The thoughts he had had in the morning of that day could not be ignored—indeed, they had to be countered—and if no new answers appeared to be available, the old insights could still be depended upon for their proven inherent power.

It has been said that Thoreau's initial interest in "pure" wildness came to be tempered by his understanding that wildness served man best only as a source of refreshment into which he ought to dip now and again. *Walden,* therefore, would represent what Sherman Paul calls a "chastened primitivism," a mode which others have seen as a necessary next step after the encounter on Ktaadn.[9] As Charles Anderson has argued, "it is this modified concept of the wild, symbolic instead of literal, which found its way into *Walden.*"[10] Yet it is doubtful if the wild was ever, except once, exclusively literal for Thoreau. Part of the problem at Ktaadn was that Thoreau had always *used* wildness to one degree or another, finding some way to relate it to his perpetual examination of the order of self and its relation to the order of nature. It was this attitude—in which nature was always, at some level, not literal but a trope—that had trapped him up at Ktaadn. There, nature refused to be anything but its own very strange self, overwhelmingly literal, and his habitual bent toward the figurative was shown to be an irrelevance. But both Sherman Paul and Charles Anderson are surely correct in pointing out that one has to distinguish the temperate wildness expressed in *Walden* from the mind-shattering sort Thoreau spoke of in the essay on "Ktaadn, and the Maine Woods," which he published in the *Union Magazine of Literature and Art* in 1848. And there is a clear move toward temperateness between "Ktaadn" and "Chesuncook," which recorded Thoreau's second trip to Maine in 1853. There he encounters the continuing primitive in the form of an incomprehensible Indian language, "the language which has been spoken in New England who shall say how long?" *(Maine Woods,* 136). As in other, similar Romantic encounters, Thoreau's first reaction is to verify the existential presence, the actual being of another kind of person: "It took me by surprise, though I had found so many arrow-heads, and convinced me that the Indian was not the invention of historians and poets" (136). (Compare Wordsworth's meeting with the leech gatherer.) But though he achieves this sense of presence, the strangeness of the unknowable language serves to distance him from the source of wildness, the Indians themselves, at the same time as he gets into as proximate a relationship to their presence as a white man can: "I felt that I stood, or rather lay, as near to the primitive man of America, that night, as any of its discoverers ever did" (137).[11] (Compare Wordsworth's reaction to the song of the solitary reaper.) In effect, this is a rehearsal for the experience on his third journey in which Thoreau and his companions watched an Indian approach a state of pure animal wildness by imitating the squeak of a musquash. In these instances, as at Ktaadn, the genuinely wild is something one nears but cannot possibly assimilate. The later versions of that attitude undoubtedly owed much to the Ktaadn experience itself: though Thoreau finds no ferocity or bizarre landscapes in these new meetings, the quality of otherness associated with the primitive has intensified and become its dominant characteristic. Still, before and long after "Chesuncook"—that is, from at least 1841 until the final version of "Walking"—Thoreau extolled a savage American wildness which, at its most primitive, took its tone from the Hottentots who devoured the raw marrow of koodoos *(Excursions,* 225).

Only a year before the second trip to Maine, and six years after the first one, Thoreau wrote his wonderful journal entry comparing the tameness of the European nightingale with the wildness of the American thrush, much to the detriment of the former. As late as February 16, 1859, Thoreau was still praising immediate natural wildness, and, though it was nothing like Ktaadn, there was nothing chastened in some of the things he saw. He admires the wildness of the hen hawk which "settles with confidence on a white pine top and not upon your weathercock. That bird will not be poultry of yours" *(J,* XI, 450). The wildness which the hen hawk represents is characterized primarily by its resistance to taming, to the imposition of human dominance over the foreign and independent order of the primitive: "What we call wildness is a civilization other than our own," a remark which directly recalls Montaigne's comment that *"chacun appelle barbarie ce qui n'est pas de son usage."* [12] Redemption of such material is neither possible nor desirable. At the end of the entry Thoreau shapes out an analogy of the hawk with untamable genius which "can never be poet laureate, to say 'Pretty Poll' and 'Polly want a cracker' " (451). These last comments, an excellent find, save his image of genius from conventional low-Romantic attitudes which were long since seen as tawdry. Thoreau turns a neat trick in this entry: he argues for the unconquerable otherness of wild nature and shows it in the hawk; and he argues against our ability to tame the wild whose strangeness some regard as though it were a sin.

Yet there is a most important sense in which Thoreau does use the wild here for the benefit of man, permitting each to retain its integrity: his imagination draws on the untamableness of the hawk and turns the bird and its autonomy into an image of wild, independent human genius. This is Thoreau's way of showing how natural objects can be used (not subjugated) by the mind without the danger of violation by the sort of unsympathetic man who "has always a charge in his gun ready for their extermination" (450). (Of course there is nothing here of the final degree of strangeness he experienced at Ktaadn. If there were, Thoreau's imagination could not have worked at all.) With perfect cunning Thoreau allows the unredeemable hen hawk to be fully itself but to be something for him as well. Exactly a year later, on February 12, 1860, he came at the same problem from a different direction, discussing a form of imposition associated with one of man's most important redemptive tools, the naming capacity of language:

> Whatever aid is to be derived from the use of a scientific term, we can never begin to see anything as it is so long as we remember the scientific term which always our ignorance has imposed on it. Natural objects and phenomena are in this sense forever wild and unnamed by us. (*J*, XIII, 141)

Nature is admirably and permanently elusive, forever escaping the entrapment of language or any other form of the artifices of consciousness; but Thoreau had known that even in *Walden,* when he tried to chase the wild loon which always slipped away laughing.

The fluctuations and uneasiness which emerge through the flood of facts in the later journals show that half-wildness, a "chastened primitivism," could not finally be a sufficient resting place for Thoreau. Even at the time he was writing *Walden* he had begun to feel that the imagination was a more fertile and daring creator than nature itself. On the other hand—and this point is not quite contradictory—nature had offered him several resounding defeats, in part because it was always struggling to go on being itself. Sherman Paul's observation that Thoreau may have started his late technical studies of the Indian because of his "growing awareness of his inability to master the wild" is well taken.[13] The great passage on the hen hawk is as much about defeat as a special kind of victory. When Thoreau began to mull over the insufficiencies of nature there were a great many pressures compelling him, some from long past in his experience and observable as early as the ending of the *Week.* He had long suspected—and the suspicion grew with time—that the clearing in the forest, man's life in the woods of this world, was not the best that the imagination could envision for him. The radical cadences of his thought, the advance and sidestep through which a position is promoted and then qualified, work here as well. The structures of consciousness which gave form to Thoreau's worldly experience were lovely in themselves and useful for him, the fruitful discoveries of an extraordinarily flexible imagination. The structures were formative and cohesive because they participated in all aspects of his life in this world and served to give unity to the complex diversity of his explorations. But their inseparability from his earthly business, as it turned out, could be a drawback as well as a positive factor for his shaping spirit: for if nature was seen, at times, to be less than he could conceive it to be, insufficient for the fullest reach of his imagination, then the forms so closely involved with nature might themselves be less than he finally needed, sufficient though they were for his life in this world. He had to go one step further and find forms which would give due acknowledgment to the pull of nature and yet realize that it was not enough. That was the ultimate dilemma for the adequacy of his imagination.

5.

A Tangent to this Sphere

In the spring of 1852 Thoreau announced to his journal that he had come to a new awareness about the shape of the year: "For the first time I perceive this spring that the year is a circle. I see distinctly the spring arc thus far. It is drawn with a firm line" (*J*, III, 438). This venerable trope could be immensely reassuring because it guaranteed Thoreau what it had meant, immemorially, for most religions and myths—the revivification and continuity of the natural world. It seems odd, however, that Thoreau discovered it at so late a date, although he said in 1860 that "it takes us many years to find out that Nature repeats herself annually" (*J*, XIII, 279). After all, Thoreau always reveled in the return of natural warmth. As *Walden* shows, his fascination with the bleak shapes of winter could never qualify his welcome of spring, when he felt an exceptional joy which was both source and reflection of the joy he saw in the outer world: "From whatever source the light and heat come, thither we look with love" (*J*, XII, 67).

One may ask, therefore, why Thoreau took until 1852 to discover a specific and most useful pattern which, considering only his reading in Eastern religions, should have come to him long before. We can only conclude that, if he really did not know it before, he found it when he needed it; and many examples of his concern, during those years, with the relations of self and nature show that he often required the reassurance of the circular pattern, the round of nature in which he was enclosed. Early in the same year Thoreau pondered the dead stalks of a series of annuals. In the January chill he wondered what they were still doing there, and he moved from that question directly to the inevitable correspondence with the affairs of man. Man is obviously more durable than an ephemeral annual because "he sees the annual plants wither" while he contemplates their death and his own survival (*J*, III, 188). But he is not like the trees, either, because his own run of sap continues to flow in the winter, however sluggishly, until "on the approach of spring there is an increased flow of spirits, of blood, in his veins" (189). Man is therefore in one way better off than the annuals, and in an important way better off than the perennial plants with which he shares a greater con-tinuity. Best of all, the cycle of the year is a firm guarantee that he will continue to go on in his own way, freed every spring from the deep chill of the winter. The round of nature was therefore redemptive, and it was redemptive because it was a round. Linear movements leave their participants behind.

If Thoreau had already been meditating these matters in January, it is evident that what he discovered in the spring of 1852 was not the continuity of natural events but their form, the circular shape through which he could envision the continuity. And it is equally evident, by this point, that the redemptive round of nature is analogous in structure to the redeemed enclosure, the clearing in the forest which is the shape of each man's world. Each of these forms recalls and implicates the other through their configuration as enclosures and their mutual concern with terrestrial redemption. But there are other homologous forms in Thoreau's experience; for example, the dots of enclosed clearing, studded throughout an immense dark wilderness, which signify the redeemed areas in Thoreau's imaginative map of the American landscape. The map grew out of his intuitive reading of American experience, and it served to order his perceptions as well as to record them. Thus, the map determined Thoreau's reading of his own activities not only in his explorations around Concord but also in his deep probings of the Maine woods and every other equivalent situation.

Now we are beginning to see that there is a community of parallel forms in Thoreau's perception, a set of enclosed shapes through which he organized his interpretation of the world and the relation of his self to experience. In each case the enclosure has the same function for Thoreau: it signifies an act of terrestrial redemption, an act which is not concluded until the enclosure is completed. One realizes that an enclosure is an image of wholeness and completion because one can start anywhere on its circumference and return eventually to where one began: spring leads again to spring; a point at the edge of the clearing is met again after a full perambulation of the edge. The relation of these forms to the circle and sphere, the basic Transcendental images of unity and perfection, is clear and, for Thoreau, quite comforting. Further, each form is opposed to the unformed, to the wild in each instance of human endeavor, to the chaos before Genesis in the instance of the regularity of the seasons. (Thoreau spoke of pure wildness as chaos when he was up on Ktaadn.) Nearly all have to do with the economy of the imagination because they are instances of the imagination's ability to make profitable use out of the materials it receives from the experience of America. With the exception of the round of nature and its diurnal equivalent, which man does not create but discovers, the forms are the product of man's capacity to clean up a piece of experience and make it fully his own, won from the world around him. Skillfully ordered through the energy of consciousness, each form is a gesture of the mind, confirming the imagination's adequacy in its perpetual encounter with the wilderness that reaches up to the edge of its confines. Each, then, is a record of success, an achieved terrestrial redemption.

Let us add some other examples to the set of enclosed shapes. In the last chapter of *Walden* Thoreau states that "our voyaging is only great-circle sailing" because we return home eventually and inevitably, having carved the image of an orb out of the world through which we have been traveling *(Walden,* 320). That circle defines the form of our movements as well as the fact that we have to swing back finally to the point of origin. Such voyages are obviously macrocosmic versions of Thoreau's perambulations at home. All those strolls about the bounds of the town, "the confines of the actual Concord," are also circular in form, as Thoreau points out in "Walking" *(Excursions,* 217). The pattern he describes in his habitual walks is therefore identical with the shape of great-circle sailing, and both take part in the community of analogous forms we have been observing.

The round of nature which Thoreau says he became aware of in 1852 is, in its shape and completeness, a grand echo of all the other redemptive forms through which he conducted the deepest business of his life. But it is an echo with a difference because some of those forms are more nearly equivalent than others. The round of nature was technically as redemptive as any other in the set, but what it redeemed him to was essentially just more of the same; and we have now seen so much evidence of Thoreau's mature dissatisfaction with the cyclical that we can specify one basic reason for his discernible uneasiness: a redemption within the round of nature was finally no real redemption at all. At best it would be as incomplete as nature itself had come to seem. His recognition of the insufficiency of natural redemption necessarily followed after his recognition of the ultimate insufficiency of nature. Nature never ceased to be lovely, a prime source for immense satisfactions. No man or creed ever matched what it could do for Thoreau, and though he sometimes wavered he continued to be intensely attracted to it up to the end of his life. To be redeemed back into nature would be a guarantee of certain future satisfactions. Yet nature would still seem incomplete, still be incommensurate with the capacities of the mind, still be the place of transient springs; and *those* facts grew to be more and more significant in the last eight years of Thoreau's life. If he managed to outlive the annuals and the winter chill that killed them, he was still locked within the round of nature which enfolded every creature. All of the enclosed forms which determine so much of the shape of Thoreau's world are redemptive because they are enclosed. To be redeemed within nature was therefore to be a lucky prisoner of the world, both beneficiary and victim at once. Thoreau's need to discover or create enclosures was countered by his concern over their potential for confinement. Nothing defines his uneasiness more precisely than his ambivalence over the effects of the redeeming round of nature.

It should be remembered that one of Thoreau's most startling assertions about the inadequacies of nature ("we soon get through with Nature") was written into the journal while *Walden* was being published. Even as he was putting out his major statement on the shaping of human experience through the predictable sequence of natural cycles—an affirmation intended to give the greatest degree of comfort—Thoreau was making other statements which severely qualify the value of the round of nature for man. This was a time of triumph studded with moments of uneasiness which cannot be ignored or minimalized as temporary aberrations. The knowledge attained in *Walden* did not come easily, and the strength of the affirmations at the end of the book speaks to the sturdiness of the consciousness which made them. But those affirmations were not useful for, or even applicable to, the dilemmas revealed by this journal entry, and his quandaries recurred thereafter with a frequency that reveals a considerable disturbance. Thoreau had learned to move with the rhythms of nature, to draw sustenance from its circular patterns of return, but he had stopped hearing the music of complete redemption within it. Two years after the publication of *Walden* he put his contradictory assertions into the separate halves of a single entry. What had been a "maimed and imperfect nature" on the morning of March 23, 1856, becomes in the afternoon, thanks to nature's cyclical form, a guarantee of his own recovery. But in the morning he had longed for "an entire heaven and an entire earth"; and the comeback in the afternoon, however comforting in natural terms, could not promise him more than the sort of imperfect wholeness achieved when the round of nature, "an entire earth," was fully enclosed.

There is evidence of the meaning (i.e., the incompleteness) of natural redemption everywhere, even in the great passages on nature's creative return in the chapter on "Spring" in *Walden*. The thawing sandbank, which echoes corresponding forms that are repeated all through nature and up the natural segment of the chain of being, is mixed with a bit of clay. Man, looked at in his relation to these corresponding shapes, is himself "but a mass of thawing clay" (307). The whole complex of forms is "somewhat excrementitious in its character," but that is still further evidence that Nature "is mother of humanity" (308). Insofar as we are natural we are clay and excrement, sharing in spring's joyful recognition that "there is nothing inorganic" (308). What Thoreau witnesses in the sandbank is the redemption of himself as clay and excrement, himself as he is part of "an entire earth." There is nothing here about the other, companion longing for "an entire heaven." Of course Thoreau was asking for more from the cycle of nature than he was from any of the other shapes of redemption, but that was only reasonable since nature had already given him more than anything else had ever done. His problem was that nature had given him all that it could. He was left thereafter with a paradox of deficient completeness, a whole which was not nearly enough. That point, as we shall see, was also recognized in *Walden*.

Thoreau never ceased to extol all the forms of natural redemption even as he looked for ways to overcome their limitations. Eleven days after the entry about that imperfect nature which was still, somehow, a model, he announced that "I revive with Nature; her victory is mine" (*J*, VIII, 244). Later, on a bleak January afternoon in 1858, he reflected on the scarcity of berries in the woods and what that seemed to show of nature's wintry niggardliness. Then a snowflake fell on his coat: "This little object, which, with many of its fellows, rested unmelting on my coat, so perfect and beautiful, reminded me that Nature had not lost her pristine vigor yet, and why should man lose heart?" (*J*, X, 239). Four days after that, still thinking of berries, he found in them even more evidence of an eventual realization of desire: "If you are sick and despairing, go forth in winter and see the red alder catkins dangling at the extremities of the twigs, all in the wintry air, like long, hard mulberries, promising a new spring and the fulfillment of all our hopes" (*J*, X, 242-43). The promised redemption, guaranteed by the vigor that holds through the winter, is a renewal into more of the same, "a new spring." It ensures the revival of our damped-down forces. The last words, however, seem to approach the language of total redemption, foreseeing the ultimate coalescence of desire and capability, when all that we ask for and all that we can have become the same. But Thoreau does not force the point. His rhetoric is bland, perhaps deliberately so. Though there are hints of transcendence in the last words, the berries are never pressured into the intensity of an emblem. Encouraging as these statements were, they were largely no more than reaffirmations of the cyclical enclosure of nature, ending with a tag containing some vague hints of other possibilities, and Thoreau may well have wanted them exactly that way. He was, after all, still very fond of the woods of the world and could not dispense with them easily. He was trying hard to find ways of reconciling their capacities and his own desires.

Some of the modes of reconciliation during those years took the form of conventional Transcendental assumptions about the relations of consciousness and nature; but Thoreau put the familiar to work in uncommon ways which corresponded to the singularity of his problems. One of the most significant attempts, recorded on June 6, 1857, derives from an equally important entry of the day before. On the previous afternoon Thoreau had pondered the simultaneous familiarity and strangeness of local plants: "They are cohabitants with me of this part of the planet, and they bear familiar names. Yet how essentially wild they are! as wild, really, as those strange fossil plants whose impressions I see on my coal" (*J*, IX, 406). The plants are part of his world, but their forms of being exist in a forever unavailable wildness. What Thoreau senses in these plants has nothing of the grotesqueness of Ktaadn's wildness, but this kind is equally impervious to every effort of consciousness to overcome the gap. No ontological leaps are possible in a world so peopled with strangeness. Still, Thoreau's recognition of distance appears, for most of the entry, to be cool and self-possessed, undoubtedly because this is not the total rebuff he received on Ktaadn. In Maine his mind had struggled with the materials on the mountain but could do nothing with them except turn a few rocks into sheep. Here, in a more familiar context, he can put the things of this world to accepted Transcendental use as "a language of the sentiments," tools of the mind's impulse to find images for man in the inhuman. (Transcendentalist certainty is sometimes leavened with a deep sense of the otherness of the world.) If the strange is not fully domesticated it can at least be partly tamed. The world can be useful even while it is resistant. Yet, after all this work at a judicious balance, Thoreau's blunt final comment turns the positive emphasis around and makes the entry into an acknowledgment of partial defeat: "I assume to be acquainted with these, but what ages between me and the tree whose shade I enjoy! It is as if it stood substantially in a remote geological period," that is, as if its true substance were elsewhere.

The word "assume" initiates an interpretation of his activities which undermines all the confidence of Concord, stressing the limited adequacy of his language of the sentiments rather than its incomplete success. There is only so much that consciousness can control. He has been beaten by the wildness of the world.

On the following day Thoreau tackled the cycle of nature, using the same tools of consciousness in another effort at reconciliation. This time he tries to turn the round into a mood of the mind, in what is essentially an effort to both have the cycle and neutralize it too. In an eloquent fantasy on the brevity of the seasons Thoreau imagines that each season is merely a momentary effect in nature, "an infinitesimal point. It no sooner comes than it is gone. It has no duration" (*J*, IX, 406). The seasons touch him and then disappear, each instantaneously replaced by its successor in the cycle. Thoreau slipped into this bizarre fiction (a version of his desire for presentness) when he saw that a new summer was out there, and he felt flustered, as though he were too late to respond to it. His meditations on it became more complex until they cohered into a magnificently ironic conceit which draws on the tools of mechanism to illustrate the relations between the two major antitheses of mechanism, nature and the mind:

> Our thoughts and sentiments answer to the revolutions of the seasons, as two cog-wheels fit into each other. We are conversant with only one point of contact at a time, from which we receive a prompting and impulse and instantly pass to a new season or point of contact. (407)

But as the fantasy develops Thoreau grows less interested in the rapidity of change than in what this image implies about the interaction of mind and nature and their correspondingly hurried shifts of mood. Continuing his idealist inclinations of the day before, he picks up the point about the brief "prompting and impulse" which each season raises up in man and argues that our fluctuating sensations and thoughts have each a correspondent language in nature: "Now I am ice, now I am sorrel" (407). And he then pushes his fantasy to its most flagrant limit, asserting that "each experience reduces itself to a mood of the mind" (407). In saying that, Thoreau does not dissolve nature into a fragment or extension of the mind, an external counterpart of the ego established so that the ego can engage itself in action. He could do that only in a light spoof of extreme idealism, and this passage is very serious play indeed. Thoreau manages to have the round of nature all ways at once, granting its independent reality and the perpetual succession of changes but reducing the significance of those changes to an impulse whose main effect on him is to create new thoughts and sentiments. Whatever the season, it can do little more than "give a tone and hue to [his] thought" (406).

If Thoreau could never make the ontological leap and reach to the pure wildness of another form of being, he could transform the mode of being of the cycle of nature from objective to subjective reality. By that, of course, he would seem to lessen the hold of nature upon him; and in fact this whole fantasy dwells on the round of nature without a single hint at what the round does to mortal creatures. If his fantasy is therefore unreal, in light of his other preoccupations at that time, it is also a skillful attempt to circumvent the effect of the seasons. What is more, it cancels out some of the difficulties in the previous entry: there is no need to contact the deepest wildness in nature, since the importance of experience is not in what it is but in what it does to him. The mind is at all times adequate, since it needs only the stimulus given by a season to get its own work going. At the conclusion of this entry Thoreau returns to an old awareness whose sporadic appearances show that it had never been entirely forgotten. All he can ever really know about the human mind, he says, is the moods and thoughts which experience causes in himself. He cannot swear what experience does to anyone else, since "it would be worse than swearing *through glass*. For I only see those other facts as through a glass darkly" (407). Once again he is bottled up within his private enclosure of the self, as unable to reach the consciousness of another person as he was, on the day before, to contact the wildness of the plants. Thoreau's fantasy about the effect of cycles on the mind is in part compensatory, a finely shaped bit of imaginative play which touches on some of his most basic and persistent concerns.

One more instance will do to show how Thoreau was trying to reconcile his own interests with the realities of the round of nature. On October 31, 1857, he found an excellent incentive for not being melancholy at this season when the "spirits do flag a little [and] there is a little questioning of destiny" (*J*, X, 150). He found that the leaves of the skunk cabbage were dead but that under the leaves were the spears of new shoots which had already begun to develop toward their fulfillment in the following year. Thoreau toys with the conceit that this may be "a lie or a vain boast," a false prophecy, but that is actually part of a stratum of delicate wit that runs through the passage. Before this he had suggested a series of inspiring, commonplace mottoes for the buds, aware of the ironic function of such pedestrian catchwords in the context of skunk cabbage, one of nature's more amusing vulgarities. And that vulgarity is essential to his point: this fetid weed is part dead and part newly born, part withered and part green, the shoots demonstrative of the vigor he had spoken of five years earlier which guarantees survival through the winter and into a new spring (cf. *J*, III, 188). If an ignoble skunkweed can triumph, then men should not lie down in the winter of their discontent.

So far this is predictable, given Thoreau's penchant for such thoughts at this time. But Thoreau is especially canny here, successful not only in pressuring the cabbage to become emblematic but in managing both to have his cycle and defraud it too. He puts it this way: "Winter and death are ignored; the circle of life is complete" (151). So phrased, this issue is radically paradoxical. Winter and death are necessary to the completeness of the cycle, but as elements of the cycle they contribute to their own ultimate rejection. For it is only when the cycle is complete (and therefore redemptive) that winter and death can be ignored or passed by. It is only when they do their job that the job is superseded. We have to encounter winter and death in order to find ways to do without them. Thus, the simultaneous presence of death and rebirth within the same rank cabbage means that winter is being confirmed. These visible shoots are not implied promises but palpable and immediate proofs of next summer's fruition. An unlikely phoenix rises from its ashes before the ashes have cooled into their winter chill.

Yet the bedeviling problem of nature's insufficiency is still not cleared up, even with this dazzling display of nature's (and Thoreau's) virtuosity. Once again nature is demonstrably adequate, but it is only naturally so, and the imagination which turned the skunk cabbage into an image of terrestrial redemption had been recognizing for some time that there were vast areas of the mind's desire which even such paradoxical weeds could not fully satisfy. Thoreau's serious play with the cabbage was amusing, consoling, and challenging to the efficacy of his imagination; but when he won out in these and similar contests there was still very much to hope for beyond the promises in weeds.

Thoreau never ceased looking for compromises, but it was clear that he had to find something else because the compromises he did achieve were never sufficiently in his own favor. When he came to terms with nature in his later years—whether through delight or necessity, the pleasures of the woods or the compulsions of the cycle—the compromise was usually in favor of his natural self, and that was fine but not enough. There had been a time when nature could satisfy the spirit more than sufficiently, but there came a time when the satisfactions of the spirit began to separate more and more from nature because the spirit had other needs which grew severe in their urgency. Yet those demands could be only partly appeased, at best. Very often it seemed as though the pure forms that his spirit sought were out beyond the edge of the enclosure which enfolded him and offered him natural satisfactions. Thus, the cyclical repetition of natural processes made a closed circle whose limits would contain Thoreau so long as, and to the degree that, he was natural. In several of the examples we have looked at there is a perceptible sense of frustration which sometimes intensifies into a feeling of entrapment, of being ensnared inside an enclosure whose boundaries were absolutely binding and inflexible. The passage which evolves into the myth of the morning paradise is a prime instance of that feeling. Nature's enclosure was in part paradisiacal, often exceptionally so, but it could never be the morning paradise whose atemporal bliss is forever new and unchanging. Because Thoreau was not the kind of mystic who craves dissolution of all contact with palpable experience, the desire for compromise and the occasional feeling of entrapment could only continue.

The round of nature was not the only enclosure within which Thoreau could feel uncomfortably constricted. Several repeated patterns in his perception, and in the imagined wholes he made out of it, indicate that Thoreau had often been somewhat uneasy over confinement within boundaries, even as he was busily making or discovering clearings in the wilderness of the world. One primary example was the sense of enforced isolation which would surface now and again, the awareness of the difficulties of breaching our personal confines. We have looked at instances as late as *Walden*, and there are others as early as 1841: "How alone must our life be lived! . . . none are travelling *one* road so far as myself" (*J*, I, 239). Sometimes the entrapment is self-generated:

> I perceive that some, commonly talented, persons are enveloped and confined by a certain crust of manners, which, though it may sometimes be a fair and transparent enamel, yet only repels and saddens the beholder, since by its rigidity it seems to repress all further expansion. . . . They have, as it were, prematurely hardened both seed and shell. (*J*, IX, 265)

But there were perimeters of time and space as well as the walls set up around consciousness, and if the latter were often thought to be unbridgeable, Thoreau could find the former frustrating as well. The difference, however, is that Thoreau put a considerable amount of well-aimed and successful effort into overcoming the limitations created by time and space. For example, his parochialism in regard to Concord was offset, as has been noted, by an internationalism which made illustrations of universal activity out of affairs around Concord. Though he could state that local business was enough for him, that he would never finish working away at all that could be seen within the confines of Concord, it was Concord as microcosm that appeared finally to matter most:

> The *S. lucida* makes about the eleventh willow that I have distinguished. . . . It transports me in imagination to the Saskatchewan. It grows alike on the bank of the Concord and of the Mackenzie River, proving them a kindred soil. I see their broad and glossy leaves reflecting the autumn light this moment all along those rivers. Through this leaf I communicate with the Indians who roam the boundless Northwest. (*J*, IX, 56)

Four days earlier he had been out in a local swamp and had

come across a wild area as exciting as any in Labrador: "I have no doubt that for a moment I experience exactly the same sensations as if I were alone in a bog in Rupert's Land, and it saves me the trouble of going there" (*J,* IX, 42). The point is that Thoreau could have his Concord and the world too. The line Thoreau charted in his walks around Concord defined the margins of his daily life, the lengths to which he chose to go. But Thoreau's compulsion to turn home cosmography into a map of universal experience meant that he could refute the confinements of a single place although he simultaneously enjoyed his restriction to it. At times he argued that the spirit has no fixed home, which is to say that it is at home everywhere. Events of the spirit—one's own or the universal form—ignore the material locales in which they occur because the actions of the spirit ultimately have nothing to do with mundane places. They teach another geography: "The Great Spirit makes indifferent all times and places. The place where he is seen is always the same, and indescribably pleasant to all our senses" (*J,* I, 363); "Any prospect of awakening or coming to life to a dead man makes indifferent all times and places. The place where that may occur is always the same, and indescribably pleasant to all our senses" (*Walden,* 134). The congruence of these quotations shows that the Great Spirit may awaken a man anywhere; and the imagination, through its ability to redeem time and place, will show that the event actually occurs everywhere. Thoreau's imagination was always impatient with perimeters, even as he continued to value what the mind could make out of an enclosed space such as the bounds around Concord. The ideal was an imagination so supple that it resisted the fixity which could turn a lovely, redeemed enclosure into a prison:

> Ever and anon something will occur which my philosophy has not dreamed of. The limits of the actual are set some thoughts further off. That which had seemed a rigid wall of vast thickness unexpectedly proves a thin and undulating drapery. The boundaries of the actual are no more fixed and rigid than the elasticity of our imaginations. (*J,* V, 203)

He had said the same, with less grace, several years earlier: "The excursions of the imagination are so boundless, the limits of towns are so petty" (*J*, III, 5). That was the coda to a complaint we have already inspected, his grumble over the events of the previous week, "after having been perambulating the bounds of the town all the week, and dealing with the most commonplace and worldly-minded men, and emphatically *trivial* things" (5). Here he argues that he can survive spiritually only by going out of bounds, transgressing the limits of the town's life—a transgression which it is a sin not to perform. He is driven by the strength of his genius, which refuses to be rigidly encompassed: "Genius has evanescent boundaries, like an altar from which incense rises" (*J*, IX, 265).

But of course Thoreau had been passing beyond boundaries all along: his fracture of the confines of place was paralleled by his recurrent interest in modes of perception which could overcome the limits and costs of sequential time. By sharing in the thoughts of Sadi, Thoreau had dissolved all barriers of distance between them. That was a way of bridging personal as well as temporal gulfs, partaking in the (apparently inaccessible) innermost life of a long-dead thinker who was still his contemporary. When Thoreau thought like Sadi he was no longer locked within the limits of his self or the present moment. Yet, paradoxically, there were other forms of the refutation of time which gloried in presentness, collapsing the boundaries between now and all other times by bringing them all, simultaneously, into temporal immediacy: "In eternity there is indeed something true and sublime. But all these times and places and occasions are now and here. God himself culminates in the present moment" (*Walden*, 97). In this refutation of time we must also include every form of the ritual work at the margin, every mode of redeeming the past into the present, whether it is the recovery of old artifacts, the blending of the dust of previous inhabitants, a repetition of immemorial actions, or even the uncovering of an ancient species of salamander. All those places with fuzzy margins—the bean field, the house that was near to dissolving into a natural object—are visible, tangible products of the same activity, the shattering of divisions, temporal or spatial, between where we are and where we want to be.

Thoreau's awareness of the enclosures that cycles make, and of the possibilities of establishing countermovements to those cycles, appears as early as the *Week*. That is, his understanding of all the implications of enclosing forms was not exclusively a product of his later years but was broached in his earliest writings. If the *Week* is like *Walden* in being organized, for the most part, on the structure of a major cycle, it also anticipates *Walden* in that it contains a counterpoint of rhythms which gives the book its radical energy of movement. In fact, the design of the *Week* is unsurpassed in Thoreau's work for the complex counterpoint of its components. To begin with, there is the major cycle of the journey, the movement from Concord, Massachusetts, and back again. In "Concord River," the introductory chapter, the flow of the stream which they journey upon is identified as "an emblem of all progress, following the same law with the system, with time, and all that is made"; and one instance of what is made are the weeds, "still planted where their seeds had sunk, but ere long to die and go down likewise" (*Week*, 11). The progress of the water is as cyclical as the travelers' journey because it goes down to the sea and returns, in clouds, to the mountains from which it began. If the movement of the weeds themselves is linear, that only demonstrates that the participants in the cycle are less durable than the cycle itself. Accompanying the shapes of the voyage and the stream are the cycles of the day, the week, and—not apparent until the end of the book—the seasons as well, all together establishing a pattern of mirrors in which going and returning are acknowledged to be the major cadences of natural experience. Several smaller versions, such as the ascent and descent of mountains, occur frequently enough throughout the *Week* to anchor those rhythms at every level of the book's imaginative life.

Yet there are other movements which go counter to the natural rhythms of progression and recurrence in which man and all other creatures take part. The forward flow of time and the river is opposed by the narrator's persistent impulse to dwell on historical events which have occurred at the places which they pass. The natural movements which push him forward are continually offset by countervailing movements of consciousness which reach backward, recovering that which is no longer there and bringing it into relationship with the flowing immediacy of the present. Nature cannot make such retrograde gestures but men can, in deliberate counternatural actions. As it turns out, there are various contrary actions running throughout the *Week*, setting up opposites to the sweep of natural rhythms and the cycles which structure them. In every case the countermovement is associated, in some way, with the antithesis of natural experience. For example, Thoreau describes his ascent of Saddle-Back in terms of two movements: one forced upon him by the limitations of his capacities; the other a potential action which will occur only when his insufficiencies are transcended. At the top of the mountain he has visions of paradise and a transformed earth. Where he stands is a "new platform," a halfway point from which he can guess what the rest of the journey would be like: "As I had climbed above storm and cloud, so by successive days' journeys I might reach the region of eternal day, beyond the tapering shadow of the earth" (198). But, facing the perennial Romantic conflict between desire and capability, he is not yet able to travel on this one-way excursion, an undeviating movement that would take him where even the earth's shadow could not touch him. The fault is within himself: "owing, as I think, to some unworthiness in myself, my private sun did stain himself" and "I sank down again into that 'forlorn world,' from which the celestial sun had hid his visage" (199). In returning he completes the cycle of his journey, and his return is to the world of the cycle—the same distinction he was to work out between the world of the town and the place of the morning paradise.

The ascent of Saddle-Back is a skillfully ordered prefiguration of the ascent of the mountain near the end of the *Week;* but further, in its organization and aims it takes part in the same complex of rhythms which controls the book as a whole. The purpose of their trip is to go up to the mountain in New Hampshire which holds the source of the Merrimack River. In order to do so, Thoreau and his companion have to work against the natural flow of the river (and life) which would take them down to the sea. They descend the Concord River until it intersects with the Merrimack and then travel up the Merrimack into New Hampshire. Of course there is more effort involved in this retrograde movement than in the natural progressive one; but there is more effort in climbing a mountain (and having a vision of the heavenly source) than in descending it and returning to the town. Their movement is contranatural, an effort of the human will analogous to the retrograde efforts that consciousness makes in recovering the historical associations of the scenes they pass by.

But their trip to the source of the Merrimack River takes them even further back in time than their meditations on history can take them, because the travelers are going back to the center of origin, a point which is beyond time because it is the place from which the flow begins. (In the *Week* Thoreau climbs up to the primal source, while in *Walden* he digs down to it.) But they are compelled to return, as Thoreau did from the top of Saddle-Back and every other comparable journey; and when they do so they receive a not-so-subtle reminder of their current evanescent status and the cost of experience. They return to the world of natural cycles and find themselves much further along in nature's seasons, and their own, than they had been when they left. On their last day they became aware of decline: "That night was the turning-point in the season. We had gone to bed in summer, and we awoke in autumn; for summer passes into autumn in some unimaginable point of time, like the turning of a leaf" (365). In the counterpoint of rhythms nature has won out, for now.

At the end of the *Week* Thoreau calls for a Blakean cleansing of the doors of perception. Like Wordsworth he argues that men must make their homes in the world because "here or nowhere is our heaven" (405). It is time for a personal terrestrial renewal: "We have need to be earth-born as well as heaven-born" (406). That will be accomplished only by working on what we already have and perfecting our terrestrial capacities until they can provide all that we desire:

> We need pray for no higher heaven than the pure senses can furnish, a *purely* sensuous life. Our present senses are but the rudiments of what they are destined to become. . . . Is not Nature, rightly read, that of which she is commonly taken to be the symbol merely? . . . What is it, then, to educate but to develop these divine germs called the senses? (408)

After that, with startling promptness, Thoreau proceeds to qualify and contradict most of these urgent exhortations. He offers a poem in which he compares himself to "a bunch of violets without their roots/And sorrel intermixed,/Encircled by a wisp of straw/Once coiled about their shoots,/The law/By which I'm fixed" (410). The law which encloses and secures him is the cycle which binds him around. (It is Thoreau's gentler version of "this heavy chain/That does freeze [Earth's] bones around" in Blake's "Earth's Answer.") Snatched out of the Elysian fields by Time, he "was not plucked for naught" because "stock thus thinned will soon redeem its hours,/And by another year,/Such as God knows, with freer air,/More fruits and fairer flowers/Will bear,/While I droop here." At the end there will be a freer season for what is left. This is hardly an exhortation to transform the earth by purifying the senses, but quite a different sort of attitude to terrestrial experience: we are, after all, rootless and bound, part of what has to be brought out of paradise and into the world in order to redeem the time for "more fruits and fairer flowers."

That life in nature which had once been a promise of heaven, if we earned it, is now viewed as a sacrifice for the sake of a better stock. There is nothing in the poem, or in the comments which follow it, about the benefits of purified seeing. We are tied up by earthly life and can only look forward to our leaving it. These radically opposed methods of evaluating natural experience are not productively paired contraries, because nothing positive comes out of their opposition. Nor is there any dialectic leading to an encompassing third term, because there is no way in which these attitudes could come together to create a reconciling position. Thoreau is beset by warring impulses, eager to embrace the earth because that is our chance to find heaven around us, yet arguing also that we have been sorted out and bound down here, plucked from another place where we had our roots.

The remainder of the chapter continues this contranatural development with a dense series of assertions and images which lead Thoreau out of terrestrial immediacy. Modern astronomy affects him as did "those faint revelations of the Real" of which he has heard; and the practices of astronomy hint at modes of perception which can help us to penetrate "the immaterial starry system," that is, "the spaces of the real, the substantial, the eternal" (411-12). But the astronomer can show us even more. He exemplifies the capacity of the redemptive imagination to break the confining cycles (the orbits) which bind us. After that the imagination can lead us to those ultimate spaces we know are there:

In what inclosures does the astronomer loiter! His skies are shoal, and imagination, like a thirsty traveler, pants to be through their desert. The roving mind impatiently bursts the fetters of astronomical orbits, like cobwebs in a corner of the universe, and launches itself to where distance fails to follow, and law, such as science has discovered, grows weak and weary. (413)

This movement which fulfills desire is the same as the one he foresaw on Saddle-Back which would take him "beyond the tapering shadow of the earth." It is the linear antithesis to the cyclical, the movement of desire as opposed to the movement of necessity. His rejection of the earthly experience which he had just embraced is now complete: "I have interest but for six feet of star, and that interest is transient. Then farewell to all ye bodies, such as I have known ye" (413). He completes the pun on human and astronomical bodies two pages later with a quotation about the soul of Sadi shaking "from his plumage the dust of his body" (415). Two segments of poems, the second from Giles Fletcher, culminate this whole movement with a request to "cheat me no more with time" and a reminder that the cycle of the day is an emblem of the growth and decline of man's life. The last words of the book refer to spring, confirming by this reminiscence that they are now in a later season.

The conflux of patterns within the *Week* is obviously well controlled until the end of the book. Before that point Thoreau was able to establish the value of the cyclical and all the possibilities of experience within it, at the same time as he offered an alternative, foreseeable but not yet available, which would achieve the apotheosis of desire. At the end, however, he grandly extols the potential of our life in nature, insisting that the limitations are not in the materials but in our ability to work with them; and then he goes on to argue that it is those same materials which keep us from our grandest flights. Nature is either all potential or a weighty chain. The reconciliation of such contradictory readings was a considerable challenge to the adequacy of Thoreau's imagination. If he was only partly successful in the *Week*—or rather, successful in some places and not in others—he had at least established with absolute clarity that his problem had certain perimeters, and indeed was a problem about perimeters.

The ending of the *Week* appears, in perspective, as a rehearsal for the ending of *Walden.* In the later book Thoreau amassed a large and diverse collection of images of boundary assertion and boundary breaking, a series which is significant not only for its scope but for its strategic position in the commanding structure of his major work. The series begins near the end of the penultimate chapter with an animated paean to nature and wildness. Outside the areas which contain our village life lie "the unexplored forests and meadows which surround it" *(Walden,* 317). We are drawn by a wildness that teases us out of the town and into the mysterious and unfathomed. And in fact it ought to do so because "we need to witness our own limits transgressed, and some life pasturing freely where we never wander" (318). The potential constrictiveness of the village can be overcome only by going beyond its limits to get "the tonic of wildness," a stimulant craved incessantly because "we can never have enough of Nature" (317-18).

Coming as it does just after this chapter's glorification of the round of nature ("Walden was dead and is alive again" [311]; cf. Luke 15:24), the passage on the transgression into wildness is an appropriate capstone to Thoreau's most exuberant commentary on the meaning of nature for man. The seasons of the earth were shown to be a valuable analogy for what man wants most, a guarantee of eternal continuity: "There needs no stronger proof of immortality. All things must live in such a light. O Death, where was thy sting? O Grave, where was thy victory, then?" (317). That recognition was a moment of equal triumph for both nature and consciousness: most of the organization of *Walden* echoes, in a construct of the mind, both the form and promise perceptible in the round of nature. This was not merely a convenient fiction, fabricated until something better comes along, but a veritable and hard-won rendering of Thoreau's reading of reality. When the passage on wildness and the transgression of our limits follows on the recognition of analogy it serves as an apt coda, reminding us that nature's value is autotelic as well as imagistic, in itself as well as in what it can represent for man.

Thoreau continues his boundary-breaking on the first page of the "Conclusion," which follows immediately after these passages.

He supplies some home-grown images to objectify his chiding of Concord: "we think that if rail-fences are pulled down, and stone-walls piled up on our farms, bounds are henceforth set to our lives and our fates decided" (320). To show the breadth of the world outside of our private enclosures Thoreau lists all sorts of exotica that could never be found in the environs of Concord. The solution, of course, is to transgress those environs; but in doing so (Concord is now behind us and the sea under us) "we should oftener look over the tafferel of our craft [because] our voyaging is only great-circle sailing" (320). Thoreau patterns this discourse so as to move gracefully from a small, parochial enclosure, which we are encouraged to rupture, to the shape of the great circle, whose rupturing cannot now be achieved because that would require a transcendence of the earthly. The move is from the minute and local, the stone walls which surround our farms and our lives, to the sublimest of all natural circles, the longest walk of all. Yet the purpose of the great circle is to remind us that when we complete it we have in fact returned home; and the most useful map of all will delineate home cosmography, the microcosmic enclosure of the self.[1] Exploration in those inner latitudes may well require provisioning analogous to the sort that Mungo Park and other macrocosmic explorers used. After all, "were preserved meats invented to preserve meat merely?" (321). But once we are on the seas of our subjective geography we may find them to be very wide indeed, so broad that we shall never have to return in a circle but can go on until even the earth itself disappears:

> Start now on that farthest western way, which does not pause at the Mississippi or the Pacific, nor conduct toward a worn-out China or Japan, but leads on direct a tangent to this sphere, summer and winter, day and night, sun down, moon down, and at last earth down too. (322) [2]

Several other elaborate instances of the transgression of boundaries, as well as some passing references, follow on this clustered pattern. The passage on *"Extra vagance"* has Thoreau seeking adequacy of expression by wandering "far enough beyond the narrow limits of my daily experience," like a cow which kicks over its pail and "leaps the cow-yard fence" running after her calf

(324). He wants our outlines in front to be dim and misty, not precise and confining, so that we can wander extravagantly in search of the truest expression. Several pages later Thoreau offers the story of the artist of Kouroo, a fable of the time-transcending activities of the perfectionist. This craftsman, shaping the perfect staff, is untouched by the seasons and therefore by the round of nature. His work has redeemed him out of time, so that he has no need of liberating release into one more spring. At his moment of ultimate purity all the previous lapses of time are seen to have been an illusion, just enough "for a single scintillation from the brain of Brahma to fall on and inflame the tinder of a mortal brain" (327). With this parable of purity and apotheosis Thoreau ends the series of enclosures and transgressions which began with the glorification of the round of nature near the end of the previous chapter.

It is possible to examine this set of materials in several ways: (1) we can begin with the passage on the stone walls around our lives, which would keep the set contained within the final chapter; and (2) we can begin with the exuberant affirmation of the meaning of the round of nature toward the end of the penultimate chapter. In the first case there is a movement which goes from the constrictiveness of our local lives and daily business up to a myth about a craftsmanship so subtle and productive that the bounds of the diurnal are unconsciously transcended. The second alternative includes the first as a subtheme but moves from a declaration of the possibilities of redemption within natural time to an allegory of the higher redemption outside it. Either alternative is consonant with the material in the text and with the overall context of Thoreau's imagination. What is more, either one offers a lovely, unsettling complication to the structure which is being fulfilled here, toward the end of the book. No round can do its work until its shape is completed. But what we have at the end is an extraordinary cluster of closings and unclosings, so many and so varied that their interrelationships are both intricate and fertile. The images follow one after another in a complex interweaving and mirroring in which shapes echo each other and in turn are contradicted by their contrasts and antitheses. The effect is, in general, to affirm the major round which has reached its most crucial stage in the book, its moment of completion. But all the unclosings and questionings of the various rounds, going from the leap out of the cowyard to the embarkation on a tangent which never returns, make the affirmation of the major round somewhat less than total.

Of all the unclosings in this series the most blatant refutations of the redemptive round of nature occur in the fable of the artist of Kouroo and the passage on the voyage within. The fable needs little explication, since its transcendence of natural time is obvious. All that the cycle of nature can do is bring on more springs which, for the individual, will eventually have to run out. But the craftsman has earned eternal youth, an exact parallel to the eternal freshness in the myth of the morning paradise that also transcends the diurnal round of Concord. The other passage urges us to "start now on that farthest western way" which will eventually take us "at last earth down too." This is not an isolated exhortation but the culmination of an intricate movement which began with the leaping of Concord's bounds and sent us into the complexities of subjective geography. On the way Thoreau dropped a remark about preserved meats and the meat of our bodies which recalls the distaste for the flesh seen in "Higher Laws." The journey within, for Thoreau the most productive of all, has nothing to do with our meat, our natural constitution. Eventually this journey takes us not only beyond our natural selves but beyond the circle of our terrestrial travels, and, finally, even beyond the round of the earth itself. In the context of the concluding pages of *Walden* the fable of Kouroo completes a sequence going from the timely to the timeless. In that same context the series of passages on subjective geography clarifies an even more complex set of contraries. There had been an embrace of the earth and its wildness, yet there is also this desire to escape from it. There had been a love of the texture and forms of nature, yet there is also this disgust with the body's meat. None of these contraries cancels any of the others out. All stand simultaneously as actual, current assertions. Their presence together, in this crucial location within the narrative, is the most compelling confirmation available of the ambiguities Thoreau had to live with in his embrace of the round of nature.

These difficulties are compounded in the final words of the book, which are separated by a few pages from the series we have been inspecting but are nevertheless closely related to them. Thoreau's last instance of a birth into a new life—the story of "a strong and beautiful bug which came out of the dry leaf of an old table of apple-tree wood"—refers openly to the cycles; yet it does so in a context that does not affirm the round of nature but rejects it (333). The egg had been imprisoned in matter for ages, and those ages are discernible by the rings of the trees, the annual layers which are the sign of nature's incessant cycles. When the bug hatches and begins to eat his way out of the table (the clog of matter), he does so to escape from this imprisonment to ultimate freedom. When he is out he is no longer covered by the hard skins of time which the annual cycles have put over them. For Thoreau this story is emblematic of an emergence into a supernatural scheme, characterized by immortality: "Who does not feel his faith in a resurrection and immortality strengthened by hearing of this?" (333). To have such an antinatural story at the end of a book whose main structure is based upon the redemptive form of the seasons is, to say the least, to question the *full* efficacy of nature as a system of analogies. All of Thoreau's complaints about soon getting through with nature are implicit in this unequivocal story at the end of *Walden*.

Ultimately one has to say that, in the overall context, the round of nature is extolled, its symbolic import put forth with considerable enthusiasm; but at the same time Thoreau shows that, though nature is satisfying in itself, it is not satisfying enough. Indeed, nature is most useful when it contributes to its own cancellation. Natural processes signify the promise of an eventual redemption, but that redemption will take man beyond nature and everything it contains that is both lovely and repellent. The mediating instrument is indispensable as a tool to shape our visions, but when the visions are fully realized, the instrument—which is a clog and a hindrance as well as a tool—is gladly discarded. Of course this view of nature's usefulness and current dominance did not resolve the militant antinaturalism in the story of the beautiful bug; but in the context of the book as a whole, especially the relation of the ending to the shape of the whole, naturalism and antinaturalism work together most productively. The strategic placement of these concluding passages—especially the exhortation to go earth-down, the fable of Kouroo, the story of the bug—establishes a complex perspective on all that had preceded them. In effect, the passages leave *Walden* open-ended, so that Thoreau's commitment to nature and its cycles remains firm but with a qualifier added on that would permit other moves in other directions. One has to break the hold of the cycle in order to fulfill the promise which the cycle embodies. And in fact this ultimate openness is more subtly and specifically true to the facts of Thoreau's total experience than a rigidly cyclical structure, without qualifications, could ever be. The latter, with its explicit praise of nature, could never include the disgust for the natural flesh that sounds out of "Higher Laws," or Thoreau's comment in that chapter that he was looking forward to a transcendence of "this or any vegetable wilderness" (212). Thoreau knew that there were discrepancies and discontinuities between body and spirit which had to be taken into account, and he was too finely attuned to all the intricacies of his private experience to disregard them.

Those discontinuities had been apparent to him from his earliest examination of the relations of consciousness and nature, though he could take different attitudes to the question at different times. On March 3, 1839, with full-blown Transcendental rhetoric, Thoreau argued that the poet "must be something more than natural . . . his thought is one world, hers another" (*J,* I, 74-75). Thirteen years later, his arrogance long past, he had become aware of another kind of distancing, this one engendered by the realities of temporal experience:

> Too late now for the morning influence and inspiration. The birds sing not so earnestly and joyously; there is a blurring ripple on the surface of the lake. How few valuable observations can we make in youth! What if there were united the susceptibility of youth with the discrimination of age? Once I was part and parcel of Nature; now I am observant of her. (*J,* III, 378)

There is more here than the passing of the morning of the day; it is later in the cycle of Thoreau's life as well. He can look back with all the finesse of maturity, but he can do so only at the price of separation. This is the argument of Wordsworth's "Immortality" ode, and with all the attendant ambiguities. That seasoned sort of separateness gives an ironic twist to the related passage in the chapter on "Solitude" about the aloofness of the spectatorial consciousness. There, Thoreau stated that "with thinking we may be beside ourselves in a sane sense" because "we are not wholly involved with Nature" *(Walden,* 134-35). In the "D" text of *Walden,* written late in 1851 and early 1852 (i.e., about the same time as the journal passage about his separateness from nature), Thoreau had worked out a nearly finished version of the comments on the spectatorial consciousness, but the line "we are not wholly involved with Nature" was not yet there.[3] The line was therefore a late product, and so were the passages in the "Conclusion" about the preserved meats and traveling earth-down (see note 2). As he got close to the final version of *Walden* Thoreau's sense of his partial aloofness from nature coalesced with his awareness that the cycles do bind us down but cannot hold down every aspect of us. Part of what we are is spectatorial,

> sharing no experience but taking note of it; and that is no more I than it is you. When the play, it may be the tragedy, of life is over, the spectator goes his way. It was a kind of fiction, a work of the imagination only, so far as he was concerned. (135)

The movements described in the "Conclusion" are the journeys of the immortal spectator that is in all of us, taking his leave from the scene of the play.

Thoreau was an organicist, an extoller of the closed system of nature, who had a profound, ironic recognition of the problems engendered by natural experience. At the ending of *Walden* he left room for his awareness that the recurrent rebirth into spring does not preclude the possibility of a final rebirth into the gloriously uncyclical. In so combining wholeness and open-endedness, Thoreau shaped a structure which is even more complex and useful than the echoing of a cycle. *Walden* contains the shape of the closed round of nature, but the structure of the book as a whole, from first to last page, is not identical with that shape. The shape is completed in the penultimate chapter, and it is qualified in the "Conclusion." What happens at the end has the same effect as the opening of an enclosure because it permits an escape from the round, but Thoreau handles all this so skillfully that he has, within his book, both the completed enclosure and the opening as well.

He manages to have both continuity and discontinuity, repetition and an irreversible journey to the west, all at once. What he has to live with is justifiably dominant, but what he will eventually want is allowed to claim a carefully defined place in the total context.

Thoreau does not have to make a choice between these contraries since his mode of organizing his materials makes it possible for the alternatives to function separately and productively within the same framework. Blake's language describes Thoreau's situation precisely: "these two classes ... are always upon the earth, & they should be enemies; whoever tries to reconcile them seeks to destroy existence." [4] A rigidly binary structure that would force Thoreau to cherish the flesh *or* to flee it would be untrue to the wholeness of his experience, however contradictory its parts may have been on repeated occasions. The only viable alternative to a binary structure is this version of the rhythm of advance and sidestep which he had long ago perfected, the cadences of consciousness which permit him to make an elaborately supported assertion, show how useful it is for the living of a life, and then qualify the assertion by showing its inherent limitations. The assertion is never denied or canceled but put in the fullest possible perspective. That is the rhythm which ends *Walden*. An earlier understanding of those cadences would have brought the *Week* to a more successful conclusion.

The counterpoint of attitudes which results from the cadences clarifies a surprising perception which had been implicit elsewhere in Thoreau, certainly in the *Week*, but was rarely so distinct as it was at the end of *Walden:* the breaking of an enclosure is as positive an act as the making of one, and it is at least as redemptive. That is one major reason why Thoreau did not feel compelled to make a choice at this point in *Walden*, deciding to become naturalist or antinaturalist. Though he was immersed in the immanent he could counter its embrace with an antiform which showed the way to an escape toward the gloriously transcendental, the morning paradise, which is beyond all movement. The vernal warmth and morning brightness of Thoreau's paradise are static and perpetual. It is not a place one passes through but a state one gets to after all journeys, cyclical or otherwise, have run their course.

In his essay on Thoreau in *The Machine in the Garden* Leo Marx argues that the organization of *Walden* according to a seasonal pattern "affirms the possibility of redemption from time, the movement away from Concord time, defined by the clock, toward nature's time, the daily and seasonal life cycle." [5] The shift from clock time to natural time is a transition from the urban to the wild, from the saved world of Concord and its constrictiveness to the unredeemed forms of natural experience with their freedom and openness. The paradox implicit in the shift is basic to Thoreau: this is a self-generated redemption from the fixities and hindrances of the civilized world, a world that had itself been redeemed from nature at an earlier point. (As surveyor Thoreau continues to do more redeeming for Concord, though he cannot finally approve of all that Concord does with what it has won.) We can call this transition from clock time to natural time a primary act of redemption, since it is the first gesture of escape into freedom that Thoreau made, the requisite initial movement that he was to continue making all through his life. Yet it does not accomplish a "redemption from time," as Marx argues, but a redemption into another mode of time, one that has larger and more fluent rhythms which permit an expansiveness that the clocks of Concord could never condone. The shift from clock time to natural time creates a difference in degree, but not in kind. As Thoreau puts it in *Walden,* "the day is an epitome of the year," not its opposite (301). The cycle and its participants always return to a point of new beginning.

The conclusions of the *Week* and *Walden,* as well as all the allied passages in the journal, show that Thoreau grew to see the need of a secondary act of redemption, a gesture that would break not only the hold of all cycles but also the pressures of time that underlie them. This act is more radical than its primary counterpart because the latter not only kept him within the framework of time but assumed that Thoreau would have to return to the clock world of the village at the end of his walk into the wild. Thoreau knew that the movement into the woods was only half a gesture. It could be completed either by going back to Concord or—but this was only in fantasy—by going forward to a final place. Sometimes he allowed himself to imagine the latter alternative:

How different the ramrod jingle of the chewink or any

bird's note sounds now at 5 P.M. . . . A certain lateness in the sound, pleasing to hear, which releases me from the obligation to return in any particular season. I have passed the Rubicon of staying out. I have said to myself, that way is not homeward; I will wander further from what I have called my home—to the home which is forever inviting me. (*J*, V, 186-87)

There are different homes corresponding to the different shapes of movement. The course one follows after leaving the breached enclosure takes the form of a parabola, a nonreturning curve which is an eternal arc, neither perfectly linear nor disappointingly circular. The "farthest western way" that Thoreau mentions in the "Conclusion" to *Walden,* the way which leads "earth down," is an arc of that sort, a "tangent to this sphere" which eventually leaves the sphere behind. Thoreau had prefigured the image of the parabola in the chapter on "Sounds," where he speaks of a train moving off "like a comet, for the beholder knows not if with that velocity and with that direction it will ever revisit this system, since its orbit does not look like a returning curve" (116). The archsymbol of contemporary civilization, the machine which invaded the garden, shares in the image which describes the way out of the earth and its civilization. This ironic pattern of echoes was probably unconscious, but it has a subtle and incisive effect in the overall context, because included in the entire pattern are several of the major modes of redemption available to Thoreau and his contemporaries: the train helped men buy their way out of wildness, but the comet with its nonreturning curve left behind it every kind of terrestrial salvation, from the seasonal round to the new world of the train.[6] This is one more instance of Thoreau's tendency to turn the images of modern mechanism into testimony of the world beyond the machine. The timeliness of the modern train, itself a symbol of civilization's concern with punctuality, takes its place in a total scheme whose goal is an escape from time. But that departure is as yet only a promise: all he can see now is a "train of clouds stretching far behind and rising higher and higher, going to heaven while the cars are going to Boston" (116).

There is a deep pattern in Thoreau's experience of his world which can be interpreted as though it were in the form of a narrative. The activities are Thoreau's, but they are also characteristic of his time and his country, of Romantic as well as American experience. The main actor in the narrative is mind, understood in general terms as the human desire and capacity to organize intellection/imagination so as to control experience for the benefit of man. Specific exemplifications of the actor elsewhere include Coleridge's "shaping spirit" (both as the primary and secondary imagination); the Puritan urge to assert the value of spiritual election in this strange new country; and the impetus behind Melville's voyages, even the vengeful ones. The locale of the action, which is also the object of the action, is nature and especially the wild. The latter is defined most generally so as to include the woods outside Concord, the summit of Ktaadn, the dark forests outside Salem, and the seas of Coleridge's and Melville's mariners; that is, that which is not mind but which mind wants to visit and work on so as to take it over for man. The activity of taking over by the mind can be understood as some synonym of the verb "to redeem," Thoreau's personal favorite as the term for this practice.

Thoreau sets out on his afternoon walks or into the Maine woods; the Puritans go into the wilderness to face the satanic images that are disguised as Indians; Ahab pushes into the South Seas; Coleridge's mariner finds himself sailing through a land of ice and snow. In Thoreau's case the narrative contains those actions which led him to draw up his imagined map of American experience. The map is the graphic, static record of the activities in the narrative of redemption, what the mind has done in making a place for itself in the New World's vastness. Like all maps it is essentially a chart of relationships—of the redeemed to the unredeemed, of consciousness to nature, of the self to experience, of civilized America to wild America. These figured relationships are a synchronic way of looking at the diachronic patterns which inform the essential Thoreauvian narrative. But since the narrative is Melvillean as well as Thoreauvian, and the model can be found in Hawthorne and Cooper (even in Crèvecoeur and Parkman, who were uneasy with frontier brutality), it confirms the prevalence of the deep pattern throughout a broad sweep of American experience. The Puritan version of the quest form which this narrative usually takes was the errand into the wilderness. Because that was ultimately a search for personal salvation (the darkness of the wilderness reflected the darkness in the soul), the redemption of the heathen was, analogically, a salvation of self through a purification of the dark forces within.[7] Thoreau shared the Puritan sense of the kindred wildness in the soul and the woods, but his own quests were never so dark, though he worked with the same model. Yet he did know that the model had national as well as personal relevance: the narrative underlies most of the patriotic exhortations in "Walking," and that essay as a whole is based on the applicability of the model to large national movements as well as to his own private affairs.

But Thoreau found more and more often that it was not always possible to complete the narrative, or that if one did so the completed narrative remained strangely unsatisfactory, as though it ought to have had more meaning than it turned out to have. In the first case the elements were not able to fulfill all their functions, and therefore the full potential of meaning was never achieved. In the second the functions were completed, but the result was disappointing or even frustrating. If the goal of the actor's activities was the indomitable top of Ktaadn, then all pressure the actor exerts through those activities will be useless, the narrative incomplete, because mind and this piece of nature are incommensurate. If one should say "the mind redeems nature at the top of Ktaadn," the statement would be nonsensical: nature at the top of Ktaadn cannot be redeemed by the mind, and the statement cannot, therefore, point to the results of any possible narrative. Of course one can say, "the mind cannot redeem nature at the top of Ktaadn," and indeed that is what Thoreau had to say; but it was not what he wanted to hear. He was not at all pleased when his radical narrative model had to be summed up by a negative statement. The myriad of disturbing reminiscences of Ktaadn, or of nature's stubborn facticity, or its mysteriousness, all fall into this frustrated or negative pattern. Whether the wildness outside the clearing was frighteningly or impressively impossible to handle, the fact of negativity or incompleteness remains the same. (In a Puritan version this resistance to spirit would corroborate the existence of satanic evil in the woods and the heathen who inhabited them.)

On the other hand, there is the increasingly more frequent

version of the narrative which is complete but still not enough, all those instances of nature's insufficiency which compel us soon to get through with it. Mind and nature are incommensurate because the actor can imagine more than the locale can offer him, and the activity he performs has more potential than the locale can absorb. In each of these cases, whether complete or incomplete, the actor is defeated, either by his own insufficiencies or by those of his locale. I noted much earlier that the drive into the wild is an attempt to reach the creative center of being, the point of pure potential from which all vitality comes. To touch at that center was to claim some of its energy for man. A walk into the heart of the swamp was an invigorating investigation of absolute potential. The last third of the many volumes of the journals offer increasingly saddening evidence that these struggles to win a piece of the ultimate stratum for man were no longer successful. Thoreau was asking for more from nature's wildness than he could find in it. Whether the cause was in his weakened receptivity or in the greater stretch of his consciousness—it seems to have been in both—the fact of incommensurateness was everywhere apparent.

There is a third version of the radical narrative in which the roles shift and what had been the actor becomes the object of action. This is a later case, emergent when Thoreau was looking for consolation during his wintry decline and found that the round of nature which brought him into decline was bound to bring him out of it soon, to redeem him into a temporary renewal. The abstract model remains the same, but the components exchange functions. This version would have to be disconcerting at some level because it is clearly a violation of basic premises involved in the previous versions: it runs into all the accepted Transcendental assertions about the primacy of consciousness or spirit. Thoreau's role and status as a human being are defined in considerable part by the function of consciousness as actor in his redemptive narrative. But in this version consciousness shifts to become that which is acted upon, the recipient rather than the giver, the object and not the agent. Consciousness could tolerate this when it had to, since there was no other way of affirming natural renewal. But it could not endure this status permanently, because, after all, nature was sufficient for cyclical promises (and for a great deal of delight) but not for the fullest redemption. Only the mind, as agent, could offer that.

The answer was to reorder the functions within the model and make mind both actor and object of action, acting upon and saving itself by taking itself earth-down on the ultimate parabola. This is the stage of secondary redemption in which the mind rejects nature as the object of action and sets up a more efficient set of narrative components—mind, redemption, and mind. In effect, what Thoreau does is to change the object of action into something more amenable to permanent redemption by the mind; and what could fill that bill better than the mind itself? The old order was forever dissolved by eliminating one element and duplicating another. This was the second time the components had shifted, and it was necessarily the last. Of course this ultimate pattern of the redemptive narrative could not be actualized or completed in Thoreau's natural state, but he could at least sketch out various possibilities of expressing it. He showed it happening in the fable of the artist of Kouroo. In fact, the conclusion to *Walden* is a collection of images and stories which *are* those very possibilities of expression, figurative versions of the final set of components.

The reiteration of all these dichotomies lasted until the end of Thoreau's life, and it appears in some of the last work that was published. Several months before his death he revised for publication a number of the lectures he had been giving during the fifties. Among them was the final version of the essay that was to appear posthumously in the *Atlantic Monthly* for June 1862 as "Walking, or the Wild." It had begun as a lecture on "The Wild," first delivered at the Concord Lyceum on April 23, 1851, with an introduction which referred to Wordsworth's "Stepping Westward" and inserted some apologetic lines about Thoreau not speaking on "the Fugitive Slave Law on which every man is bound to express a distinct opinion." [8] None of these passages is in the final version, though the first could have been, and Wordsworth's poem may have contributed to the ending of the essay. After mentioning Wordsworth in his initial lecture Thoreau adds that "for want of a better rallying cry" these sentences from his journal "may accept the words 'stepping westward.' " [9] Even at that point the associations of westering and wilderness were clear in Thoreau's mind, and Wordsworth's heavenward "stepping" was the way of getting there, what Thoreau was later to change to the less idiomatic "walking." That change, however, was not toward the banal and general but toward the precise definition of an activity whose meaning touched on most elements of Thoreau's experience.

During the decade, as the work of his redemptive imagination became more difficult and complex, Thoreau's lecture was confirming the hypothesis that walking was the mode and the wild was the object which fitted best with the redemptive bent of his mind. By 1856 his exploration of these ideas had resulted in a lecture so large that he had to break it into two *(Correspondence,* 465). When he revised the material for publication, he put it all back together as a marvelously coherent package of Thoreauvian preoccupations, though its length led him to suggest to the publisher that it could easily be divided into installments *(Correspondence,* 640). The coherence of the final product did not preclude an ultimate ambivalence. Indeed, some of the same imagery which fostered the coherence of the various themes—especially the cyclical structure of his walks and the association of the West with Eden—also contributed to the ambivalence which appears at crucial points in the essay. "Walking" is second only to *Walden* in its clear understanding of the equivocal status of some of Thoreau's most essential assertions.

The ambiguities are telegraphed near the beginning of the essay, in a passage whose complex import is not fully perceptible until the essay is completed:

> Our expeditions are but tours, and come round again at evening to the old hearth-side from which we set out. Half the walk is but retracing our steps. We should go forth on the shortest walk, perchance, in the spirit of undying adventure, never to return,—prepared to send back our embalmed hearts only as relics to our desolate kingdoms. *(Excursions,* 206)

The circle described in those tours which come round again is that of the circuitous journey. Elsewhere in the essay Thoreau remarks that he goes into the wild to "recreate" himself, and the return to the town brings him back, as similar journeys often bring their participants, to the source from which he set out. Circuitous journeys are not always such simple returns. In their redemptive form they are like spirals, journeys around and upward through versions of the fall, along the hard road through experience, and to the conclusion of the quest at another and higher Eden, a different Grasmere that is yet the same, a New Jerusalem surpassing the Old, the world of the highest Innocence.[10]

Concord is like none of these goals. Thoreau has been purified but the town has not. It is Concord from which he had been forced to flee and cleanse himself in the first place, and when he returns it is to more of the same old style. To put the problem another way, his circuitous journey involves a return to the east, and that movement goes against all his natural impulses: "Eastward I go only by force; but westward I go free" (217). He returned in an ambivalent mood that combined compulsion and refreshment; and though those contraries do not quite negate each other they confirm once again that his great-circle sailing was not always the perfectly happy form that it was supposed to be. If his journey brought him back to the town, the return showed that he had been regenerated but only partly redeemed. As he put it in a journal entry in 1859, "though you may have sauntered near to heaven's gate, when at length you return toward the village you give up the enterprise a little, and you begin to fall into the old ruts of thought, like a regular roadster" (*J*, XII, 347). Like the day, Thoreau would have to do it all over again tomorrow, which meant that his redemption was diurnal or, in the terms I have been using, primary. The regeneration or re-creation was therefore itself only temporary, limited by the same forces that limited his redemption to the primary stage.

In part, it would seem, the problem is within ourselves, a point Thoreau had implied in describing his descent from Saddle-Back. Our expeditions ought not to be rounded tours but "persevering, never-ending enterprises" designed to accomplish an ultimate act of redemption: "For every walk is a sort of crusade, preached by some Peter the Hermit in us, to go forth and reconquer this Holy Land from the hands of the Infidels" (*Excursions*, 206). But we do not adventure in that way because "we are but faint-hearted crusaders." On the level of the imagery of the journey to the Holy Land, then, it is our timidity which is at fault. The passage implies that we need only will the never-ending enterprise to make it happen. Yet if our incapacity for such errantry betrays our spiritual insufficiency, there is another level of journeying which complicates these matters somewhat more. Within a few paragraphs Thoreau shifts back to the dominant mode of journeying in the essay, the walks into the wildness around Concord. There, the emphasis is not on redeeming the Holy Land but on the necessity of cleansing ourselves: "I think that I cannot preserve my health and spirits, unless I spend four hours a day at least—and it is commonly more than that—sauntering through the woods and over the hills and fields" (207). If we are ever to blame for our insufficiency in this matter, that would come only from an occasional tendency to procrastinate: "sometimes I have stolen forth for a walk at the eleventh hour, or four o'clock in the afternoon, too late to redeem the day" (208). Yet even on our lengthiest and most productive walks, when the bogs have cleansed us of Concord, there is no way of doing as the crusaders did, going "forth . . . never to return" (206). Though we know how to walk very well, we always have to come back to the town. We are bound to Concord though we may want to be bound for somewhere else, and Thoreau—no wild man of the woods—knew that we have no other choice in this world.

Nor are we at fault if the regeneration wears off quickly, and the small-circle sailing has to begin again with another trip out to the wild. Diurnal redemption is for the day only. If the source of that redemption, the wild around Concord, were more effective, the redemption would not be so fragile, so easily worn down by the town; but of course that is asking for more from nature than it could ever give. Once again we face the fact that "we soon get through with nature" and require something else that is more adequate to our needs. The wild is lovely and extraordinarily satisfying, but it is so much a part of the cyclical, so deeply involved with temporality, that its effects can only be temporary. The pattern of his regeneration, which grows and declines, is as cyclical as nature itself; and in order to be regenerated he has to go out and back, completing another kind of round. We are bound to the energy of the wild and the dryness of Concord, but most of all we are bound to the cycles which contain them both. Thoreau knows this well, and he embodies that knowledge not only in the language of the Crusades but in a figure which he had already used for the same purpose in *Walden:*

> The future lies [westward] to me, and the earth seems more unexhausted and richer on that side. The outline which would bound my walks would be, not a circle, but a parabola, or rather like one of those cometary orbits which have been thought to be non-returning curves. (217)

Coleridge had worked with the same set of figures some thirty years earlier: "Man does not move in cycles, though nature does. Man's course is like that of an arrow; for the portion of the great cometary ellipse which he occupies is no more than a needle's length to a mile." [11] But Thoreau's commentary differs radically from that of Coleridge because Thoreau acknowledges that man is indeed involved with cycles and has to find a way of giving them their due without giving himself fully to them. He tried out that delicate balancing act in the *Week, Walden,* and "Walking," and in all three in exactly the same way, through a version of the parabola. The parabola is a form which is curved just enough to give the impression of the arc of a circle without ever returning as the full circle does. Thoreau's move is therefore from natural rhythms and their associated economies to other rhythms which give some of the effect of the natural form without its enclosing circular shape. Thoreau does not deny the natural but looks at it somewhat differently (partially, to be sure) and in so doing he manages to transform the consequence and meaning of its shape without ever fully rejecting the shape itself. Nature is used to take him beyond nature. The cyclical is quietly transmuted into the anticyclical so as to ease the binding of his mind by old forms that are no longer perfectly congenial. In that best of all possible walks he would go on the "farthest western way" he mentioned at the end of *Walden,* the track which leads "earth-down." In "Walking" that gesture toward a separation from nature is repeated and, just as in the *Week* and *Walden,* in a context which simultaneously extols the most glorious physical qualities of the natural world. Once again Thoreau manages to have it most ways at once. His imagination was always eager to find advantage for itself without discrediting the world he associated with, and it does so in

"Walking" through a series of analogies that are absolutely adequate to all that he asks of them.

The final analogy was prefigured at the beginning of the essay. The impulse not to return leads him to move happily and inexorably toward what we should have to call, according to one pattern embedded in the essay, the ultimate of all fertile layers. But according to another pattern the perfect movement figured in the parabola leads toward paradise, the West which holds the location of the eternal city. In a journal passage from 1851 Thoreau had written about his vision of "the eternal city of the west, the phantom city, in whose streets no traveller has trod, over whose pavements the horses of the sun have already hurried, some Salamanca of the imagination" (*J*, II, 296). "Walking" is framed by such visions of the Holy Land. It begins with an elaborate pun on the meaning of sauntering: Thoreau claims that the word is derived from those who go *à la Sainte Terre*, to the Holy Land. Saunterers are Holy Landers, that is, crusaders, and that analogy permits Thoreau to move on to the exhortation concerning the "persevering, never-ending enterprises" which we ought to undertake. Thus, the association of walking and redemption has been solidly established at the beginning; and hints of the relationship surface often enough throughout the essay for the reader to keep the association clearly, if at times subliminally, in mind. It reappears in the last words of the essay, in a description of sunset:

> The west side of every wood and rising ground gleamed like the boundary of Elysium, and the sun on our backs seemed like a gentle herdsman driving us home at evening.
>
> So we saunter toward the Holy Land, till one day the sun shall shine more brightly than ever he has done, shall perchance shine into our minds and hearts, and light up our whole lives with a great awakening light, as warm and serene and golden as on a bankside in autumn. (247-48)

The Crusader's journey to redeem the Holy Land is echoed in the walker's tour toward the golden West, where he shall find that he has redeemed the Holy Land within himself. By Thoreau's time most of the associations of westering and the New Jerusalem had become conventional elements in America's self-awareness and description of itself. The associations were widely successful in achieving that combination of idiosyncrasy and universalism which America's mythographers seem always to have wanted. During the earliest explorations all of America had been thought of as another Eden, and when the eastern seaboard was settled the analogy inevitably shifted westward to the fertile promise of the plains and beyond. Thoreau had more than one way of putting it: "As a true patriot, I should be ashamed to think that Adam in paradise was more favorably situated on the whole than the backwoodsman in this country" (223). The overall movement described in "Walking" is therefore (in contrast to the daily return to Concord) a journey toward a new and better Eden, a New Jerusalem so far surpassing the old that it is an eternal city and a golden one, perhaps much like the garden of Hesperides, which, as Thoreau points out in "Walking," was an old form of the terrestrial paradise and the ancient's version of the Great West. From there no return would be necessary or desirable. It is the heart of the eternally new and therefore the goal of all walks that makes all walking exciting. As he had used nature to transcend nature, so does Thoreau use the American experience of westering, with its attendant myths, to lead the national into forms of the eternal and universal.

The ending of "Walking" is Thoreau's final statement on the proximity of Eden. He had lived his life with an exceptional sensitivity to confines, and here he returns for his last deep stare at the margin between where he is now and that which is, for the moment, beyond him: "The west side of every wood and rising ground gleamed like the boundary of Elysium." He had made that gesture toward the edge of a paradisiacal land many times before. In December 1856, for example, he wrote out a series of journal entries whose relationship is a complex prefiguration of the final mellowness of "Walking." Speaking of the stillness of the winter woods, Thoreau remarks that he hears "only the strokes of a lingering woodchopper at a distance, and the melodious hooting of an owl," the sort of interplay of civilizing and unredeemed sounds he responded to in Maine (*J*, IX, 172). However much the woods are cut into, the "aboriginal voice" of the owl continues to stand for those untamed areas that have still held out and are still there just beyond the margin that men have reached: "As the earth only a few inches beneath the surface is undisturbed and what it was anciently, so are heard still some primeval sounds in the air" (172). These are the materials Thoreau was always charting, with the thin surface of the civilized right up against aboriginal darkness. As for the bird who lives in the wood, if it is not permanently invisible within its domain it might as well be, since Thoreau hears it nearly every week but manages to see it only once in a decade. Even for him, its spokesman, there is a deep layer of the wild which is accessible only sporadically. And then (except for the rarest moments) it is available only indirectly, not in an immediate meeting. Thoreau could refresh himself in the wildness of the swamps, but he had to settle for mere eavesdropping on this stratum of wildness. There is no direct hint of dissatisfaction in this passage, nothing overtly frustrating about the inaccessible proximity of the owl. But this is still another instance of Thoreau's awareness that there are limitations of perception and control in man's encounter with the absolutely wild, whether here, in a mood of admiration and wonder, or at Ktaadn, in profoundest fear. Once again he acknowledges that nature can be too much as well as too little, that the commensurateness of mind and nature which he habitually assumed cannot always be guaranteed.

A few lines later Thoreau talks about the sunset and "a burnished bar of cloud" over the valley "as if it were the bar over that passage-way to Elysium" (173). Seen from the perspective of the beginning and end of "Walking," this conjunction of images of limitation and desire is not fortuitous. The quest for Elysium follows upon the recognition of present incommensurateness. And as if to underscore the significance of that combination, Thoreau repeats the pattern in another entry six days later. There he clarifies and intensifies the concatenation by bringing the hooting of the owl and the sounds of the woodchopper together in a tight sequence with "the gilded bar of cloud across the apparent outlet of the pond, conducting my thoughts into the eternal west" (182). The sequence ends with Thoreau taking a "hasty walk homeward to enjoy the long winter evening." Thus he makes the full returning tour he was to speak of in "Walking," completing that second half of the walk which was "but retracing our steps." All of the components are here in this rehearsal for "Walking," including the ultimate opening to the west. The essay put the components into their most accomplished and productive relationship.

Thoreau's skill in controlling the culminating myth of "Walking" is comparable in kind, if not in range, to his deftness at the end of *Walden*. In his book he completed the cycle of departure and return before its opposite came into play. In the essay he began with an evocation of the anticycle which associated it with the apotheosis of desire. He went on to spend most of the essay on an elaborate paean to nature's wildness and the way one gets to it, and finished with a temperate, assured version of the ideality he had postulated before. The structure is cunning enough to permit Thoreau to express all his preferences at once, even the most contradictory elements. The balance is delicate, and he brings it off nicely: his glorification of earthly wildness began only after his desire for transcendence had been stated, and the qualification that necessarily emerged was firmly, if tactfully, reinforced by the comment on the parabola and other related remarks. Thus, when he came to the coda Thoreau could allow himself a subdued rhapsody on the West and Elysium, confident that in so doing he was making a final and acceptable adjustment of perspective. This was his most effective statement about alternatives, more harmonious than the myth of the morning paradise, better integrated with current possibilities than the ending of the *Week*. He was enabled to give a more precise definition of what the parabola at the end of *Walden* was aiming for when it too would go earthdown: the result would be an ultimate transgression and a felicitous one, accomplishing the redemption of the redeemer. Since his goal was the eternal West, he would have arrived at the place of permanent newness, beyond which he could not and need not go. His map, which had shown a series of bright enclosures surrounded by darkness, would no longer be accurate. Everything would be bright and nothing would be enclosed. All of Thoreau's perceptions and images lead toward this terminal paradox—that in Elysium everything would be both new *and* redeemed—the opposite of what it could be naturally. That was the high point of the adequacy of his myth, the absolute limit of desire.

But all of this is prospective, the sketch of a future itinerary, and Thoreau has to qualify his myth with a reminder of current limitations. As the essay eases gracefully to a finish, it brings all the ideas full circle, closing up the patterns and emphasizing, by the fact of its circularity, that Thoreau is not yet ready for his parabola. Each of the major themes appears once again. A passing comment about walking on a railroad leads to an echo of the earlier point about being out on the edge of things: "I feel that with regard to Nature I live a sort of border life" (242). Then, in swift succession and in a remarkably perspicuous relationship, come the themes of living in the present; the return to one's senses; paradise in a meadow; the eternally new; and, finally, Elysium and the Holy Land toward which we saunter. This is the last scene, in which all the major characters reenter at once. The essay finishes where it must, where the rhythm of the themes had to lead him. The Holy Land emerges once more as a reminder of where he would like to go, but the circularity of the essay emblems Thoreau's unfinished state, where he has to be now. Still, "Walking" ends in warmth: the golden glow which suffuses the west woods and rises becomes, in the final paragraph, the sun associated with the Holy Land, full of unparalleled serenity and light. What he can see now in the West is a pure and bright light that gilds the withered grass, a sun which seems to be gently urging him home. In the great radiance of its light it offers him what he wanted most at the end, the sure promise of a final translucence.

Notes

Chapter One

1. Coleridge also discussed the distinctions of genius and talent at a number of points, e.g., *Table Talk,* August 20, 1833, in *The Complete Works of Samuel Taylor Coleridge,* ed. W. G. T. Shedd, Vol. VI (New York: Harper and Brothers, 1884), p. 481.
2. Emerson, of course, was obsessed with centrality. Like Thoreau, he used it as a structuring principle with which to order his perceptions, but in Emerson's case the ordering was nearly always at a more abstract level than that of Thoreau. The following, from *The Transcendentalist,* is typical: "[The idealist's] experience inclines him to behold the procession of facts you call the world, as flowing perpetually outward from an invisible, unsounded centre in himself, centre alike of him and of them, and necessitating him to regard all things as having a subjective or relative existence, relative to that aforesaid Unknown Centre of him." *The Complete Works of Ralph Waldo Emerson,* Centenary Edition, ed. Edward W. Emerson, Vol. I (Boston: Houghton Mifflin, 1903), p. 334. All further references are to this edition.
3. Compare *Correspondence,* 298-99, and the ending of the journal entry for September 29, 1854 (*J,* VII, 61).

4. Thoreau's observations should be compared to the work of Mercia Eliade on the sacred center. See *Patterns in Comparative Religion* (New York: World Publishing, 1972), pp. 374 ff.; and *The Sacred and the Profane* (New York: Harper and Row, 1961), pp. 32 ff.

5. Emerson, "The American Scholar," ed. cit., Vol. I, p. 95.

6. Compare *J*, XIV, 305-6, and Blake's use of "charter'd" in "London."

7. Emerson called all else but his soul "the NOT ME." See *Nature*, ed. cit., Vol. I, p. 4.

8. On March 30, 1842, he was confident that one could attain to "startling privacies with every person we meet" (*J*, I, 356).

9. See *Oeuvres complètes de Jean-Jacques Rousseau*, ed. Bernard Gagnebin and Marcel Raymond, Vol. I (Paris: Gallimard, 1959), p. 1793, fn. 2.

10. In his "Biographical Sketch" on Thoreau, Emerson refers to Thoreau's desire to "live as far apart as possible, and each be a man unto himself" (reprinted in Vol. I of the Walden Edition, p. xv); but in this, as in other passages in the essay, Emerson misses the profound ambiguities involved in Thoreau's position.

11. Compare, in the same entry, pp. 38-39, where Thoreau implies that this separateness is willed.

12. Ed. cit., p. 1149.

13. Ibid., p. 1153.

14. The phrase occurs in a variant passage from "Frost at Midnight." See Coleridge, *Poetical Works*, ed. Ernest Hartley Coleridge (London: Oxford University Press, 1969), p. 241.

15. *Nature*, ed. cit., Vol. I, pp. 64-65.

16. Ibid., p. 50.

17. Compare, among other instances, *J*, III, 384, and *J*, VIII, 44.

18. Ed. cit., p. 1045.

Chapter Two

1. See *Correspondence*, p. 436. In the manuscript of "Walking" in The Concord Free Public Library the phrasing goes: "For my part, I feel that with regard to Nature, whose Elysian fields never reach quite up to our doors, I live a sort of border life." There is obviously a margin between our doors and nature's Elysian fields.

2. Houghton Library manuscript of "Walking," bms AM 278.5.

3. See Henry Nash Smith, *Virgin Land* (New York: Random House, n.d.), p. 25, for a similar association made by Thomas Hart Benton.

4. Antoine Orliac speaks of two states of Romantic sensibility: *"l'un caractérisé par l'expansion éperdue de l'individu, l'autre par l'introspection artiste où il s'efforce de retrouver en profondeur ce que le jet lyrique n'a pu atteindre en hauteur."* There are numerous versions of the linking of the drives within and without in Romanticism, symbolized, for example, in the pairing of ascent and descent, mountains and caves, etc. For

Orliac see "Essai sur le tourment romantique" in *Mercure de France*, 199 (1927), 288-89.

5. I quote from the reprint of the essay in John W. McCoubrey, *American Art 1700-1960: Sources and Documents* (Englewood Cliffs, N.J.: Prentice Hall, Inc., 1965), pp. 102-3. Further page references will be noted in the text.
6. In Cole this was clearly more than obligatory. Contrast the ending of Cooper's essay "American and European Scenery Compared" in *The Home Book of the Picturesque* (1852; rpt., Gainesville, Florida: Scholars Facsimiles and Reprints, 1967).
7. Ed. cit., p. 1047.
8. From an essay on "Barbarism and Civilization" in F. B. Sanborn, *The Life of Henry David Thoreau* (1917; rpt., Detroit: Gale Research, 1968), p. 181. Compare Emerson's *Nature*, ed. cit., pp. 19-20.
9. Compare the essay on "Advantages and Disadvantages of Foreign Influences in American Literature" in Sanborn, *Life*, pp. 130-34.
10. *Essais de Michel de Montaigne*, ed. Albert Thibaudet (Paris: Gallimard, 1950), p. 251.
11. These attitudes should be contrasted to those of Hölderlin and other Europeans who craved the emergence in one's home ground—e.g., the localization—of divine energies that were holding themselves back.
12. See my comments on the radical Thoreauvian narrative in the last chapter and also the discussion by Richard Slotkin on "the hedged-in Puritan concept of the coastal enclave" in *Regeneration Through Violence: The Mythology of the American Frontier, 1600-1800* (Middletown: Wesleyan University Press, 1973), pp. 181 and 185.

Chapter Three

1. *Moby-Dick*, ed. Harrison Hayford and Hershel Parker (New York: W. W. Norton, 1967), p. 232. All further references will be noted in the text.
2. For commentary on Western allusions in *Moby-Dick* and Melville generally, see Edwin Fussell, *Frontier: American Literature and the American West* (Princeton: Princeton University Press, 1965).
3. Sherman Paul, *The Shores of America: Thoreau's Inward Exploration* (Urbana: University of Illinois Press, 1972), p. 108.
4. *The Writings of Herman Melville*, Vol. I, *Typee*, ed. Harrison Hayford, Hershel Parker, and G. Thomas Tanselle (Evanston and Chicago: Northwestern University Press and The Newberry Library, 1968), p. 56.
5. The Centenary Edition of *The Works of Nathaniel Hawthorne*, Vol. I, *The Scarlet Letter*, ed. William Charvat and Fredson Bowers (Colum-

bus: Ohio State University Press, 1962), p. 215. Further references in the text.

6. See above, chapter 2, note 11.
7. Compare Slotkin, pp. 66, 75-77, 104, and his material on Hawthorne.
8. See *J*, XIII, 141, for comments by Thoreau on naming and the wild.
9. In "Chesuncook" (99-100) and "The Allegash and East Branch" (203) Thoreau records aural versions of the mind's impulse to find evidence of civilization in the woods. "Chesuncook" also shows Thoreau, in a dream state, turning the woods into Broadway (118). For a different perspective see "A Winter Walk," where Thoreau speaks of how an ax sound enhances the wildness of the woods while "the elements strive to naturalize the sound" *(Excursions,* 173).
10. Emerson, ed. cit., p. 52.
11. *Biographia Literaria,* ed. J. Shawcross (London: Oxford University Press, 1954), Vol. I, p. 58. (Compare Keats's letter to Benjamin Bailey of March 13, 1818.) In the *Notebooks* Coleridge talks of rocks and stones putting on "a vital semblance": see *The Notebooks of Samuel Taylor Coleridge,* ed. Kathleen Coburn, Vol. I (New York: Pantheon Books, 1957), no. 1189. (See also the note to this entry, referring to the lines on the "huge stone" in "Resolution and Independence.") But Coleridge, Thoreau's equal in the flexibility of the redemptive imagination, could turn the process around and make sheep into rocks: "The great tarn and the apparitions from the Sheep moving on the outward ridge—coloured as rocks. When they began to move, seemed as moving rocks" (no. 1804).
12. From Schlegel's *Ideen* in *Charakteristen und Kritiken I, 1796-1801,* ed. Hans Eichner, *Kritische Friedrich Schlegel Ausgabe,* Vol. II (München: Ferdinand Schöningh, 1967), p. 263.
13. For more instances of such domestication see the long journal entry for August 9, 1860 *(J,* XIV, 25 ff.), especially pp. 36 ff.
14. *Obermann* (Paris: Charpentier, 1865), p. 133 (letter XXXVI). ·
15. Paul, 263-64.
16. See Paul's comments on this issue, pp. 361-62.
17. On October 10, 1858, Thoreau supplemented the material on the finger mountains. The smallest fungus, unlike a mere mass of earth, is related to us because it is organic. It is the expression of an idea or a law, "not raw, but inspired, appropriated by spirit" *(J,* XI, 204).
18. Compare *J,* IV, 472, where he associates "the rottenness of human relations" with the rankness of death and decay.
19. On March 25, 1859, Thoreau wrote of setting his own kind of subjective traps so that "my intellectual part may taste some venison and be invigorated" *(J,* XII, 82-83). Here the ingestion is through consciousness.
20. Huntington Library manuscript HM 924.

21. In "Walking" Thoreau takes the diametrically opposite tack, arguing that "how near to good is what is *wild*" *(Excursions,* 226).

22. From his *Orphic Sayings,* reprinted in *The Transcendentalists: An Anthology,* ed. Perry Miller (Cambridge, Mass.: Harvard University Press, 1971), p. 311.

23. Huntington Library manuscript HM 924.

24. Paul, p. 339, and compare p. 363.

25. *Henry David Thoreau* (New York: William Morrow, 1974), p. 108. Charles Anderson argues that there is an ascent from wildness to virtue in "Higher Laws": see *The Magic Circle of Walden* (New York: Holt, Rinehart and Winston, 1968), p. 151.

26. Emerson, ed. cit., pp. 4-5.

27. In *J,* III, 290, Thoreau refers to a fisherman who "represents the Indian still." In *J,* XI, 422-25, he continues the point in relation to musquash hunters.

Chapter Four

1. See, for example, Werther's letter of May 10, 1771.

2. *The American Adam* (Chicago: The University of Chicago Press, 1955).

3. Ibid., p. 15.

4. Emerson, ed. cit., Vol. II, p. 66.

5. Ibid., p. 67.

6. Compare *J,* XI, 5: "The wood thrush sings almost wherever I go, eternally reconsecrating the world, morning and evening, for us."

7. Emerson, in *Nature,* quotes the schoolmen as saying "the knowledge of man is an evening knowledge ... but that of God is a morning knowledge" (ed. cit., p. 73).

8. Compare *J,* IV, 126: "the perception of beauty is a moral test."

9. Paul, p. 362.

10. Anderson, p. 203.

11. Thoreau's awareness of his limitations of comprehension in regard to the Indians is referred to by Fussell, op. cit., p. 332 (see also pp. 340 ff.).

12. Montaigne, ed. cit., p. 243.

13. Paul, p. 365.

Chapter Five

1. Compare the following, from a Huntington Library manuscript of the *Week* (HM 13195): "Men make a perpetual mistake with respect to ... travelling. Who ever got nearer to Rome by aid of the most favorable winds—or the most industrious diligence? But all travelling

grows out of a wish to return home and stay at Rome—if the traveller can find it."

2. This sentence is a very late addition to the text. It does not appear in the "F" version, dated late 1853-54 (Huntington Library manuscript HM 924).

3. Huntington Library manuscript HM 924.

4. *The Marriage of Heaven and Hell* in *The Poetry and Prose of William Blake*, ed. David Erdman (Garden City, N.Y.: Doubleday, 1965), p. 39.

5. *The Machine in the Garden: Technology and the Pastoral Ideal in America* (London and New York: Oxford University Press, 1972), p. 261.

6. See Marx, op. cit., passim.

7. Compare Slotkin, op. cit., pp. 104-9.

8. Houghton Library manuscript bms Am 278.5.

9. Ibid.

10. For an elaborate analysis of these patterns see Meyer Abrams, *Natural Supernaturalism: Tradition and Revolution in Romantic Literature* (New York: W. W. Norton, 1971).

11. *Table Talk*, ed. cit., p. 249 (May 18, 1833).

Index

227